CYBERJUTSU

CYBERJUTSU

Cybersecurity for the Modern Ninja

by Ben McCarty

San Francisco

Printed in the United States of America

First printing

24 23 22 21   1 2 3 4 5 6 7 8 9

ISBN-13: 978-1-7185-0054-9 (print)
ISBN-13: 978-1-7185-0055-6 (ebook)

Publisher: William Pollock
Executive Editor: Barbara Yien
Production Editor: Rachel Monaghan
Developmental Editors: Nic Albert and Athabasca Witschi
Project Editor: Dapinder Dosanjh
Cover Design: Octopod Studios
Cover Illustrator: Rick Reese
Technical Reviewer: Ari Schloss
Copyeditor: Paula L. Fleming
Interior Design and Composition: Maureen Forys, Happenstance Type-O-Rama
Proofreader: Holly Bauer Forsyth
Indexer: Beth Nauman-Montana

For information on book distributors or translations, please contact No Starch Press, Inc. directly:
No Starch Press, Inc.
245 8th Street, San Francisco, CA 94103
phone: 1-415-863-9900; info@nostarch.com
www.nostarch.com

Library of Congress Cataloging-in-Publication Data

Names: McCarty, Ben, author.
Title: Cyberjutsu : cybersecurity for the modern ninja / Ben McCarty.
Description: San Francisco, CA : No Starch Press, [2021] | Includes bibliographical references and index. | Summary: "Teaches ancient approaches to modern information security issues based on authentic, formerly classified ninja scrolls"-- Provided by publisher.
Identifiers: LCCN 2020052832 (print) | LCCN 2020052833 (ebook) | ISBN 9781718500549 (print) | ISBN 9781718500556 (ebook)
Subjects: LCSH: Computer security. | Computer networks--Security measures. | Computer crimes--Prevention. | Ninjutsu.
Classification: LCC QA76.9.A25 M4249 2021 (print) | LCC QA76.9.A25 (ebook) | DDC 005.8--dc23
LC record available at https://lccn.loc.gov/2020052832
LC ebook record available at https://lccn.loc.gov/2020052833

To my lovely Sarah
and to those helpless organizations
afraid of new ideas
and blind to their own weaknesses
for motivating me to write this book

About the Author

Ben McCarty is an ex-NSA developer and US Army veteran. He is one of the first fully qualified Cyber Warfare Specialists (35Q) to serve in the Army Network Warfare Battalion. During his career, he has worked as a hacker, incident handler, threat hunter, malware analyst, network security engineer, compliance auditor, threat intelligence professional, and capability developer. He holds multiple security patents and certifications. He is currently a quantum security researcher in the Washington, DC, area.

About the Technical Reviewer

Ari Schloss started his cybersecurity career with the federal government at the IRS and has contracted with DHS and CMS (Medicare). He has experience in NIST 800-53/800-171 compliance, cybersecurity defense operations, and forensics. He has a master's degree in Information Assurance and an MBA. He currently serves as a security engineer at a defense contractor in Maryland.

BRIEF CONTENTS

CONTENTS IN DETAIL

7
ACCESS TO TIME 57

You should start your attack with no delay and not prematurely but perfectly on time.

8
TOOLS 63

Remember, if you use a ninja tool, be sure to use it when the wind is whistling so as to hide any sound and always retrieve it.

9
SENSORS 71

Whether day or night, scouts for a far-distance observation should be sent out.

10
BRIDGES AND LADDERS 79

There will be no wall or moat that you cannot pass, no matter how high or steep it is, particularly if you use a ninja ladder.

25
ZERO-TRUST THREAT MANAGEMENT 195

If you enter a room from the rear and if there is someone in the room who is not asleep, then they will not suspect you as an intruder. It is because those who come from the rear are not considered possible thieves or assailants.

26
SHINOBI TRADECRAFT 201

Secret techniques to infiltrate without fail are deceptive, and they are varied and flexible and are done according to opportunity. Thus, as a basis, you should embrace the old ways of the shinobi who served under ancient great generals, but remember not only to keep to these ways but to adapt them, each dependent on the situation and the moment.

FOREWORD

Cybersecurity has never been this critical to our economic prosperity and social peace. The need to protect our businesses' intellectual property and people's personal information is of utmost importance. Cybercriminals are getting faster, more creative, more organized, and more resourceful. Cybersecurity practitioners find themselves constantly discovering new threats and responding to new attacks, despite all the cyberdefense measures they have already taken. It's a cyber arms race.

In the 200 or so pages that follow, Benjamin McCarty, a brilliant cyber threat intelligence expert and an innovative security researcher whom I have known since 2017, shares how to protect your information from cyberhackers. Ben's main message is simple: think like a ninja. But what about this message justifies writing an entire book? For the full and thorough answer, you just have to read it. But I can tell you that, at a high level, the answer lies in the tactics and techniques that ninjas use to wage warfare.

When I was in graduate school 15 years ago, the first security lesson I learned in my security engineering class was to think like a hacker. Within the cybersecurity community, we have been touting this message for several years, if not decades. But judging by the number of cyberattacks that organizations continue to undergo every year, this message does not seem to have sunk in for a large number of cyberdefenders. This is understandable for two reasons. First, the message is hard to internalize because of the lack of details. And second, any details available may be very hard to grasp. Ben addresses both issues by changing the message from "Think like a hacker" to "Think like a ninja."

"How?" you might ask. Well, the answer lies in the ninja scrolls, which were scripted in medieval times but carefully kept secret until the mid-20th century. The scrolls were recently translated from Japanese to English. The translation reveals just how ninjas were trained to think, strategize, and act. Ninjas, being covert agents, cautiously kept their strategies and tactics secret. But the revelations made through the publication of their scrolls are worth a deep analysis to understand what made ninjas so successful in their espionage, deception, and surprise attack missions over centuries.

Ben's analysis of these scrolls gleans the strategies, tactics, and techniques that ninjas used to conduct their attacks. He maps these ancient tactics and techniques to the modern-day tactics, techniques, and procedures (TTPs) used by hackers to conduct cyberattacks. Reading through the playbook and procedures will help security professionals understand not only how a ninja thinks, but also how a cybercriminal thinks. With that understanding, you will be able to develop the craft of really thinking like a hacker and internalizing that security principle. Not only will that help you predict the hacker's potential next move, but it will also give you time to prepare for that move and build up your defenses to prevent the hacker from reaching their goal.

Another reason why Ben's use of the ninja scrolls to bring these TTPs closer to cyberdefenders is a very smart approach is because these scrolls deal with attacks in the physical world; that is, they reference physical objects and describe movements within a physical environment. Physical environments are much easier for our brains to visualize than cyber or virtual environments. Thinking about the hacker's tactics and techniques as they relate to tangible assets makes them more discernible. You can start envisaging how a hacker might apply a particular TTP to compromise one asset or move from one asset to another. In each chapter, Ben brilliantly takes you through a castle theory thought exercise to help you visualize those movements in a medieval castle and then translate them to a cyber environment.

Readers will greatly benefit from the wealth of tips and strategies Ben lays out. This is a timely contribution: cybersecurity is becoming one of the main pillars of our economy. Ben McCarty, with his decade-long threat intelligence experience, is exceptionally well positioned to share the practical tips of how to think like a ninja and a hacker in order to protect both your information and the digital economy at large.

MALEK BEN SALEM, PhD
Security R&D Lead
Accenture

ACKNOWLEDGMENTS

I must start by thanking my lovely Sarah. From reading early drafts to giving me advice on the cover and providing me with the freedom to write a book, thank you so much.

To Chris St. Myers, thank you for keeping me engaged and happy under your leadership while I was conducting deep threat intelligence research into cyber espionage. The experience was essential for me to saliently capture the minds of cyber espionage threat actors. You never stopped me; you only encouraged me and taught me many things along the way.

I'm eternally grateful to the US Army TRADOC cadre and DET-MEADE, who recognized my potential and placed me into the first cyberwarfare class and unit. This unique experience was especially formative for my understanding of cybersecurity and operator tradecraft.

A very special thanks to Antony Cummins and his team for translating the ninja scrolls and making them available to the English-speaking world. It is because of your efforts and infectious passion for the ninja that I found the inspiration to write this book.

To everyone at No Starch Press who helped improve the manuscript and make it into a book I am proud of, thank you.

Finally, thank you to all those who have been a part of my cybersecurity journey. Learning from other cybersecurity professionals has been a pleasure and has greatly enriched my overall knowledge and understanding of cybersecurity and threats. I needed every bit of it to write this book.

INTRODUCTION

First and foremost: I am not a ninja. Nor am I a ninja historian, a sensei, or even Japanese.

However, I did perform cyber warfare for the US Army, where my fellow soldiers often described our mission as "high-speed ninja shit." That's when I really started noticing the odd prevalence of "ninja" references in cybersecurity. I wanted to see if there was anything substantive behind the term's use. I started researching ninjas in 2012, and that's when I found recent English translations of Japanese scrolls written more than 400 years ago (more on those in the "About This Book" section that follows). These scrolls were the training manuals that ninjas used to learn their craft—not historical reports but the actual playbooks. One of these, *Bansenshūkai*, was declassified by the Japanese government and made available to the public on a limited basis only after World War II, as the information had been considered too dangerous to disseminate for almost 300 years. In medieval times, non-ninjas were never supposed to see these documents. Bold warnings in the scrolls inform readers to protect the information with their lives. At one time, simply possessing such a scroll was enough to merit execution in Japan. The taboo nature of the material added an undeniable mystique to the reading experience. I was hooked.

After reading more than 1,000 pages of translated source material, it became clear that the instructions and secret techniques meant for ninjas were essentially on-the-ground training in information assurance, security, infiltration, espionage, and destructive attacks that relied on covert access to heavily fortified organizations—many of the same concepts

I dealt with every day of my career in cybersecurity. These 400-year-old manuals were filled with insights about defensive and offensive security for which I could not find equivalents in modern information assurance practices. And because they were field guides that laid bare the tactics, techniques, and procedures (TTPs) of secret warfare, they were truly unique. In our business, nation-state cyber espionage units and other malicious actors do not hold webinars or publish playbooks that describe their TTPs. Thus, these ninja scrolls are singular and invaluable.

Cyberjutsu aims to turn the tactics, techniques, strategies, and mentalities of ancient ninjas into a practical cybersecurity field guide. Cybersecurity is relatively young and still highly reactionary. Industry professionals often spend their days defusing imminent threats or forecasting future attacks based on what just happened. I wrote this book because I believe we have much to learn by taking a long view offered in these scrolls of information security's first advanced persistent threat (APT). The information warfare TTPs practiced by ancient ninjas were perfected over hundreds of years. The TTPs worked in their time—and they could be the key to leapfrogging today's cybersecurity prevailing models, best practices, and concepts to implement more mature and time-tested ideas.

About This Book

Each chapter examines one ninja-related topic in detail, moving from a broad grounding in history and philosophy to analysis to actionable cybersecurity recommendations. For ease of use, each chapter is organized as follows:

The Ninja Scrolls A brief introduction to a tool, technique, or methodology used by ninjas.

Cybersecurity An analysis of what the ninja concept teaches us about the current cybersecurity landscape.

What You Can Do Actionable steps, derived from the preceding analysis, that you can take to secure your organization against cyber threats.

Castle Theory Thought Exercise An exercise that asks you to solve a threat scenario using what you've learned about ninja and cyber concepts.

Recommended Security Controls and Mitigations A checklist of recommended security settings and specifications, based on the NIST 800-53 standard,[1] that you can implement for compliance purposes or to conform to best practices.

This book does not seek to provide a comprehensive catalogue of ninja terminology or an extended discourse on ninja philosophy. For that, seek out the work of Antony Cummins and Yoshie Minami, who edited and translated Japan's ancient ninja scrolls for a contemporary audience. This book references the following Cummins and Minami titles (for more details on each, see the section "A Ninja Primer" on page xxiv):

- *The Book of Ninja* (ISBN 9781780284934), a translation of the *Bansenshūkai*
- *The Secret Traditions of the Shinobi* (ISBN 9781583944356), a translation of the *Shinobi Hiden* (or *Ninpiden*), *Gunpo Jiyoshu*, and *Yoshimori Hyakushu*
- *True Path of the Ninja* (ISBN 9784805314395), a translation of *Shōninki*

Cummins and Minami's work is extensive, and I highly recommend reading it in full. These collections serve not only as inspiration but as the primary sources for this book's analysis of ninjutsu, from military tactics to how to think like a ninja. Their translations contain fascinating wisdom and knowledge beyond what I could touch on in this book, and they are a thrilling window into a lost way of life. *Cyberjutsu* is greatly indebted to Cummins and Minami and their tireless efforts to bring these medieval works to the contemporary world.

A Note on the Castle Theory Thought Exercises

I believe that talking about issues in the cybersecurity industry comes with at least three baked-in problems. First, even at security organizations, nontechnical decision makers or other stakeholders are often excluded from, lied to about, or bullied out of cybersecurity conversations because they lack technical expertise. Second, many security problems are actually human problems. We already know how to implement technical solutions to many threats, but human beings get in the way with politics, ignorance, budget concerns, or other constraints. Lastly, the availability of security solutions and/or answers that can be purchased or easily discovered with internet searches has changed how people approach problems.

To address these issues, in each chapter, I have presented the central questions at the heart of the topic in the Castle Theory Thought Exercise—a mental puzzle (which you hopefully can't google) in which you try to protect your castle (network) from the dangers posed by enemy ninjas (cyber threat actors). Framing security problems in terms of defending a castle removes the technical aspects of the conversation and allows for clearer communication on the crux of the issue and collaboration between teams. Everyone can grasp the scenario in which a ninja physically infiltrates a castle, whether or not they can speak fluently about enterprise networks and hackers. Pretending to be the ruler of a castle also means you can ignore any organizational bureaucracy or political problems that come with implementing your proposed solutions. After all, kings and queens do what they want.

For Future Use

There are many cybersecurity ideas in this book. Some are lifted from the original scrolls and adapted for modern information applications. Others are proposed solutions to gaps I have identified in commercial products or services. Still other ideas are more novel or aspirational. I am not sure how the implementations would work on a technical level, but perhaps someone with better perspective and insight can develop and patent them.

If, by chance, you do patent an idea that stems from this book, please consider adding my name as a co-inventor—not for financial purposes but simply to document the origins of the idea. If you have questions about this book or would like to discuss the ideas for practical application, email me at *ben.mccarty0@gmail.com.*

A Ninja Primer

This brief primer is meant to help shift your notion of what a "ninja" is to the reality depicted in historical evidence. Try to put aside what you know about ninjas from movies and fiction. It's natural to experience some confusion, disbelief, and cognitive discomfort when confronting evidence that contradicts long-held ideas and beliefs—especially for those of us who grew up wanting to be a ninja.

The Historical Ninja

Ninja went by many names. The one we know in the 21st-century West is *ninja*, but they were also called *shinobi*, *yato*, *ninpei*, *suppa*, *kanja*, *rappa*, and *ukami*.[2,3] The many labels speak to their reputation for being elusive and mysterious, but really the profession is not hard to understand: shinobi were elite spies and warriors for hire in ancient Japan. Recruited from both the peasantry[4] and the samurai class—notable examples include Natori Masatake[5] and Hattori Hanzō[6]—they likely existed in some form for as long as Japan itself, but they don't appear much in the historical record until the 12th-century Genpei War.[7] For centuries after, Japan was beset by strife and bloodshed, during which feudal lords (daimyō[8]) employed shinobi to conduct espionage, sabotage, assassination, and warfare.[9] Even the fifth-century BCE Chinese military strategist Sun Tzu's seminal treatise, *The Art of War*, stresses the necessity of using these covert agents to achieve victory.[10]

The ninja were fiercely proficient in information espionage, infiltration of enemy encampments, and destructive attacks; shinobi were perhaps history's first advanced persistent threat (APT0, if you will). During a time of constant conflict, they opportunistically honed and matured their techniques, tactics, tools, tradecraft, and procedures, along with their theory of practice, *ninjutsu*. The *Bansenshūkai* scroll notes, "The deepest principle of ninjutsu is to avoid where the enemy is attentive and strike where he is negligent."[11] So, operating as covert agents, they traveled in disguise or by stealth to the target (such as a castle or village); collected information; assessed gaps in the target's defense; and infiltrated to perform espionage, sabotage, arson, or assassination.[12]

With the long, peaceful Edo period of the 17th century, the demand for shinobi tradecraft dwindled, driving ninjas into obscurity.[13] Though their way of life became untenable and they took up other lines of work, their methods were so impactful that even today, shinobi are mythologized as some of history's greatest warriors and information warfare specialists, even being attributed fabulous abilities such as invisibility.

The Ninja Scrolls

Shinobi knowledge was most likely passed from teacher to student, between peers, and through a number of handbooks written by practicing shinobi before and during the 17th century. These are the ninja scrolls. It's likely that families descended from shinobi possess other, undisclosed scrolls that could reveal additional secret methods, but their contents have either not been verified by historians or have not been made available to the public. The historical texts we do have are key to our understanding of shinobi, and reviewing these sources to derive evidence-based knowledge helps avoid the mythology, unverified folklore, and pop culture stereotypes that can quickly pollute the discourse around ninjas.

Among the most significant ninja scrolls are:

The *Bansenshūkai* An encyclopedic, 23-volume collection of ninja skills, tactics, and philosophy culled from multiple shinobi. Compiled in 1676 by Fujibayashi, this scroll is an attempt to preserve the skills and knowledge of ninjutsu in a time of extended peace. It is also, essentially, a job application and demonstration of skills, written by shinobi for the shogun class that might need their services in a less peaceful future.

The *Shinobi Hiden* (or *Ninpiden*) A collection of scrolls believed to have been written around 1655 and then passed down through the Hattori Hanzō family until their eventual publication to the wider world. Perhaps the most practical of the ninja manuals, these scrolls reveal the techniques and tools shinobi used on the ground, including diagrams and specifications for building weapons.

The *Gunpo Jiyoshu* (or *Shiyoshu*) A wide-ranging scroll that touches on military strategy, governance, tools, philosophy, and wartime use of shinobi. Believed to have been written by Ogasawara Saku'un in 1612, the *Gunpo Jiyoshu* also contains the *Yoshimori Hyakushu*, a collection of 100 ninja poems designed to teach shinobi the skills and wisdom necessary to succeed in their missions.

The *Shōninki* A training manual developed in 1681 by Natori Sanjuro Masatake, a samurai and innovator of warfare. A highly literary text, the *Shōninki* was likely written for those who had already become proficient in certain areas of physical and mental training but who sought knowledge refreshers and greater insight into the guiding principles and techniques of ninjutsu.

Ninja Philosophy

It is important to develop intellectual empathy with the values and mindset of the ninja, without delving into mysticism or spiritualism. I consider the ninja philosophy to border on hacker-metacognition with undertones of the yin-yang of Shinto-Buddhism enlightenment influence. While familiarity with the underlying philosophy is not necessary for understanding ninja tactics and techniques, learning from the wisdom that informs ninja applications is certainly helpful.

The Heart [of/under] an Iron Blade

The Japanese word *shinobi* (忍) is made up of the kanji characters for blade (刃) and heart (心). There are various ways to interpret its meaning.

One is that shinobi should have the heart of a blade, or make their heart into a blade. A sword blade is sharp and strong, yet flexible—a tool designed to kill humans while also acting as an extension of the user's spirit and will. This dovetails with the Japanese concept of *kokoro*, a combination of one's heart, spirit, and mind into one central essence. In this context, the iconography provides insight into the balanced mindset necessary for someone to assume the role of a ninja.

Another interpretation is of a "heart under a blade." In this reading, the blade is an existential threat. It is also not only the physical threat that endangers a shinobi's life but also a weapon that closely guards their beating heart. The *onyomi* (Chinese) reading of 忍 is "to persist," which highlights the inner strength needed to work as a spy in enemy territory, under constant threat. The shinobi had to perform life-threatening missions that sometimes meant remaining in the enemy's territory for extended periods before acting—that is, being an advanced persistent threat.

The Correct Mind

Bansenshūkai declares that shinobi must have "the correct mind" or face certain defeat. Achieving this rarified state means always being present, focused, and conscious of purpose—it is mindfulness as self-defense. Shinobi were expected to make decisions with "benevolence, righteousness, loyalty, and fidelity"[14] in mind, even though the result of their craft was often conspiracy and deception. This philosophy had the benefit of calming and focusing shinobi during moments of intense pressure, such as combat or infiltration. "When you have inner peace," *Shōninki* states, "you can fathom things that other people don't realize."[15]

"The correct mind" was also believed to make shinobi more dynamic strategists. While other warriors often rushed quickly and single-mindedly into battle, the shinobi's focus on mental acuity made them patient and flexible. They were trained to think unconventionally, questioning everything; historian Antony Cummins compares this kind of thinking to contemporary entrepreneurial disrupters. If their weapons failed, they used their words. If speech failed, they put aside their own ideas and channeled their enemy's thought processes.[16] A clear mind was the gateway to mastering their enemies, their environment, and seemingly impossible physical tasks.

Shōninki puts it succinctly: "Nothing is as amazing as the human mind."[17]

Ninja Techniques

The infiltration techniques detailed in the ninja scrolls illustrate the astonishing effectiveness of the shinobi's information-gathering processes. They practiced two primary modes of infiltration: *in-nin* ("ninjutsu of darkness") refers to sneaking somewhere under cover of darkness or being otherwise hidden to avoid detection, while *yo-nin* ("ninjutsu of light") refers to infiltration in plain sight, such as disguising oneself as a monk to avoid suspicion. Sometimes shinobi used one within the other—for instance, they might infiltrate a town in disguise, then slip away and hide in a castle's moat until the time of attack.

Regardless of whether they used *in-nin* or *yo-nin*, shinobi set out to know everything possible about their targets, and they had time-honed methods for gathering the most detailed information available. They studied the physical terrain of their target, but they also studied the local people's customs, attitudes, interests, and habits. Before attempting to infiltrate a castle, they first conducted reconnaissance to determine the size, location, and function of each room; the access points; the inhabitants and their routines; and even their pets' feeding schedules. They memorized the names, titles, and job functions of enemy guards, then used enemy flags, crests, and uniforms to sneak in openly (*yo-nin*) while conversing with their unsuspecting targets. They collected seals from various lords so they could be used in forgeries, often to issue false orders to the enemy's army. Before they engaged in battle, they researched the opposing army's size, strength, and capabilities along with their tendencies in battle, their supply lines, and their morale. If their target was a powerful lord, they sought to learn that ruler's moral code and deepest desires so that the target could be corrupted or played to.[18]

Shinobi were taught to think creatively via the "correct mind" philosophy. That training made them hyperaware of the world around them and spurred new ways of taking action in the field. For instance, the *Shōninki* taught shinobi to be more effective by observing the behavior of animals in nature. If a shinobi came to a roadblock or enemy checkpoint, they thought like a fox or a wolf: they did not go over or through it; they displayed patience and went around it, even if the bypass took many miles. Other times, it was appropriate to let themselves be led "like cattle and horses,"[19] out in the open, perhaps posing as a messenger or emissary to get close to the enemy, who was likely to overlook people of lower classes. No matter how shinobi felt—even if they were white-hot with anger—they worked to appear serene on the outside, "just as waterfowl do on a calm lake."[20] If they needed to distract a guard from his post, they could impersonate dogs by barking, howling, or shaking their kimonos to imitate the sound of a dog's shaking.[21]

Shinobi brought about battlefield innovations that armies and covert operatives still practice to this day, and those methods were successful because of how the shinobi's tireless reconnaissance and impeccable knowledge of their targets weaponized information and deception.

1

MAPPING NETWORKS

With these maps, the general can consider how to defend and attack a castle.

For moving the camp, there is a set of principles to follow about the time and the day of moving. The duty of a shinobi is to know exactly the geography of the area and the distance to the enemy.
—Yoshimori Hyakushu #9

Once you get the details and layout of the castle or the camp, all you need to do is get back with it as soon as possible, as that is what a good shinobi should do.
—Yoshimori Hyakushu #24

The very first piece of advice offered in the *Bansenshūkai*'s "A Guideline for Commanders" is to produce meticulously accurate maps that your generals can use to plan attacks against the enemy.[1] Selected poems of the *Yoshimori Hyakushu*[2] also stress the importance of drawing and maintaining maps with enough detail to be useful to both an army and an individual *shinobi.*

Commanders usually tasked shinobi with creating maps. The scrolls make clear that the skill of being able to accurately draw what you see—mountains, rivers, fields—is not the same as drawing purposeful, contextualized threat intelligence maps to aid military strategy or shinobi infiltration. The scrolls state that the following details are relevant to the tactics of war and shinobi tradecraft and thus should be included in maps:[3]

All entrances and gates of a house, castle, or fort. What types of locks, latches, and opening mechanisms are present? How difficult is it to open the gates or doors, and do they make noise when opened or closed?

The approaching roads. Are they straight or curved? Wide or narrow? Dirt or stone? Flat or inclined?

The design, makeup, and layout of the structure. What is each room's size and purpose? What is kept in each room? Do the floorboards squeak?

The inhabitants of the structure. What are their names? Do they practice any noteworthy skills or arts? How alert or suspicious is each person?

The topology of the castle and surrounding area. Are signal relays visible from inside and outside the location? Where are food, water, and firewood stored? How wide and deep are the moats? How high are the walls?

Understanding Network Maps

Network maps in cybersecurity are network topology graphs that describe the physical and/or logical relationship and configuration between *links* (communication connections) and *nodes* (devices) in the network. To better understand the concept, consider road maps or maps in an atlas. These describe physical locations, geographic features, political borders, and the natural landscape. Information about roads (links)—their name, orientation, length, and intersections between other roads—can be used to navigate between different locations (nodes). Now let's consider the following hypothetical scenario.

Imagine you live in a world where roads and buildings spontaneously appear or vanish in the blink of an eye. GPS exists, and you have the coordinates of where you are and where you want to go, but you must try to get there by following a bewildering network of constantly changing roads.

Fortunately, navigation officials (*routers*) are placed at every crossroads to help travelers like you find their way. These routers are constantly calling their neighboring routers to learn what routes and locations are open so they can update their routing table, kept on a clipboard. You must stop at every intersection and ask the router for directions to the next corner by showing them your travel card, which has your intended destination coded in GPS coordinates. The router checks their clipboard for currently open routes while making some calculations, quickly points you in a direction, stamps your travel card with the router's address, hole-punches your travel card to track the number of routers you have checked in with on your journey, and sends you off to the next router. You repeat this process until you reach your destination. Now imagine this world's cartographers, who would have likely given up on producing accurate maps, unable to keep up with the ever-changing network. These mapmakers would have to be satisfied with labeling key landmarks and points of interest with generic names and drawing fuzzy lines between these points to indicate that paths of some sort exist between them.

This hypothetical situation is in fact what exists in cyberspace, and it's why network maps are not as accurate and their maintenance is not as prioritized as it should be. The lack of high-quality, comprehensive network maps is a recognized challenge for cybersecurity organizations. If an organization has a map at all, it's typically provided to the security operations center (SOC) to illustrate where sensors or security devices are in the flow of data and to better understand packet captures, firewall rules, alerts, and system logs. However, it's probably also abstract, describing only basic features, such as boundaries for the internet, perimeter network, and intranet; the general location of edge routers or firewalls; and unspecified network boundaries and conceptual arrangements, indicated by cloudy bubbles. An example of an underdeveloped, yet common, network map available to cybersecurity and IT professionals is provided in Figure 1-1.

To describe why Figure 1-1 is a "bad" map, let's reexamine the *Bansenshūkai*'s advice on mapping in terms of the equivalent cyber details.

All access points of a node in the network. What types of interface access points are present on the device (Ethernet [e], Fast-Ethernet [fe], Gigabit-Ethernet [ge], Universal Serial Bus [USB], Console [con], Loop-back [lo], Wi-Fi [w], and so on)? Is there network access control (NAC) or media access control (MAC) address filtering? Is remote or local console access enabled or not locked down? What type of physical security is present? Are there rack door locks or even USB locks? Is interface access logging being performed? Where are the network management interface and network? What are the IP address and MAC address of each access point?

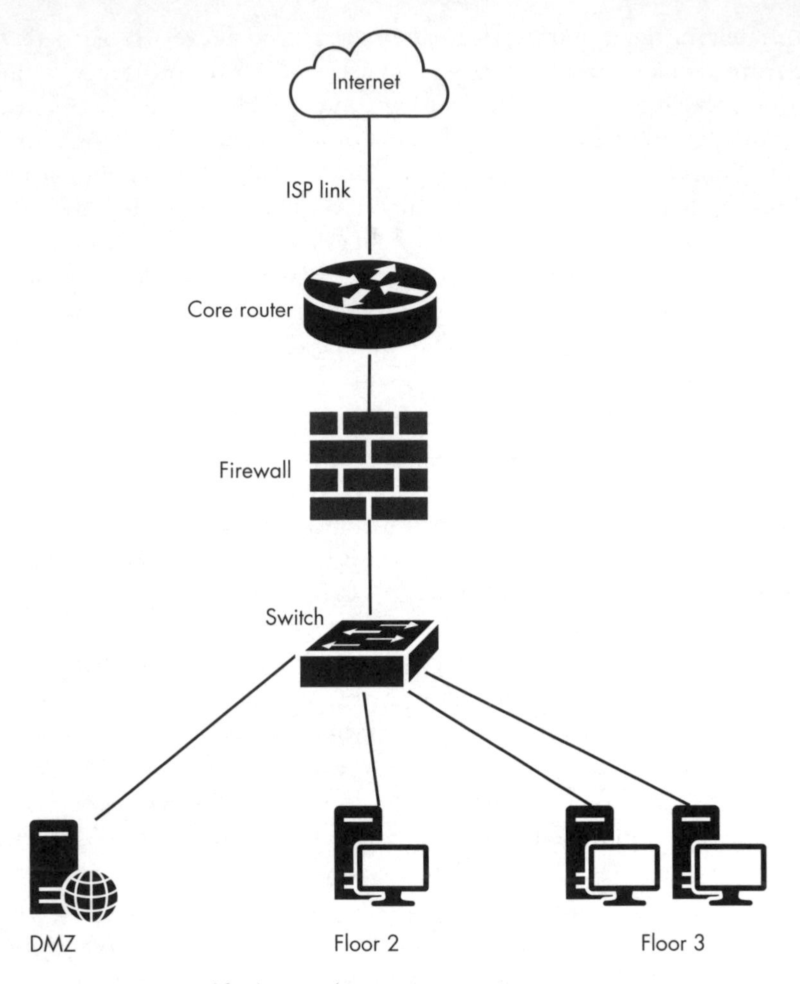

Figure 1-1: A simplified network map

The bordering gateways, hops, and egress points. Is there more than one internet service provider (ISP)? Is it a Trusted Internet Connection (TIC) or Managed Internet Service (MIS)? What is the bandwidth of the internet connection? Is the egress connection made of fiber, Ethernet, coaxial, or other media? What are the hops that approach the network? Are there satellite, microwave, laser, or Wi-Fi egress methods in or out of the network?

The design, makeup, and layout of the network. What is each subnet's name, purpose, and size (for example, Classless Inter-Domain routing [CIDR])? Are there virtual local area networks (VLANs)? Are there connection pool limits? Is the network flat or hierarchal or divided based on building structures or defense layers and/or function?

The hosts and nodes of the network. What are their names? What is their operating system (OS) version? What services/ports are they running, and which do they have open? What security controls do they have that might detect an attack? Do they have any known common vulnerability exploits (CVEs)?

The physical and logical architecture of the network and building. Where is the data center located? Are Ethernet jacks available in the lobby? Does Wi-Fi leak outside the building? Are computer screens and terminals visible from outside the building? Is security glass used in the office? Are guest/conference room networks properly segmented? What are the core access control lists (ACLs) and firewall rules of the network? Where is DNS resolved? What is available in the perimeter network or DMZ? Are external email providers or other cloud services used? How is remote access or virtual private network (VPN) architecture in the network?

Organizations without a working network map might instead reference wiring diagrams or schematics produced by their IT department. These simplified illustrations document the relative arrangement of systems, networking equipment, and device connections, and they can function as references for troubleshooting technical or operational issues within the network. However, too many organizations forego even these crude diagrams in favor of a spreadsheet that catalogs hostnames, model and serial numbers, street and IP addresses, and data center stack/rack rows for all equipment. If stakeholders can use this spreadsheet to locate assets and never have any major network issues or outages, the existence of such documentation may even discourage the creation of a network map. Appallingly, some companies rely on an architect or specialist who has a "map" in their head, and no map is ever formally—or even informally—produced.

To be fair, there are legitimate reasons for the lack of useful network maps. Building, sharing, and maintaining maps can eat up valuable time and other resources. Maps are also liable to change. Adding or removing systems to a network, changing IP addresses, reconfiguring cables, or pushing new router or firewall rules can all significantly alter the accuracy of a map, even if it was made just moments before. In addition, modern computers and networking devices run dynamic routing and host configuration protocols that automatically push information to other systems and networks without the need of a map, meaning networks can essentially autoconfigure themselves.

Of course, there's an abundance of software-based "mapping" tools, such as Nmap,[4] that scan networks to discover hosts, visualize the network via number of hops from the scanner, use Simple Network Management Protocol (SNMP) to discover and map network topology, or use router and switch configuration files to quickly generate network diagrams. Network diagrams generated by tools are convenient, but they rarely capture all the details or context needed to meet the high-quality mapping standard that a defender or adversary would want. Using a combination of mapping tools, network scans, and human knowledge to draw a software-assisted network map is likely the ideal solution—but even this approach requires the investment of significant time by someone with specialized skills to remain accurate and thus useful.

Despite these limiting factors, it is crucial that defenders maintain mapping vigilance. The example map in Figure 1-2 illustrates the level of detail a defender's map should include to protect a network.

Distinctive shapes, rather than pictograms, are used to represent devices in the network. The same shape type is repeated for similar device types. For example, the circles in Figure 1-2 represent workstations, squares represent routers, and rectangles represent servers; triangles would represent email relays or domain controllers if they were present. In addition, the shapes are empty of texture or background, allowing information written inside to be clearly legible.

Every interface (both virtual and physical) is labeled with its type and number. For example, the Ethernet interface type is labeled `eth`, and the interface is numbered the same as it would be physically labeled on the device, `eth 0/0`. Unused interfaces are also labeled. Each interface is given its assigned IP address and subnet when these are known.

Device information, such as hostname, make and model, and OS version are documented at the top of the device when known. Vulnerabilities, default credentials, known credentials, and other key flaws are notated in the center of the device. Running services, software, and open ports are documented as well. VLANs, network boundaries, layout, and structure should be designed into the network map and labeled as such, along with any noteworthy information.

Collecting Intelligence Undetected

For shinobi, collecting intelligence without being detected was an elite skill. Loitering near a castle while taking detailed measurements with a carpenter square or other device would tip off the inhabitants, exposing

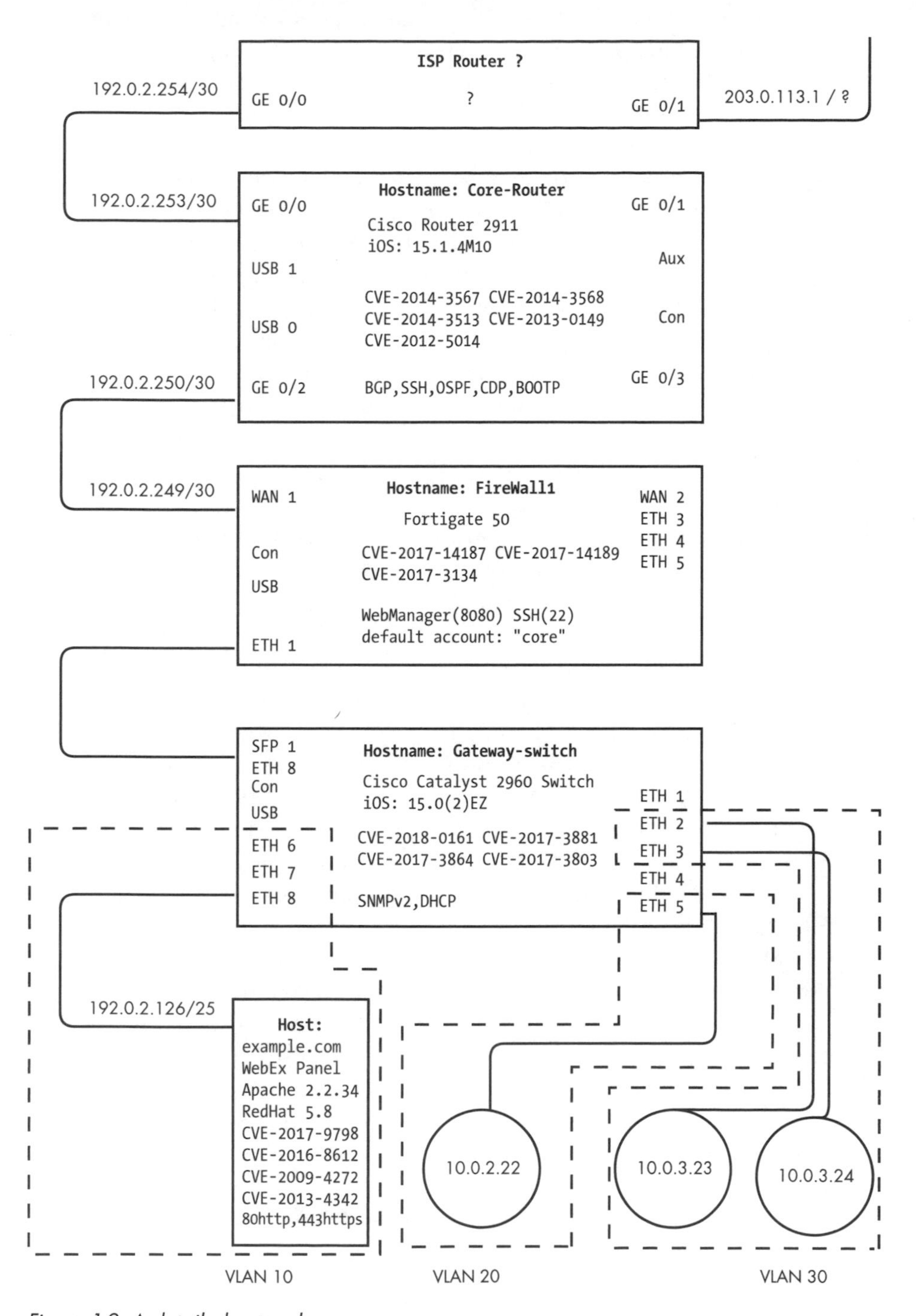

Figure 1-2: A detailed network map

the shinobi as an enemy agent. Consequently, industrious shinobi made maps during times of peace, when the occupants of fortifications lowered their guard; at these times, shinobi could travel more freely and invite less suspicion as they collected data.[5]

Often, however, shinobi had to come up with ways to furtively take measurements, note topographical features, and gather other intelligence. Tellingly, the *Bansenshūkai* includes a description of how to accurately produce maps in a section about open-disguise techniques, indicating that shinobi used deception to conduct mapping within plain sight of the enemy. The scroll references a technique called *uramittsu no jutsu*[6]—the art of estimating distance—that involves finding the distance to a familiar object using knowledge of the object's size for scale. *Uramittsu no jutsu* also incorporated clever trigonometry tricks; for example, a shinobi might lie down with their feet facing the target and use the known dimensions of their feet to take measurements, all while appearing to nap under a tree.

Collecting network bearings is one of the first things adversaries do before attacking a target network or host. Adversary-created maps have the same purpose as historical ninja maps: identifying and documenting the information necessary to infiltrate the target. This information includes all egress and ingress points to a network: ISP connections; wireless access points; UHF, microwave, radio, or satellite points; and cloud, interconnected, and external networks.

Attackers will also look for Border Gateway Protocol (BGP) gateways and routes or hops to the network. They'll look for the network's representational structure, layout, and design; network inventory including hostnames, appliance models, operating systems, open ports, running services, and vulnerabilities; and network topology such as subnets, VLANs, ACLs, and firewall rules.

Many of the network-mapping tools attackers use are "noisy," as they communicate to large numbers of hosts, use custom packets, and can be detected by internal security devices. However, attackers can mitigate these weaknesses by slowing or throttling the network mapper, using noncustom (non-suspicious) packets, and even performing manual reconnaissance with common tools that already exist on the victim host, such as `ping` or `net`. Attacks can also use innocuous reconnaissance methods, in which the attacker never touches or scans the target but instead collects information using Shodan or other previously indexed data found via internet search engines.

More sophisticated adversaries develop tradecraft to perform *passive mapping*, a tactic whereby the attacker collects information about a target without interacting directly with it (without actively scanning it with

Nmap, for example). Another passive mapping tactic is the interpretation of packets captured from a network interface in *promiscuous mode*, which configures a network interface to record and inspect all network communications; this is the opposite of *non-promiscuous mode* in which only communication the network addresses to itself is recorded and inspected. You would use promiscuous mode to gain an understanding of the neighboring hosts, traffic flow, services, and protocols used on the network without ever actively interacting with it.

Another method for mapping a network without directly interacting with it is to collect a network admin's emails as they leave the network, searching for network maps of the target in an external file storage-sharing environment, or looking in third-party troubleshooting help forums where the admin may post logs/errors, router configurations, network debugging/tracert/ping, or other technical details that disclose the layout and configuration of the network. Much like the ninja's *uramittsu no jutsu* technique, the exploitation of observable information from a target's network can be used to map it without alerting the target. Passive mapping can include measuring the latency of recorded tracerts from the network to identify satellite hops (for example, the presence of a satellite is indicated by a sudden 500-millisecond increase in communication delay) or detecting a firewall system's deep-packet processing (for example, the preprocessor recognizes a potential malicious attack and adds perceptible delays to specially crafted communication). Passive mapping might also include information disclosure of the internal network from external DNS zones and record responses; public procurement orders and purchase requests for certain software/hardware; or even job postings for network/IT admins with experience in a specific technology, networking equipment, or hardware/software.

After the attacker has spent so much time developing them, their maps may be more complete than the target's own—the adversary may know more about the target's network than the target does. To offset any such advantage, network defenders should strive to develop and maintain superior maps and keep them highly protected.

Creating Your Map

The map creation process can happen in three general steps:

1. Make the necessary investment to create a comprehensive, accurate map that can be easily updated and securely stored. It should contain the information necessary for each team's use case (such as IT, network operations center [NOC], and SOC). Consider

hiring a dedicated person or team, or an outside vendor, to make and analyze the map.

2. Make the map, including the types of precise details specified in the beginning of this chapter.
3. Request that the map be peer reviewed as part of change management requests, as well as whenever anyone notices an incongruity in or divergence from the map.

Let's take a closer look at the second step: making the map.

After you have identified all key stakeholders and persuaded them that this project should be a priority, the first step is to gather anything and everything your organization has internally that could help with the mapping process. This includes wiring diagrams, old network architecture project plans, vulnerability scans, asset inventory lists, inventory audits of the data center, DHCP leases, DNS records, SNMP network management data, endpoint agent records, packet captures (PCAP), SIEM logs, router configurations, firewall rules, and network scans. Router configurations should be the primary source for constructing the major architecture and layout of your network map; consider starting by putting your core/central router(s) in the middle of your map and branching out from there. PCAP captures can reveal endpoints communicating on the network that may not respond to network scans or that cannot be reached by scans due to network filtering. After you allow select systems to collect PCAP for an extended period in promiscuous mode, it will be possible to review the list of endpoints found in the PCAP, as seen in Figure 1-3.

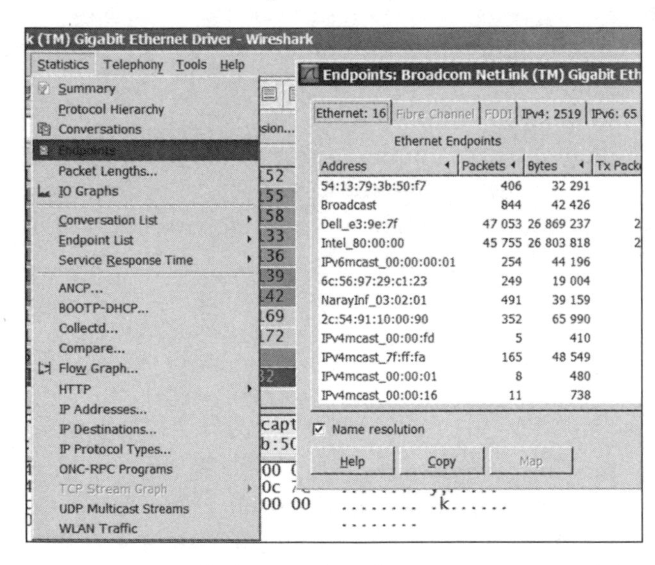

Figure 1-3: Wireshark screenshot of endpoints discovered during PCAP collection

Ideally, PCAP collection should occur during network scans to validate the reach of the scans. Also, multiple network scans should be conducted, with a minimum of one endpoint per subnetwork conducting a scan of its subnet; these scans can be manually stitched together into a network map topology, as shown in Figure 1-4. Identify items that can be automated so this process is easier to repeat in the future.

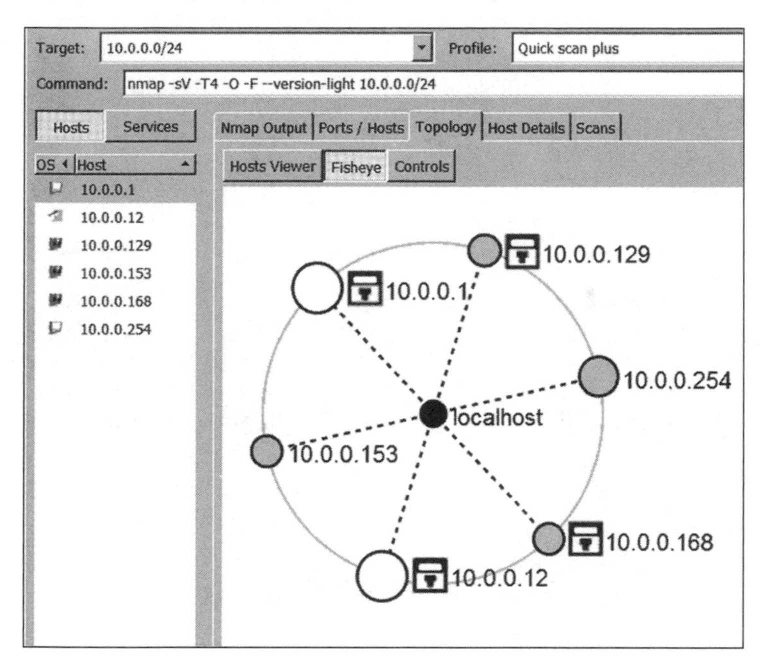

Figure 1-4: The Zenmap topology view of a scan of the 10.0.0.0/24 subnet

Once all the data has been collected, it will need to be processed, analyzed, and merged. It will be useful to find out which source of data is the most accurate as well as to identify data sources with unique and helpful information (for example, the last-seen-time of a device) before consolidating all the data. Also, any incongruities and discrepancies should be investigated. These might include devices missing from the network, rogue devices in the network, and strange network behavior or connections. If you discover that your network scanners were not able to penetrate certain enclaves or subnets due to IP rules or intrusion prevention systems (IPSes), consider requesting network changes to allow deeper and more comprehensive scanning. A key outcome from this stage of the project is the identification and location of all authorized and unauthorized devices connected to your network—a huge accomplishment.

Evaluate software-mapping tools that can automatically ingest SNMP data, network scans, and vulnerability scans and allow manual editing to incorporate any additional data. The tool you choose should produce a comprehensive, accurate, and detailed network map that meets your stakeholders' needs. Pick the best solution that will handle your data and meet your budget.

Produce the map and test it. Test its usefulness during change management meetings/security incidents and network outage/debugging events. Does it help resolve issues and find problems faster? Test its accuracy with traceroutes and tcpdumps over interfaces. To test the accuracy with traceroutes, conduct internal and external traceroutes from different network locations to see whether the hop points (routers) are present in the map and flow logically according to your map. An example traceroute is seen in Figure 1-5.

```
C:\Users\benm>tracert -4 example.com

Tracing route to example.com [93.184.216.34]
over a maximum of 30 hops:

  1     2 ms     1 ms     1 ms  10.0.0.1
  2    18 ms    10 ms     9 ms  96.120.106.61
  3     9 ms    10 ms     9 ms  xe-5-2-0-sur01.newmexiconw.dc.bad.comcast.net [162.151.98.145]
  4    18 ms    10 ms    11 ms  ge-1-21-ur02.waldorf.md.bad.comcast.net [68.87.135.97]
  5    41 ms    11 ms    10 ms  ae-13-ar01.capitolhghts.md.bad.comcast.net [68.87.168.61]
  6    13 ms    14 ms    14 ms  be-33657-cr02.ashburn.va.ibone.comcast.net [68.86.90.57]
  7    11 ms    12 ms    12 ms  be-10142-pe01.ashburn.va.ibone.comcast.net [68.86.86.34]
  8    12 ms    12 ms    12 ms  as27471-2-c.350ecermak.il.ibone.comcast.net [173.167.57.50]
  9    11 ms    11 ms    13 ms  152.195.64.133
 10    11 ms    10 ms    11 ms  93.184.216.34

Trace complete.

C:\Users\benm>
```

Figure 1-5: A Windows traceroute to example.com

See what your red team and blue team can do with your map. Collect feedback and perform the mapping process again with the goal of producing an even better map in less time.

CASTLE THEORY THOUGHT EXERCISE

Consider the scenario in which you are the ruler of a medieval castle with valuable information, treasure, and people within your stronghold. You receive credible threat intelligence that a ninja has thoroughly mapped your castle and surrounding area, though it is unclear whether this activity was part of active targeting or just passive reconnaissance. You don't know what the map looks like or how detailed it is. Your only map of the castle is an architectural design plan that was used during initial construction—and was designed for the builders and not for other users—but has since become out of date.

What does the ninja's map likely include that your map doesn't? What would the ninja know about your castle that you don't, and how could that information be used for infiltration? Who in your fiefdom would benefit from access to the ninja's map? Whom would you trust to map your castle in the same way the ninja did, allowing you to see what the ninja sees?

Recommended Security Controls and Mitigations

Where relevant, each recommendation is presented with an applicable security control from the NIST 800-53 standard, and it should be evaluated with the idea of maps in mind.

1. Assign responsibilities for documenting a network map. Implement policies and procedures to coordinate updates of the map between teams. [CM-1: Configuration Management Policy and Procedures; CM-3: Configuration Change Control | (4) Security Representative; CM-9: Configuration Management Plan]
2. To establish a baseline, document the configuration of the network's topology, architecture, logical placement, and information systems. [CM-2: Baseline Configuration]
3. Incorporate flaw identification (such as map inaccuracies) and remediation (for example, of vulnerabilities inherent in the network architecture) into the network-mapping process. [SI-2: Flaw Remediation]

Debrief

In this chapter, you got a review of shinobi mapping objectives, map standards, and mapping techniques as well as an overview of modern network-mapping practices and technologies. Considering the importance of network maps, how to create (good) maps, and how attackers collect intelligence on your system may have sparked your imagination, and you may have thought of new data sources or techniques you could use to map your own network and others' networks.

In the next chapter, you will get a chance to use your network map as a type of data flow diagram (DFD) to perform threat modeling. This means you'll identify areas in your network where a threat actor is likely to attack it or bypass your defenses to infiltrate it. I'll discuss the novel ninja security technique of "guarding," which can be used to defend these weak points in your network.

2

GUARDING WITH SPECIAL CARE

Even castles with strong fortifications should be guarded, paying particular attention to the recessed corners.

What shinobi should keep in mind when stealing into a castle or camp are the naturally fortified and difficult directions, the woods, and blind spots.
—Yoshimori Hyakushu #10

Shinobi were historically proficient infiltrators. The ancient scrolls describe how to quickly identify and brutally exploit weak spots in an enemy's fortifications. The scrolls also stress that shinobi should use higher-order thinking to creatively apply their knowledge when building their own defenses. *Bansenshūkai* advises commanders tasked with defending a camp or castle to identify, inspect, and guard with special care the areas where shinobi are most likely to attempt entry, such as the recessed corners of a castle's stone walls, rubbish disposal areas, water pipes, and nearby woods or bushes.[1]

Understanding Attack Vectors

Consider the castle's wall an *attack surface* and weak points in the castle's wall (for example, the water pipe or poorly placed stones in the wall that provide footholds) *attack vectors*. The term *attack surface* refers to all the software, networks, and systems that the adversary has the opportunity to attack. Any point within the attack surface can be an attack vector, or the means an attacker uses to gain access. In cybersecurity, it's always advisable to reduce your attack surface. That said, while reducing the castle footprint would shrink the attack surface that needs to be defended, it wouldn't mitigate the amount of damage the adversary could inflict or prevent any given attack vector from being exploited. Nonetheless, attack surface reduction can make guarding the target easier.

Bansenshūkai's volume on hidden infiltration includes a list of well-intentioned defensive techniques, weapons, and modes of thought that can actually expose a camp to risk. It implores commanders to consider how everything in their environment could be used against them. For example, the scroll instructs infiltrators to look for *shinobi-gaeshi*, spikes set up around an enemy's encampment to deter would-be attackers.[2] Because defenders placed these spikes in locations they considered vulnerable, the spikes' presence told enemy shinobi where the defenses were inadequate; defenders were essentially broadcasting their insecurities. Shinobi knew they could remove these spikes—doing so was relatively easy, as they were almost always attached as an afterthought—and gain passage through the weakest spot in the target's perimeter.[3]

A succinct example of such security that is "bolted on" as an afterthought is found in Microsoft Windows' PowerShell. The multitude of security features added on top of the .NET framework with each new version of PowerShell do not address the product's core flaws and, in fact, have allowed threat actors to create an armory of tools and weapons that can be used to infiltrate systems that support PowerShell. This is an excellent case study for any security researcher wishing to examine *shinobi-gaeshi* more closely.

The ancient castles still standing in Japan are not typically adorned with spikes, but they do tend to have water pipes that are too small for a human to climb through, perimeters cleared of vegetation, and no recessed corners in the outer walls—all of which suggest that emperors, taking their cues from shinobi, made efforts over time to eliminate these vulnerabilities. However, while it is ideal to eliminate weaknesses so they do not require guarding, it is not always possible.

In this chapter, we'll discuss the concept of guarding and its proposed place within the five functions of cybersecurity. We will then discuss how to identify the vulnerable areas that may require guarding with threat modeling.

The Concept of Guarding

Guarding is the act of exercising protective control over assets by observing the environment, detecting threats, and taking preventative action. For example, the lord of a castle identifies a fairly large water drainage pipe in the castle wall as a weak point. The lord retains the pipe, which performs an important function in allowing water to exit, but requires a guard to stand nearby, preventing attackers from using the pipe as a means of access.

In general, organizations tend to keep cybersecurity staff in the dark about weak systems, network blind spots, or vulnerable attack vectors that should be guarded with special care. Some organizations assume it's entirely the cybersecurity staff's responsibility to discover security flaws in the network. Many stakeholders have not identified these attack vectors in the first place, or if no commercial solution exists or no commonly accepted countermeasure can be applied easily, they simply ignore the weaknesses and hope they will not be exploited.

In some instances, management directs security personnel *not* to perform basic logging, scanning, or patching of legacy systems for fear that touching them will disrupt business operations. In more political organizations, it's common for a threat to not be recognized as a valid concern unless it's identified through a formal documentation process. Imagine seeing that a castle is missing its west wall, reporting this obvious vulnerability to the king, and having the king dismiss your concerns because his guards have not mentioned it in their official reports.

Guarding Within a Cybersecurity Framework

The *National Institute of Standards and Technology (NIST) Cybersecurity Framework*[4] seeks to prevent these common missteps and improve organizations' resilience to cyber threats through five core cybersecurity functions: identify, protect, detect, respond, and recover. These functions help identify vulnerabilities in networks and systems by using common information security tools and processes.

For instance, most organizations begin the process of identifying weaknesses by conducting vulnerability or application scans of systems on their network—this is the *identify* function. Effective and reliable, these scans identify obvious security issues such as unpatched software, active accounts with blank passwords, default factory credentials, unparameterized input, and SSH ports open to the internet. Next comes the *protect* function. Upon discovery of an unsecured system, the scanner documents the problem, and then security staff fixes or mitigates the vulnerability with patches; configuration changes; or long-term architectural, security system, or software implementations.

If the security staff is unable to protect a system that has been identified as an attack vector, I believe they should *guard* it through human controls. However, a guard function is missing from the NIST framework. Instead, we move straight to the *detect* function: the security staff attempts to detect an adversary by monitoring and investigating anomalous events. Once the security staff detects infiltration, only then do they execute the *respond* function by containing the threat, neutralizing the threat, and reporting it.

Last is the *recovery* function: restoring the systems and data to operational status, as well as improving their ability to resist future attacks.

While essential to a robust security profile, these safeguards are prevention-, protection-, or response-based functions. The cybersecurity industry rarely applies the concept of guarding—using human controls and protection—to information systems, because it's not feasible for a human defender to manually inspect and approve every email, web page, file, or packet that leaves or enters the environment in the way that a gate guard could watch people or packages entering a building.

For example, computers with 1GB network connections can process more than 100,000 packets per second, far more than any human could inspect. Instead of using human guards, defenders either rely heavily on automated security controls or simply accept/ignore risk as part of doing business. Guarding can still be feasible within a modern digital network, however, if guards are inserted only into areas that need special care and attention, such as the most likely attack vectors. This is why threat modeling to identify these areas in your organization will be useful.

Threat Modeling

The closest thing to guarding in cybersecurity is *threat hunting*, which involves vigorously seeking out indicators of infiltration in logs, forensic data, and other observable evidence. Few organizations perform threat hunting, and even in those that do, a hunter's job is to detect, not guard.

Nonetheless, it's important that cyber defenders go beyond the conventional framework, continually imagining new ways in which networks and information systems could be attacked, and implement the necessary defenses. To this end, defenders can use threat modeling to implement information flow controls and design safeguards against threats rather than simply react to them.

Typically performed only by cyber-mature organizations, threat modeling involves documenting a *data flow diagram (DFD)*, which describes the flow of data and processes inside systems. DFDs are typically documented as a type of flowchart, but can be roughly represented by a detailed network map. A DFD can be used as a tool for structured analysis of your attack surface that allows you to think of attack scenarios within the parameters of the documented information systems. It doesn't require vulnerability scanning, proving of the attack scenario by red teams, or validation from a compliance framework, and organizations don't need to wait for a security incident to prove a threat model before acting to guard against the vulnerability.

Understanding the modern cyber equivalents to "recessed corners of a castle's stone walls, rubbish disposal areas, water pipes, and nearby woods or bushes" of your environment could help you identify attack vectors that may need guarding with special care.

Consider this example: as part of their nightly duties, a security guard pulls on every doorknob in an office to make sure the doors are locked. If they find an unlocked door, they lock it, secure the keys, and file a security incident ticket.

It is later determined that a security incident occurred because door keys were copied or stolen, so the organization adds a second-level authenticator control (such as a keypad or badge reader) to the doors, changes the locks, and issues new keys. These new preventive security controls satisfy compliance auditors, and the ticket reporting the unsecured doors is closed. The chief information security officer (CISO) even hires a red team to perform a narrow-scope physical penetration test of the new door-locking mechanisms, and the team confirms that they were denied access because of the enhanced security measures.

However, once we conduct threat-modeling exercises, we identify that it's possible to push moveable ceiling tiles out of the way and climb over the office wall, bypassing the new security measures altogether. To counteract this, we could add controls, such as security cameras or motion detectors in the ceiling crawl space, or we could install solid, tunnel-resistant ceilings and floors. Guards could even be hired and trained to look for evidence of disturbed ceiling tiles, ceiling particulate on the floor, or footprints on the walls. Guarding against this threat would require that guards be posted inside the room or stationed within the ceiling crawl space, armed with the authority and tools to protect the room from intruders.

The feasibility of implementing such countermeasures is low—you might be laughed out of your manager's office for even suggesting them. It's easy to see why organizations are more likely to accept or ignore certain threats than attempt to repel them, and this is likely why the NIST Cybersecurity Framework doesn't include a guard function. If thoughtfully informed by detailed threat modeling and carefully implemented in a creative and deliberate manner, however, this guard-centric mode of thinking can bolster the security of information systems and networks.

An example of a scenario suitable for the implementation of the guard function is in *jump boxes*. Jump boxes are systems that span two or more network boundaries, allowing administrators to log in remotely to the jump box from one network and "jump" to another network to gain access to it. The conventional cybersecurity framework advises hardening jump box systems by patching all known vulnerabilities, restricting access with various firewall rules, and monitoring audit logs for anomalous events such as unauthorized access. However, such technical controls are often attacked or bypassed. A guard, on the other hand, could physically disconnect the internal network cable from the other network and connect it directly only after verifying with the administrator that they have approval to execute remote commands against these systems. The guard could also actively monitor actions on the machine in real time and forcibly terminate the session anytime they observe malicious or unauthorized actions. Implementing the guard function in this way might mean hiring a human guard to sit in the data center to protect both physical and remote access to these sensitive systems.

Using Threat Modeling to Find Potential Attack Vectors

The basic steps for identifying attack vectors are to follow the guidelines for threat modeling, starting with creating a DFD. Once potential attack vectors are identified from the DFD, the shinobi scrolls recommend inspecting them to determine what technical security controls can be implemented to protect them. Then, as a last resort, use guards to defend these areas as well. You can use the network map you made in the previous chapter to help create the DFD or use it as a rough substitute.

1. *Model your information systems.* Create an accurate DFD with the help of your organization's network, security, development, business, and other IT system owners and experts. It does not need to use Unified Modeling Language (UML) or other advanced

concepts—it simply needs to accurately represent your systems and the information within them. Note that large, complex systems can easily take a team more than six months to diagram.

2. *STRIDE and guard.* STRIDE is a threat-modeling methodology developed by Microsoft[5] to describe what could go wrong in an information system. The acronym comes from the ways in which an attacker could violate six properties of the system:

Spoofing Identity	=	Authentication
Tampering with Data	=	Integrity
Repudiation/Deniability	=	Nonrepudiation
Information Disclosure	=	Confidentiality
Denial of Service	=	Availability
Elevation of Privilege	=	Authorization

To use STRIDE, you will review your DFD and, at every point where there is data input, data processing, data output, or other data flows/rules, hypothesize how an adversary may threaten it. For example, if a system requires a thumbprint to verify a user's identity before allowing access to the system, you might consider how they could spoof the thumbprint to impersonate a different user. Similarly, you could think about ways they could tamper with the fingerprint database to insert their print, or you could explore a scenario in which the attacker causes the fingerprint scanner to go down, allowing unauthorized access through a weaker authentication process.

After learning this framework, you can use it to challenge any imagined threat models that do not accurately represent your systems or scenarios that do not describe how a plausible threat impacts a specific component, surface, or vector. This may require inviting technical subject matter experts to threat-modeling sessions.

Suppose, for example, that an organizational threat-modeling session produces the following scenario: "The threat of malware compromises the integrity of internal databases."

This threat is not properly modeled. Among other pieces of critical information, the scenario does not describe how malware could be delivered and installed. Nor does it describe how the malware would compromise the integrity of the database: does it encrypt, delete, or corrupt data? It does not describe which vectors allow the threat to impact the system, and it doesn't consider the information flow and controls currently in place or provide realistic countermeasures. If, for example, we determined that the most plausible way to infect an internal business database with malware would be through a malicious USB drive, then security may need to draft policies detailing how staff must use USB drives or install cameras to monitor access to USB ports. The organization might decide to grant security the ability to turn USBs on or off, dictate which drives can interface with USBs, control the information flow and direction of USB ports, inspect the files on USB drives before granting access to the requestor, control access with hardware or software locks, or even hot-glue the USB ports shut. Such measures, resulting from thorough threat modeling, allow security personnel to guard against specific threats with special care, rather than having to accept the risk or being limited to protect and detect functions.

3. *Do not advertise bolted-on security.* Threat modeling is an iterative, infinite process of evaluating new threats and developing protective countermeasures. In your haste to protect your systems, avoid the use of *shinobi-gaeshi* security controls—defensive efforts that may backfire by drawing attention to your vulnerable areas. Often because of time, resource, or operational restrictions, you may have taken only half measures that a motivated, sophisticated threat actor can defeat. For example, hot glue in a USB port can be removed with isopropyl alcohol. Where possible, assess the viability of a pure security-first defense approach.

   In the USB threat example, the USB interacts with the hardware abstraction layer (HAL) that sits below the OS kernel. It cannot be fully protected or mitigated with software and policy controls, as those exist above the kernel and can be bypassed. Therefore, a more complete solution might be to implement a motherboard and chassis configuration in which USB ports do not even exist. In contrast, hot glue in the USB port advertises to motivated threat actors that you have not properly addressed the security of USBs, and it will likely be a successful attack vector for them should they be able to pull it free—just as the shinobi pulled out the spikes bolted onto pipes and walls in ancient times.

> **CASTLE THEORY THOUGHT EXERCISE**
>
> Consider the scenario in which you are the ruler of a medieval castle with valuable assets within your stronghold. You receive credible threat intelligence that a ninja plans to infiltrate your castle and set fire to the food supply in your dungeon. The dungeon has multiple ingress/egress points whereby staff transport food, moving freely and without monitoring.
>
> Consider what measures guards could take to protect food from a fire in the basement. What staffing changes could you implement to control human interactions with the food and protect it from harm? What measures would ensure that guards could quickly observe, report, and respond to fire in the basement? How could guards detect a ninja infiltrating the basement, and what architectural changes could be made to mitigate blind spots that allow access to the food?
>
> Note that while it would be advisable to have backup food supplies in alternate locations or to store the food within fire-resistant material, for this exercise, consider how guards could control and protect the food rather than directly address the fire threat.

Recommended Security Controls and Mitigations

Where relevant, each recommendation is presented with an applicable security control from the NIST 800-53 standard, and it should be evaluated through the lens of guarding with special care.

1. Review the results of auditors, red team assessments, vulnerability scans, and incident reports to find vulnerabilities in your environment that cannot be easily patched or mitigated with controls (that is, those that require special guarding). [CA-2: Security Assessments; CA-8: Penetration Testing; IR-6: Incident Reporting | (2) Vulnerabilities Related to Incidents; RA-5: Vulnerability Scanning]
2. Perform threat modeling of your environment to identify vulnerabilities. Then determine which ones can be designed out of your environment. Explore the concept of guarding security functions and apply those controls to threats that cannot be easily purged. [SA-8: Security Engineering Principles; SA-14: Criticality Analysis; SA-15: Development Process, Standards, and Tools | (4) Threat Modeling/Vulnerability Analysis; SA-17: Developer Security Architecture and Design]

3. To deter, protect against, and ensure rapid response to threats, hire real-time security personnel as guards and integrate them into vulnerable areas of business operations. [IR-10: Integrated Information Security Analysis Team]

Debrief

This chapter has helped you think about the places in a network environment that an adversary is likely to target for infiltration. You have also been introduced to the concept of guarding with direct human interaction between information systems and processes. You may have utilized your network map from the previous chapter or created your own data flow diagram (DFD) as a representation of your environment to identify likely attack vectors and potential STRIDE threats that could be mitigated with guards.

In the next chapter, we'll explore a "xenophobic" security concept used by the ancient ninja that may hinder adversaries from finding any common ground or footholds in your environment to even start their attack vector process.

3

XENOPHOBIC SECURITY

If you accept strangers without much thought, the enemy shinobi may come in disguised as a stranger and seek information from the inside.

If beggars or outcasts come near the guardhouse,
treat them in a rough way and clear them off.
—Yoshimori Hyakushu #91

In this chapter, we'll explore the concept of *xenophobic security*—or security based on a distrust of outsiders—and how it can be applied as a type of anti-privilege protection domain. To illustrate this idea, we'll consider the hostile environment that shinobi had to navigate.

Shinobi trying to infiltrate villages and gather information in plain sight faced a ubiquitous challenge: the pervasive xenophobia of the medieval Japanese. The isolation of the country's villages gave rise to unique dialects, hairstyles, clothing, and other customs that made each community its own social ecosystem.[1] The small populations in these remote locales meant everyone usually knew everyone else and an outsider obviously did not fit in.[2]

As outsiders, the shinobi were routinely viewed with suspicion and followed. They could not move freely around town, and they were often prevented from renting rooms and purchasing food. Certainly, villagers would not share information with them. The community's xenophobia reduced the shinobi to anti-privileged status.

Understanding Anti-Privilege

To grasp the significance of anti-privilege, let's first examine the concept of *privilege*, which in cybersecurity refers to the permissions a user has to perform actions, such as reading or deleting a file. Modern computer systems have a ringed architecture with different levels of privilege:

ring4 Default (unprivileged)

ring3 Normal user (least privileged)

ring2 Superuser (admin)

ring1 Root (elevated privilege)

ring0 Kernel (system)

For example, a common villager (least privileged) or a cat (unprivileged) may be able to leave the town any time they want. A village chief with elevated privilege has the additional permissions to lock the town gates at will. However, a foreigner suspected of mischief (anti-privilege) could have less permission than a stray cat (unprivileged) and therefore would not be allowed to leave the village.

This distinction between anti-privileged and unprivileged status is important. In some computer systems, actions such as logging out are considered unprivileged and are given by default to actors in all rings. Untrustworthy processes/users can use these default unprivileged capabilities to enable more malicious actions or operate somewhat freely to further more sophisticated goals. On the other hand, by denying an anti-privileged process from logging out, you may prevent it from clearing its session history or evidence of its existence in the first place. Consider if computer systems could adopt a ring5 (anti-privilege) security control. Using our village as an example, one could speculatively force a suspected shinobi to submit to searches and interrogation before being allowed to leave the village. In this way, the village could catch thieves and spies. Furthermore, by making infiltrators' jobs that much more risky and expensive, villages undoubtedly deterred hostile activity.

To infiltrate such a xenophobic village, a shinobi first had to memorize and practice a range of culturally distinct disguises, becoming fluent in the style of dress, dialect, grooming techniques, monetary customs, and social mores unique to the location.

When the cultural disguise was mastered, the shinobi still needed to have a convincing reason to be in the village; usually this was job related. The *Ninpiden* describes how shinobi could appropriate a generic cover story, perhaps claiming to be a monk on a spiritual journey, a merchant, a beggar, or even a samurai traveling on orders from his lord. (Though also recognized by villagers as an outsider, a samurai did not incur the same level of distrust as a potential fugitive or bandit.)

While in disguise around people of the same job, class, or caste, shinobi were advised to demonstrate enough knowledge to appear believable in the profession but also to act dumb and in need of help to perform common tasks. Feigning ignorance served to deceive a target about the shinobi's true intelligence while flattering the target's own, causing them to lower their guard and offer information freely. The *Ninpiden* lists specific targets shinobi should attempt to win over with these tactics, such as local deputies, magistrates, doctors, monks, and others who may work in the presence of the local lord or authority. These targets typically had information valuable to the mission.[3]

Note that the social hierarchies of the medieval Japanese village resemble the privilege ring structure in modern computer systems, or even the layered segmentation of computer networks in which the outside layers, like a DMZ, are the least trusted. Likewise, normal villagers (the least privileged) would be unable to interact with the lord who is at the center, or ring0.

We can apply the way shinobi identified likely targets to a cybersecurity context. Just as shinobi targeted those who were, metaphorically, closer to ring0 or who had access to ring0, so will modern threat actors target privileged classes of systems/users. Thus, defenders should consider what the computer equivalents of such high-status individuals as monks and magistrates are in their systems. Furthermore, you should consider what disguises a modern threat actor might use to approach the more privileged systems/users.

The Problem with Interoperability and Universal Standards

Whether they consciously think about it or not, *interoperability* is a top priority for technology consumers: people expect their devices, apps, systems, and software to work seamlessly with new and old versions and across different platforms, as well as interchangeably with other makes and models. The International Organization for Standardization (ISO), the International Electrotechnical Commission (IEC), the Internet

Engineering Task Force (IETF), the Internet Society (ISOC), and other governing bodies have established widely agreed-upon standards for how technology is designed and should operate and integrate.

These efforts have produced many of the ISO standards, Request for Comments (RFC), and other interoperability protocols that make computers more accessible, not to mention easier to build, manage, diagnose, repair, program, network, and run. A prime example is the Plug and Play (PnP) standard introduced in 1995, which directs a host system to detect and accept any foreign device plugged into it via USB, PCI, PCMCIA, PCIe, FireWire, Thunderbolt, or other means and then autoconfigure, load, install, and interface automatically.

Unfortunately, when the goals are to establish functionality and maintain its operability, security is almost never a priority. In fact, the PnP standard—which facilitates the trust and acceptance of unfamiliar entities—was built to the exact opposite of the xenophobic security standard held by the medieval Japanese. For example, an unfamiliar system can connect to a network as an outsider and request an IP address from Dynamic Host Configuration Protocol (DHCP), ask for directions from the local router, query the authoritative DNS server for the names of other devices, and obtain local information from Address Resolution Protocol (ARP), Server Message Block (SMB), Web Proxy Auto Discovery (WPAD), and other protocols designed to ease the burden of compatibility. You plug the system into the network and it works, demonstrating behavior users expect and desire. However, the cybersecurity industry would benefit from being more "xenophobic" in its networking protocols.

To mitigate weaknesses resulting from PnP-like accessibility, security controls such as Network Access Control (NAC) and Group Policy Objects (GPO) have been introduced. On host systems, these technologies safeguard against potentially malicious foreign devices that physically connect to internal networks or systems.

NACs typically lock down the DHCP, assigning unrecognized computers to guest IP subnets or unprivileged VLANs. This allows foreign systems to connect to the internet for general access but segments them from the rest of the trusted network. Such behavior is especially desirable for conference rooms and lobbies so that external business partners and vendors can operate without exposing the network to threats.

GPO on local hosts enforces what types of devices—external hard drives, USBs, media readers, and the like—can be configured and installed on a system. GPO can even whitelist known applications within an organization while simultaneously blocking all unfamiliar software from downloading or installing on the host system.

However, these security controls are notable exceptions. From RJ45 Ethernet jacks using the EIA/TIA-561 and Yost standards to packet-based networking using the IEEE 802 standards—and everything in between—most technologies are built with transparent, widely known, default standards that ensure quick and easy use across foreign systems and networks, leaving them vulnerable to unauthorized rogue systems that may conduct network discovery, reconnaissance, sniffing, and communication.

Developing Unique Characteristics for Your Environment

Having unique properties and characteristics in your IT inventory will help to distinguish your assets from rogue assets that may enter your environment and even protect your network from compromise. These characteristics are observable through inspection or analysis, but their use should not be publicly disclosed, as such disclosure would defeat the countermeasures. Most elements within modern IT systems and software are configurable, and such configuration changes effectively create a xenophobic IT model in your systems.

Recently introduced commercial products that use a zero-trust model can help make your network or systems "xenophobic" to unfamiliar systems, software, and devices through a combination of technical protocols and distrust. Strict whitelists and authentication/authorization procedures can achieve similar results, but a proper solution would introduce a computer version of "dialects"—settings, customs, and other unique characteristics that deviate from universal computing standards. Systems or devices connecting to your internal network would need to be "indoctrinated" to the unique culture of your organization, while unindoctrinated servers, components, networking devices, and protocols would distrust or reject the unfamiliar foreign agent and alert the security team to its presence.

With some creativity and engineering, these cultural computer identifiers could be implemented at any layer of the Open Systems Interconnection (OSI) model (application, presentation, session, transport, networking, data link, physical) to identify network outsiders and provide an additional layer of defense against adversaries. Whether it's transposing certain wires in hidden adapters of RJ45 jacks, expecting secret handshakes (SYN, SYN ACK, ACK-PUSH) at the TCP/IP level, or using reserved bits in the Ethernet header, a xenophobic solution should be modular, customizable, and unique per instance.

> **CASTLE THEORY THOUGHT EXERCISE**
>
> Consider the scenario in which you're the ruler of a medieval castle with valuable assets within. You notice that one of the local fishermen, who sells fish to your cooks, preserves the fish in an unfamiliar fashion and has a strange dialect. When asked about his unique storage methods, he claims he does it that way because the fish tastes better. He doesn't have a surname you recognize.
>
> What culturally unique identifiers could you use to determine whether the fisherman is an outsider, and how might you apply that test? If the fisherman claimed he was born in your village but temporarily moved away, how would you verify his story? If you couldn't verify his story and suspected him of being a spy, how would you manage the threat without exiling or executing a potentially innocent fisherman? To answer these questions, you'll need to consider three scenarios: the fisherman is indeed a spy, the fisherman is not a spy, and the fisherman's purpose is impossible to know. You can ask a partner to play the part of the strange fisherman by secretly choosing one of the roles beforehand, or you can play both roles of interrogator and fisherman in your head.
>
> This exercise helps you think deeply about asset identification using xenophobic mental models while avoiding technical discussions of computer standards and inventory control. While the scenario is fictitious, shinobi likely disguised themselves as fishermen sometimes, as such a cover would give them an excuse to loiter for hours, chat with locals, and perform reconnaissance on targets.

Recommended Security Controls and Mitigations

Where relevant, the following recommendations are presented with an applicable security control from the NIST 800-53 standard. Each should be evaluated with the concept of xenophobic security in mind.

1. Inspect systems to determine whether their specifications or requirements deviate from the previously agreed-upon baseline configuration. [CM-2: Baseline Configuration]
2. Maintain documentation of all information systems in your organization so you can more readily identify foreign systems in your environment. [CM-8: Information System Inventory]
3. Use encrypted information, embedded data, special data types, or metadata (for example, padding all packets to be a certain size) as special identifiers in communications so that filters can

identify and restrict unfamiliar traffic. [AC-4: Information Flow Enforcement; SA-4: Acquisition Process]

4. Restrict the implementation and knowledge of xenophobic identifiers to newly acquired systems and devices. [SA-4: Acquisition Process]
5. Embed xenophobic inspection as a security control for identifying and authenticating systems and devices in your organization. [IA-3: Device Identification and Authentication]

Debrief

This chapter described the historically xenophobic environment for shinobi that required the investment of time and effort, as well as advanced techniques, to perform preparatory reconnaissance using open disguise tactics before actual target reconnaissance could begin. You learned the concept of anti-privilege and how to create unique internal characteristics to identify rogue assets or users in your environment. Now you may be able to identify key resources or people who are likely targets in your environment that you perhaps hadn't considered as attack vectors from previous threat-modeling exercises, and you can then consider the systems or accounts that work closely with these potential targets.

However, by using the correct insignia, clothing, hairstyle, accent, and other characteristics, shinobi could evade the xenophobic inspections detailed in this chapter. Therefore, in the next chapter, we'll explore the matched-pair security technique historically used by Japanese lords to detect shinobi who might otherwise infiltrate their fortification by using a disguise.

IDENTIFICATION CHALLENGE

Though there are ancient ways for identifying marks, passwords, and certificates, unless you invent new ones and rotate them, the enemy will manage to infiltrate by having similar fake ones.

During a night attack, you may have the enemy follow you and get into the ranks of your allies. To prevent this, have a prearranged policy—a way to identify your allies.
—Yoshimori Hyakushu #27

Imagine the following historical scenario: after dispatching a large group of troops on a night raid, a military commander must open the gates to allow them back inside their fortification. Night raids helped win battles, but they also presented opportunities for a counterattack. An enemy shinobi could forge or steal a uniform from the attacking troops and blend into their formation as they returned to their base.

To combat this threat, commanders implemented a onetime password for the raiders to use before they could pass through the gate—but this password was easily defeated: the disguised shinobi would overhear the password when it was spoken by the soldier ahead of them in line. So commanders tried other identification methods. Some required the raiders to all wear underwear of a certain secret color that could be inspected upon their return, but clever shinobi would carry or wear undergarments in multiple colors, then selectively pull back layers of underwear so only the correct color would be visible during inspection. Additional countermeasures included changing passwords multiple times per day (which still didn't prevent a shinobi from overhearing the current password) and unique uniform insignia or tokens (which a shinobi could steal from the corpse of a dead soldier after the raid).

The shinobi categorized these techniques as either the art of open disguise (*yo-nin*, which translates literally to "light shinobi") or the art of hidden infiltration (*in-nin*, which translates literally to "dark shinobi"). In this case, *open* refers to being plainly visible; for example, the attacker could wear the uniform of a defending soldier, fully expecting to be seen. *Hidden*, on the other hand, refers to trying not be seen, such as by using camouflage or blending into the shadows. Many of the assorted open disguise techniques described in *Bansenshūkai* could be used both offensively and defensively. Shinobi knew not only how to use these techniques for their own attacks but also how to spot enemy infiltrators. It was common for spies to replicate uniforms and crests or overhear passwords, so shinobi developed identification countermeasures to distinguish their allies from enemies.

One such identification technique was *matched pairs*, word combination challenges used to authenticate allies.[1] This technique is also known as *countersigns* or *challenge-response authentication*. The matched-pairs technique worked as follows: an unidentified person approached a guard at the gate of a castle and requested entry. The guard first checked to ensure that the stranger was wearing the correct uniform and bearing the proper crest. If they were, then the guard uttered a word—"tree," for example. If the stranger did not respond with the correct prearranged match—"forest"—the guard knew they were dealing with an enemy. While the *Bansenshūkai* states that matched-pair phrases should be simple enough that "lower-rank" people can remember them, it advises against using common associations that an adversary might guess. So, instead of "snow" and "mountain," a more desirable pair might be "snow" and "Mount Fuji." The scroll recommends that shinobi work with commanders to generate 100 different pairs of matching words every 100 days and use a new pair every day.[2] This large number of matching pairs would allow a sentry to rotate randomly through the list (if necessary) as each troop approached, making it unlikely that a disguised enemy could overhear the answer to the challenge word they would receive.

Matched pairs were used to reveal possible infiltrators. If the stranger answered the challenge incorrectly, they were quickly detained, interrogated, and possibly killed. Knowing these consequences, *Bansenshūkai* recommends that shinobi attempting to infiltrate an enemy camp style their appearance, behavior, and speech as that of a slovenly or lower-class soldier. This way, if they were asked to answer a matched-pair challenge they didn't know, they could convincingly claim ignorance.[3] Some readers may note that their financial institution has started implementing matched-word or image pairs for online authentication, but it should be noted that these websites do not require 100 different pairs and do not update them frequently, if at all. A small pool of static matched pairs makes it possible for an adversary to observe all the pairs and then perform unauthorized actions with the stolen authentication responses.

These historical examples underscore the challenges in trying to safeguard authentication from an advanced and dynamic adversary. In this chapter, we will touch on how difficult it can be to prove your identity, along with the various factors used in information assurance (IA) to authenticate someone's identity. I will mention some of the techniques that modern cyber threat actors use to thwart the best efforts to authenticate only the correct people and highlight analogous shinobi tactics that illustrate why authentication will be a challenge for the foreseeable future. I will also provide readers with guidance on how they might apply shinobi authentication techniques to modern applications. The overall goal of this chapter is to help readers grasp the essential issues involved in this identification problem rather than getting lost in the expansive knowledge domain that authentication and cryptography have become.

Understanding Authentication

Authentication is the process of confirming a user's identity before granting access to information systems, data, networks, physical grounds, and other resources. Authentication processes confirm user identities by asking for something the user knows, something the user has, or something the user is. For example, an authenticator might ask for a password (something the user knows), a token (something the user has), or a biometric (something the user is). Depending on the level of security necessary, organizations require *single-factor*, *two-factor*, or *multifactor* authentication.

Mature organizations might also use *strong authentication*, which uses multiple layers of multifactor credentials. For example, the first step of strong authentication might require a username, password, and fingerprint, while the second step authenticates with a token and a onetime code sent over SMS. Increasingly, industry professionals are contemplating the feasibility of a fourth factor, such as a trusted person in the organization who would confirm the user's identity. Interestingly, the matched-pair shinobi scenario starts with this test; the challenge is used only if no one in the area can validate the stranger's identity.

Authentication failure is a critical security flaw. Users' authenticated identities are tied to permissions that allow them to perform specific, often privileged, actions. An adversary who successfully piggybacks on a valid user's authenticated connection has free access to the user's resources and can conduct malicious activities on information systems, data, and networks.

Unfortunately, the authentication process is imperfect. Despite a slew of cyber authentication measures, it's currently not possible to verify the identity of a user or process with complete certainty, as nearly every existing verification test can be spoofed (*spoofing* is the use of false data to impersonate another entity) or compromised. Adversaries use numerous techniques to steal passwords, intercept tokens, copy authentication hashes or tickets, and forge biometrics. If attackers gain unauthorized access to identity management systems, such as domain controllers, they can create and authenticate to fraudulently forged accounts. After users authenticate, their identities are rarely challenged during a session, unless password reentry is required to conduct privileged tasks. Similarly, shinobi in disguise could wander around the inside of a castle without being challenged—in both cases, it's assumed those inside have been authenticated.

Security technologies are evolving to fight authentication threats. One emerging solution, called *continuous authentication* or *active authentication*, constantly verifies user identities after the initial login. However, because continuous authentication dialogs might hinder the user experience, techniques are also being developed to monitor authentication through typing style, mouse movement, or other behavioral traits associated with user identities. Such techniques would catch adversaries who were physically accessing logged-in systems that had been left unattended, locking them out. This would also work with unauthorized remote access methods, such as Remote Desktop Protocol (RDP) sessions. Such techniques could identify attackers even if they used valid credentials and authenticators to log in. Of course, a person's behavior may change. Moreover, even specific behaviors can be mimicked or simulated by sophisticated adversaries by incorporating user behavior reconnaissance into their attacks.

One possible implementation of the matched-pair model involves a human-machine interface that uses passive brainwave sensors connected to a system that verifies identity based on how the user thinks. Research demonstrates that humans generate unique brain patterns when they see an object with which they have interacted before or have a specific thought association. As such, showing a user controlled stimuli (such as matched-pair word or image combinations), monitoring the brain's electrical responses, and matching them to a user profile could accurately authenticate the user. With enough unique challenge pairs dynamically generated with stylized permutations, it's unlikely that adversaries could replay or simulate a user's brainwave activity when prompted.

In the next section, we'll discuss some techniques you can use for matched-pair authentications.

Developing Matched-Pair Authenticators

Following are a few suggestions for developing matched-pair authenticators and ideas for applying them.

Work with the right commercial authentication vendors. Seek out vendors that use challenge phrase authentication that is distinct from a user's password, account name, or other identifying information that an adversary could compromise. While some financial organizations use matched-pair challenge phrases before they authorize account changes, unfortunately this method is typically used only when the user reports they've lost or forgotten their password, and the challenge phrases are static and don't change.

Develop new authentication systems. An authentication product might integrate with identity controls to present a matched-pair challenge to an authenticated user whenever they attempt to perform privileged actions, such as admin/root/system commands. Under this protocol, even if adversaries observed one or several challenge pairs, their request to perform privileged actions would be denied.

An ideal product uses two forms of matched-pair challenges: daily and user preset. The daily challenge, disseminated nondigitally in areas that are visible only to authorized personnel, challenges on-premise authentication requests with a word or image and asks the user to respond with the match. All other employees, including remote/VPN employees, establish a large set of matching word pairs that are not likely to be forgotten or misinterpreted. The organization chooses the pairs at random or rotates them to quickly pinpoint unauthorized users that have been authenticated on the network. (Note that to prevent an adversary from inserting their own matched pairs for compromised or spoofed credentials, there must be secured transmission, storage, and auditing of new matched pairs to the active challenge system.) Consider using a one-way interface to insert matched pairs in a secure controlled information facility (SCIF) or segmented room that requires manual authentication and authorization to enter and use. Other mechanisms could allow organizations to ambush an unidentified user by requiring access to their microphone, camera, location, running processes, running memory or cache, desktop screenshot, and other information on their connecting system, thereby better identifying the origin and identity of the threat.

> **CASTLE THEORY THOUGHT EXERCISE**
>
> Consider the scenario in which you are the ruler of a medieval castle with valuable assets within. You successfully complete a raid on an enemy army and return to your castle. A soldier in your army wishes to approach you and present the severed head of an enemy commander you defeated in battle, as is traditional. This warrior wears your uniform and displays the correct crest, knows the password of the day, appears to know their way around the interior of your castle, and waits for permission to enter your inner stronghold to pay their respects.
>
> Consider how you might handle suspicious individuals who pass normal authentication checks requesting privileged access. What existing security protocols or authentication processes would help you determine whether this warrior is an enemy shinobi in disguise who intends to do you harm? Other than outright rejecting the warrior's request, how might you mitigate the risk if you cannot verify their identity?

Recommended Security Controls and Mitigations

Where relevant, recommendations are presented with an applicable security control from the NIST 800-53 standard. Each should be evaluated in the context of matched-pair identification and authentication challenge responses.

1. Implement session locks after set periods of time for privileged accounts, upon privileged user requests, or in reaction to suspicious behavior. Only reestablish access after the user provides a matched-pair challenge response. (A session lock may be preferable to a normal password lock because the challenge pair match is a single click or a simpler word than the user's account password.) [AC-11: Session Lock; IA-2: Identification and Authentication (Organizational Users) | (1) Network Access to Privileged Accounts | (3) Local Access to Privileged Accounts;

IA-10: Adaptive Identification and Authentication; IA-11: Re-Authentication]

2. Identify, document, and enforce security controls on which user actions may be performed on a system without passing the matched-pair challenge response—for example, contacting technical support or making emergency calls. [AC-14: Permitted Actions Without Identification or Authentication]
3. Develop matched-pair authentication processes that are resistant to replay attacks by establishing large sets of onetime challenge response authenticators. [IA-2: Identification and Authentication (Organizational Users) | (8) Network Access to Privileged Accounts—Replay Resistant]
4. Capture information that uniquely identifies user devices requesting authentication to gain intelligence on unidentified adversaries who fail the matched-pair challenge response. [IA-3: Device Identification and Authentication | (4) Device Attestation]
5. Require in-person matched-pair input to mitigate compromise of the challenge response identification system. [IA-4: Identifier Management | (7) In-Person Registration]
6. Physically and logically segregate the matched-pair challenge response system and enforce strict access controls to safeguard it against compromise. [IA-5: Authenticator Management | (6) Protection of Authenticators]

Debrief

This chapter highlighted the challenges faced by commanders who needed to verify the identity of their troops to prevent disguised shinobi from infiltrating their fortifications. You learned about the matched-pair identification technique, both how it was used by shinobi to detect enemies and what safeguards shinobi took against the technique when on the offensive. You also saw the modern analogs of this technique in computer security authentication and identification.

In the next chapter, you will use your understanding of authentication factors and historical challenge response to learn how two-step authentication is different from but complementary to matched pairs. I will discuss a concealed shinobi authentication technique, the double-sealed password, which can be used to detect sophisticated infiltrators.

5

DOUBLE-SEALED PASSWORD

Sometimes, a set of signs such as pinching the nose or holding the ear should be used with these passwords.

Aikei *identifying signs include techniques of* tachisuguri isuguri*—that is, standing and sitting while giving passwords.*
—Bansenshūkai, Yo-Nin II

Both *Bansenshūkai* and the *Gunpo Jiyoshu* scrolls describe an open-disguise detection protocol supposedly devised by 14th-century samurai Kusunoki Masashige.[1] *Tachisuguri isuguri* signal techniques use gestures, posture, or body positioning as a secret authentication factor, thus adding a layer of security to the password verification process. These techniques form what's called a *double-sealing*[2] password system, designed to catch disguised enemy shinobi, even if they could pass other authentication challenges with stolen passwords, identifying marks, and correct challenge response words.

In the most common example of tachisuguri isuguri, a person bearing the correct uniform and crest approaches a gate for entry. Not recognizing the stranger, the guard chooses to either sit or stand, then whispers a challenge word. If the visitor is an ally who has been briefed on the tachisuguri isuguri identification protocol, they perform the prearranged corresponding action in response—a non-obvious signal such as touching their nose or ear—and whisper the matching code word. The guard permits entry only if the stranger answers with both the correct code word and the correct physical movement. (There may be multiple ways to implement tachisuguri isuguri besides having the guard stand or sit, but unfortunately those methods are believed to be recorded in the *Teikairon* scroll, a lost supplemental section of *Bansenshūkai*.)[3]

The simple brilliance of this technique is that the act of standing or sitting is usually not given a passing thought. Even a malicious observer trying to impersonate authorized personnel would likely fail to notice this second, silent challenge response. They may watch 100 people enter a gate using the same passphrase while the guard sits (because he recognizes them all), and thus they will not see how the interaction differs when the guard stands. Tachisuguri isuguri was successful enough that even other shinobi did not have adequate countermeasures to thwart it, though *Bansenshūkai* instructs shinobi to mirror what guards do and say at all checkpoints, even if the guards seem to be acting without conscious intent;[4] if nothing else, this could confuse the guard into believing the shinobi is disorganized or simply stupid. The scrolls also provide this helpful advice to any shinobi who fails an unknown tachisuguri isuguri challenge: either think fast and talk fast—or run for your life.[5]

While the shinobi scrolls are not explicit in their definition of *double-sealing* and I have no evidence that the following hypothetical example actually occurred, I still feel it's a plausible illustration of the concept. Seals, often impressed into wax, have been used since ancient times to secure the content of a letter or scroll. Ideally, each sender of communications had a unique metal stamp and so was the only person who could make a particular mark, thus verifying a document's authenticity. In addition, if anyone other than the intended recipient were to open the letter or scroll, the seal would break, indicating that tampering had taken place.

However, spies learned that with special heating techniques, they could loosen the wax, remove the seal intact without harming the paper, read the missive's contents, and then reseal the original document or affix the seal to a newly forged document that included misinformation. A counter to the technique of melting the paper side of the wax seal may have been to "double-seal" the wax. Imagine that instead of a single metal stamp, the author used a clamp or vice-like device with both a front and back stamp. The underside of the wax wafer would be given a hidden seal on the underside of the paper that could be inspected only by ripping the document open. Attempts at melting the seal off the paper might preserve the top seal but would destroy the second hidden seal, thus making the communication double-sealed.

You can see why double-sealing was adopted as an effective countermeasure against attempts to penetrate a single seal and how it helped detect the activity of enemy shinobi. In this chapter, I will note the difference between two-factor authentication and second-step authentication. I'll also discuss how a modern second-step authenticator could be double-sealed to improve its effectiveness. I will then describe what I believe are the requirements and criteria for implementing double-sealed passwords, along with implementations that use existing authenticators and technology. My hope is that after performing the thought exercises and seeing my examples for implementations of double-sealed passwords, you will appreciate the genius of Kusunoki Masashige and try this highly intuitive idea out yourself.

A Concealed 2-Step Authentication

Increasingly, more cyber authentication and identification protocols require a layer of security on top of a password. This is called *2-step authentication*: the second step requires a user to perform an additional authentication action, such as providing a secret code or clicking a button on an *out-of-band device* (that is, one not involved in the rest of the authentication process). Note the slight difference from last chapter's two-*factor* authentication, which is used to prevent an adversary from accessing an account with stolen login credentials.

While the secret code (second step) can be randomized through software applications, it is typically generated each time using the same procedure. Unfortunately, this procedural rigidity gives adversaries a number of opportunities to compromise 2-step authentication methods. For example, a 2-step authentication code is typically sent in a cleartext, unsecured message that can be intercepted via phone cloning. In this case, a user who receives the code 12345 and enters that sequence at the passcode prompt also inadvertently provides the code to the adversary. The device used to authenticate—often a phone—can be stolen, hijacked via call forwarding, or cloned and used by the adversary to complete the authentication. Similarly, the out-of-band device established for delivering 2-step codes could be lost or stolen and used to bypass the authentication process, allowing the adversary to steal user-provided backup codes.

A 2-step code that was double-sealed with a tachisuguri isuguri technique could mitigate some of the weaknesses inherent in authentication procedures. Each user should be able to establish a prearranged tachisuguri isuguri identifier that is unique and meaningful to them. For instance, suppose a user has been instructed, either orally or by another secure method, to transpose the digits in their 2-step code across the number 5 on the keypad—1 becomes 9, 2 becomes 8, and so on[6]—but only when the code displays in red font rather than the normal green. This color change is the silent tachisuguri isuguri factor, triggered when the system finds the authentication request suspicious due to the odd hour, an unrecognized device or different IP address making the request, or other criteria. (To conceal it from adversaries who may be observing logins, this protocol should not be used too frequently.) Now, when the legitimate user receives the red code 12345, they know to respond 98765, while an adversary who has stolen the user's credentials but is not aware of the concealed rule enters 12345. This halts the authentication process, flags the account for investigation, and adds a 2-step authentication failure to the session. The 2-step authenticator then sends a hint—"Use authenticator protocol #5," perhaps along with another red code, such as 64831 (to which the user should respond 46279). Another incorrect response triggers further alerts or account lockout.

Developing Double-Sealed Passwords

A double-sealed security solution that integrates with industry-standard authorization controls would do the following:

1. Be used only when the user's identity is suspect, such as when users:
    - Log in from a new device, location, IP address, or time window
    - Report that their mobile device has been stolen or compromised
    - Lose their backup token, code, or password and need to reset their password
2. Use an out-of-band or side-channel communication method.
3. Use a secret, rule-based knowledge factor. Each user should be able to customize the protocol to create a unique set of concealed rules.
4. Leverage authentication factors that are easy to understand and remember, yet not obvious.
5. Allow rules to be stacked on top of each other in the case of wrong consecutive guesses or enough time passing between authentication attempts.

6. Enable the restriction, freezing, or locking out of an account that has failed authentication too many times. Most applications have a lockout after consecutive wrong passwords but not consecutive wrong 2-step authentication attempts.
7. Not be described in any help desk SOPs or other documentation. Employees should also refrain from talking openly about the double-sealed security layer.

Popularizing double-sealed security requires designers, engineers, and users to explore what is technically feasible and apply creative thinking. For example, consider the various input variations that can be used on existing mobile devices with a 2-step authentication app and require only that the user press Yes or No buttons to verify their identity. Following are some examples to demonstrate the range of possible responses when the user is given the tachisuguri isuguri signal in their 2-step authentication app:

1. The user rotates their screen upside down before selecting Yes, and the app performs a silent inspection of the DeviceOrientation status to test whether it equals `portraitUpsideDown`.
2. The user manipulates the physical volume buttons on the mobile device to set the `OutputVolume` to 0.0 (silent) or 1.0 (max) before selecting Yes, and the app performs a silent get of the volume float value to test whether it matches the intended value.
3. The user waits to select Yes until they observe the mobile device clock roll over to the next minute, when they immediately select Yes. The app performs a silent timestamp request to compare the time of selection to HH:MM:0*X*, where *X* is less than 3 seconds.
4. The user uses excessive pressure when selecting Yes on the mobile device, and the app performs a silent get of the `UITouch.force` of the event to determine whether it was greater than a preset threshold.
5. The user performs multiple quick taps of the Yes button on the mobile device, and the app performs a silent get of the `tapCount` of the `UIEvent` to determine if it is less than 2.
6. The user performs a gesture while selecting the Yes button on the mobile device, and the app performs a silent get of the `UIGestureRecognizer` to determine whether it was a `Pinch`, `LongPress`, `Swipe` (up, down, left, right), or `Rotation`.

CASTLE THEORY THOUGHT EXERCISE

Consider the scenario in which you are the ruler of a medieval castle with valuable assets within your stronghold. You've been told that your identifying marks, crests, secret signals, and other identification methods have been disclosed to enemy shinobi, who can replicate them and gain entry to your castle. You already change these passwords and signs three times a day, but you are told that shinobi can keep up with these changes, even though you are unsure how.

Consider how you might implement tachisuguri isuguri to catch enemy shinobi. Could you create nonbinary tachisuguri isuguri—in other words, concealed rules more complex than sitting or standing? How would you protect the tachisuguri isuguri authentication process to prevent the enemy shinobi from learning it? How could you layer tachisuguri isuguri to perform a test for operational security leaks among your personnel?

Recommended Security Controls and Mitigations

Where relevant, recommendations are presented with an applicable security control from the NIST 800-53 standard. Each should be evaluated in terms of 2-step (double-sealed) authentication.

1. Utilize Out-of-Band Authentication (OOBA) through a separate communication path to verify that authentication requests originate from verified users. [IA-2: Identification and Authentication | (13) Out-Of-Band Authentication]
2. Ensure that staff do not disclose the existence of concealed rules for 2-step authentication. [IA-5: Authenticator Management | (6) Protection of Authenticators]
3. Establish multiple double-sealed rules so the tachisuguri isuguri is not static. [IA-5: Authenticator Management | (7) No Embedded Unencrypted Static Authenticators]
4. Implement out-of-band communication and establish double-sealed rules to maintain confidentiality. [SC-37: Out-Of-Band Channels]
5. Carefully design error messages for failed authentication attempts so they do not reveal double-sealed password information that an adversary could exploit. [SI-11: Error Handling]

Debrief

In this chapter, you learned about an anti-shinobi authentication technique called the double-sealed password or tachisuguri isuguri. We covered the distinction between factors and steps in the identity verification process. Then we undertook a brief analysis of the criteria for a good tachisuguri isuguri authenticator along with several examples.

In the following chapter, we will discuss a shinobi concept called the hours of infiltration. You'll learn how certain hours of the day provide advantageous opportunities for infiltration. Understanding these time-based opportunities may help you choose when to implement or trigger tachisuguri isuguri authenticators in your organization, such as only during certain hours or on specific dates, to minimize the use of tachisuguri isuguri and safeguard its secrecy.

6

HOURS OF INFILTRATION

After waiting until the hour of Ox, the ninja realized that the guard had fallen asleep; everything was dead quiet, and the fire was out leaving all in darkness.

For a shinobi, it is essential to know the proper time. It always should be when the enemy is tired or has let their guard down.
—Yoshimori Hyakushu #5

When planning theft, espionage, sabotage, assassination, or other attacks, shinobi were not burdened by the spirit of good sportsmanship or fair play. To the contrary, they carefully considered the most "advisable times and advantageous positions"[1] to strike. The *Shoninki* stresses the importance of waiting to infiltrate until a target is distracted, lethargic, likely to be hasty in judgment, drinking and carousing, or simply exhausted; *Yoshimori Hyakushu* poem 63 states that one's tiredness "could be the cause of a serious blunder."[2] Shinobi were keen observers of such behavior and would often infiltrate when an enemy was cutting down trees, focused on setting up their own position, feeling tired after a fight, or changing guards.[3]

In studying their enemies' behavior, shinobi noticed that predictable human routines created windows of opportunity for attack. The scrolls divide the day into two-hour blocks and recommend planning infiltration during the blocks that tend to align with waking, eating, and sleeping. The appropriate hour depends on the type of attack. Night attacks, for instance, are best undertaken during the hours of the Boar (9:00 PM–11:00 PM), the Rat (11:00 PM–1:00 AM), and the Hare (5:00 AM–7:00 AM), animals of the Chinese zodiac.[4]

In addition, *Bansenshūkai* notes that some generals believed in "lucky days,"[5] divined through Chinese astrology. On these dates, attacks were thought predestined for victory. If shinobi could identify enemy commanders who believed these superstitions, they could use that information—for example, by predicting troop movements based on what the commander believed to be a lucky or unlucky day to leave camp. When it comes to predictable patterns of behavior, not much has changed. In this chapter, we'll discuss how the cyber equivalents of time-scheduled events can be targeted by threat actors.

Understanding Time and Opportunities

Because people still rise, work, eat, relax, and sleep on roughly the same schedule as the feudal Japanese, the hours of infiltration suggested by the scrolls align closely with when employees are distracted, exhausted, or made careless by the challenges of a modern workday—in other words, the times they're most vulnerable to attack. Consider the scrolls' time blocks in the context of network and information system activity and usage patterns:

Hour of the Hare (5:00 AM–7:00 AM) Users wake up and log in for the first time that day. Automated and manual systems boot up, causing spikes in event logs and syslogs.

Hour of the Horse (11:00 AM–1:00 PM) Many users take lunch breaks, meaning they log out of their systems or are timed out for being idle. They may also surf the web for personal reasons—they read the news, shop, check personal email, post to social media, or perform other activities that might trigger anomaly detection systems.

Hour of the Cock (5:00 PM–7:00 PM) Users find stopping points for their work. They save files and perhaps rush to finish, greatly increasing the risk of making mistakes in both their work and their cybersecurity vigilance. For example, a worker might unthinkingly open an attachment from an email that seems urgent. Users log out of accounts and systems en masse, but some are simply abandoned, left to time out and disconnect.

Hour of the Boar (9:00 PM–11:00 PM) Most users are away from work. Whether they're at home, out socializing, or getting ready for bed, the security of their work accounts and systems is probably not at the front of their minds. Organizations with staffed overnight SOC coverage typically see a shift change during this time, creating a window for attackers to strike between user logins or while SOC users are getting up to speed for the evening. The later the hour, the greater the possibility that users—even those used to late hours—get sleepy or let their guard down because things seem quiet.

Hour of the Rat (11:00 PM–1:00 AM) Networks and systems run backups or other scheduled maintenance, generating noise in network sensors and SIEMs. SOC users might have completed their daily security and maintenance tasks and could be immersed in project work.

Hour of the Tiger (3:00 AM–5:00 AM) Batch jobs, including processing log files, running diagnostics, and initiating software builds, typically execute during this time. Aside from SOC personnel, most users sink into the deepest part of their sleep cycle and are not active on their accounts.

Lucky Days There are also specific days, weeks, and months when adversaries are likely to target systems and users. While most organizational leaders don't base activity on "lucky days," threat actors are certainly aware of regularly scheduled upgrades or maintenance, when organizations take their defenses offline, and of three-day weekends and company holidays, when systems and accounts go largely unchecked. If potential threats have not been considered, irregularities in network traffic and system logs could go unnoticed during these windows of opportunity, allowing adversaries to conduct attacks, perform reconnaissance or command and control (C2) communication, spread malware, or execute data exfiltration.

Developing Time-Based Security Controls and Anomaly Detectors

You can use the framework of the shinobi's hours of infiltration to develop time-based security that takes into account the baseline states of the network at various times, deviations from baseline, and business requirements. Applying time-based security is broadly achieved through three steps:

1. Determine the activity baseline for each hour.
2. Train personnel to monitor activity and become very familiar with typical activity during their assigned hours.
3. Assess the business needs for each hour. Based on this assessment, create business logic and security axioms to further mitigate threats and detect anomalies.

First, consider dividing your network and system logs into one- or two-hour segments. Review the historical trends and activity levels of your network and systems to establish a baseline, a critical metric for threat hunting and identifying cyberhygiene issues. Pay special attention to times when attacks have occurred, as well as times that may be routinely vulnerable to attack as determined by the organization's circumstances, threat modeling, and experience.

Once all the data has been segmented and baselined, train analysts, system administrators, and security professionals to become extremely familiar with your network's activity patterns. They should also be aware of the security gaps that organizational routines create. The shinobi scrolls instruct guards to scrutinize every irregularity and incongruity during their shift. For instance, they are expected to notice when a fisherman arrives later than normal or if an unfamiliar bird calls at an odd hour. Having security personnel similarly attuned to incongruities could prompt them to look twice at an abnormal event, which could reveal a security incident. Developing this deep expertise might require assigning security to monitor a sector—for instance, a single system that is considered a likely target—become extremely familiar with it, and then review every log and event from that system for a two-hour time frame during their eight-hour shift. This strategy is in stark contrast to the "monitor everything at all times" mentality of most SOCs—a mentality that causes alert fatigue, overload, and burnout. It should also mitigate the problems of many automated anomaly detection systems, which need a human to follow up on every anomaly and provide feedback and investigation. These systems quickly become overwhelming and the data inscrutable to security personnel who review anomalies on a daily or weekly basis.

Note that security logs are not ephemeral, like sounds in the night, but are available for future analysis. It is plausible that a sophisticated adversary might alter or eliminate security logs, filter traffic from network taps and sensors, or otherwise compromise the systems intended to log their intrusion and alert security. However, these actions should disrupt a system's normal behavior enough that an astute security analyst takes notice.

Next, you will want to ask yourself two questions:

- When are your users and systems active?
- When could the adversary be active?

Understanding how and when users log into and operate your systems helps you strategically constrain access, making it more difficult for an external or internal threat to infiltrate at your most vulnerable times. For example, if a system is not in use between 8:00 PM and 8:00 AM, turn off that system during those hours. If users have no business need to access their systems on Saturdays, then disable access to those systems for all users on Saturdays. Disabling systems at scheduled times also helps train your SOC staff to detect anomalies during specific hours, as there will be fewer alerts and systems to review. NIST standards suggest implementing such access controls, but many organizations choose instead to prioritize certain scenarios for operational convenience in emergencies, however unlikely these occurrences may be.

CASTLE THEORY THOUGHT EXERCISE

Consider this scenario: you are the ruler of a medieval castle with valuable information, treasure, and people inside. You receive credible intelligence that a shinobi plans to infiltrate your castle. Imagine that your guards have perfect knowledge of time but can enforce only the following rules:

- When any gate or door (interior or exterior) can be locked and unlocked
- Curfews, after which anyone found in the halls will be detained

Consider what level of integrity, assurance, and security you might achieve with the strict exercise of only those two time-based controls. How would you train castle residents to operate within these strictures (how will they use latrines at night, clean the premises while others sleep, take night deliveries, and so on)? What compromises do you expect to make for your security controls to be functional?

For this exercise, it is useful to draw a map of the imaginary castle or your office building. Or you can use an abstracted layout of your network map or data-flow diagram (DFD) as a "building," where switches are hallways, routers/firewalls are doors, systems are rooms, and VPNs/egress points are gates.

Recommended Security Controls and Mitigations

Where relevant, recommendations are presented with an applicable security control from the NIST 800-53 standard. Each should be evaluated with the idea of hours of infiltration in mind. (Note that applications of these techniques require that logs and alerts have timestamps and that time across all systems be in sync. See AU-8: Time Stamps.)

1. Evaluate your hours of operation and perform threat modeling. When are you most vulnerable to attack? What can you do to train your staff to be prepared? [NIST SP 800-154: Guide to Data-Centric System Threat Modeling][6]
2. Implement time-based privilege controls on accounts based on users' business and operational needs. For example, restrict certain users' ability to send or receive work email after 7:00 PM. [AC-2: Account Management | (6) Dynamic Privilege Management]
3. Restrict the ability to log into or use specific accounts during certain hours. For example, when there is an attempt to perform unauthorized actions on an inactive account between 9:00 PM and 11:00 PM, alert the user immediately to verify their identity. If they are unresponsive or their authentication fails, alert the SOC. [AC-2: Account Management | (11) Usage Conditions]
4. Leverage heuristic analysis systems to detect abnormal system access or usage patterns during set times. Users should voluntarily document and provide insight into their "typical usage" patterns to help model their expected behavior during their workday. [AC-2: Account Management | (12) Account monitoring for A-typical Usage]
5. Require system owners and users to document when systems are expected to be in use and when they could be powered off. [AC-3: Access Enforcement | (5) Security Relevant Information]
6. Shrink the time frame during which adversaries can operate. Define a strategic enterprise policy whereby sensitive or proprietary information should be accessed only during set times—for instance, between 11:00 AM and 3:00 PM on weekdays. [AC-17: Remote Access | (9) Disconnect/Disable Access]
7. Inform the account holder when they have successfully or unsuccessfully logged in, including the time and date of last login. Tracking this information helps a user alert the SOC if their account has been compromised and tell the SOC when the

unauthorized access occurred. [AC-9: Previous Login (Access) Notification | (4) Additional Logon Information]

8. After establishing times of operation, configure user devices and systems to automatically lock at a specified time, terminating all sessions. [AC-11: Session Lock]
9. Document a policy that communicates the times and dates that changes to infrastructure and systems are allowed. This assists the SOC when evaluating network and configuration changes on an hour-by-hour basis. [AU-12: Audit Generation | (1) System Wide and Time Audit Correlation Trail; CM-5: Access Restrictions for Change]

Debrief

In this chapter, you learned about the traditional Japanese time based on Chinese zodiac animals, Chinese astrology's influence on divination, and how shinobi likely used these to seize opportunities to infiltrate or outmaneuver a target. You have considered how network activity may vary depending on the time of day and how you can reduce attack opportunity through time-based controls. You became familiar with the shinobi's security standard. Specifically, you learned that a security guard was expected to notice the smallest incongruity in their scanning sector—anything that might indicate the presence of an adversary. In addition, you reviewed guidance on how to apply some of these concepts to your threat hunting, security operation processes, and anomaly detection systems.

In the next chapter, we will review an application of time confidentiality, keeping the time a secret from malware, which may allow defenders to exercise particular detection and defense options.

7

ACCESS TO TIME

You should start your attack with no delay and not prematurely but perfectly on time.

If you are going to set fire to the enemy's castle or camp, you need to prearrange the ignition time with your allies.
—Yoshimori Hyakushu #83

When shinobi were on a mission, particularly at night, one of their most crucial and complex duties was keeping track of time. If this task seems simple, remember that shinobi did not have watches or clocks. They didn't even have sand hourglasses until the early 1600s.[1] To send and receive signals at the proper time, coordinate attacks, know when the enemy would be vulnerable, and more, shinobi had to develop methods to tell time reliably.

Historically, one way to mark the hours involved lighting incense or candles known to burn at a constant rate, then ringing a bell at certain intervals to announce the time. *Bansenshūkai* recommends using environmental cues, such as the movement of the stars, or weight-based instruments to tell time.[2] These weight-based instruments were likely water clocks, sometimes called *clepsydras*, that used balance and water flow/weight mechanisms to accurately signal time intervals. Other scrolls include more abstruse options, such as tracking the change in dilation of a cat's iris throughout the day or the subtle thermal expansions of a dwelling during the night, as these align with particular hours.[3] Shinobi were even taught to derive the hour by being mindful of which nostril they were more actively breathing through. The scrolls explain how breath comes prominently in and out of one nostril, then alternates to the other, in regular intervals that can be used to track time. While this idea might seem like pseudoscience, in 1895, German scientist Richard Kayser observed and documented that during the day, blood pools on different sides of a person's nose, causing a noticeable reduction in airflow in one of the nostrils, before alternating to the other nostril.[4] Not only did the shinobi's acute observational skills identify this phenomenon more than 300 years before its scientific publication in the West, but they also developed a practical application for it. For example, they might need to lie down in the crawl space of a floor beneath their target, where they would be unable to light candles or incense, use instruments to track time, or even dare open their eyes should the glint from their eye catch the target's attention through the cracks of the floor. Under these uncomfortable circumstances, they would lie still and pay attention to their nose breath until the time to attack came—a stellar example of the shinobi's discipline, ingenuity, and creativity.

The multitude of references to time in the shinobi scrolls, combined with the arduous methods developed to track time, suggests that these techniques would not have been developed if keeping track of time were not crucial for a threat actor to operate effectively. The ubiquity of cheap, easy, and reliable ways of telling time in modern society has almost certainly conditioned us to take time and its measurement for granted.

In this chapter, we'll reconsider the value and importance of time in digital systems while briefly reviewing how it is generated, used, and secured with existing best practices. Then we will ask: if accurate time is so important to an adversary, what might happen if we could keep time secret from them? Or deny the adversary access to time? Or even deceive them with an inaccurate time?

The Importance of Time

Time is necessary for the operation of almost every modern computer system. By synchronizing sequential logic and generating a clock signal that dictates intervals of function, computers establish finite pulses of time. These pulses are like the ticking of a clock in which systems perform operations on data in stable, reliable input/output environments. The vast, intricate networks and systems that run our governments, economies, businesses, and personal lives operate on these pulses, requesting the time continuously. They could not function without their clocks.

Numerous security controls exist to protect time data. Identity authentication on Network Time Protocol (NTP) servers verifies that an attacker is not spoofing a system's trusted source of time. Encryption and checksums—encryption encodes the communication, and checksums serve to detect errors during transmission—on the NTP server's time data verify its integrity and protect it from tampering. Nonce is an arbitrary randomized number added to the time communication to prevent repeated-transmission errors. Timestamps and time synchronization logging compare the system's time to that reported by an authoritative time source. NTP stays available and fault tolerant by leveraging multiple time sources and alternate propagation methods, and if access to NTP is denied or unavailable, backup methods can accurately estimate time based on the last synchronization. Additional security best practices call for timestamping audit records, locking out sessions based on inactivity, restricting access to accounts based on the time of day, assessing the validity of security certificates and keys based on time and date information, establishing when to create backups, and measuring how long to keep cached records.

These controls protect the integrity and availability of time data, but rarely is enough consideration given to protecting time data's confidentiality. Almost any modern application can request the time at any moment, and it is generally permitted access not only to the date and time but also to clock libraries and functions. While NTP can encrypt the time data it communicates to a system, there is a notable lack of controls around restricting access to the current system time. Identifying this control gap is important because time is a critical piece of information adversaries use to spread malware. The destructive Shamoon malware,[5] for instance, was set to execute at the start of the Saudi Arabian weekend to inflict maximum damage; it was designed to wipe all infected systems before anyone would notice.

Other common attacks include disclosing confidential information, causing race conditions, forcing deadlocks, manipulating information states, and performing timing attacks to discover cryptography secrets. More sophisticated malware can use its access to time to:

- Sleep for a set period to avoid detection
- Measure pi to 10 million digits, timing how long the calculation takes to determine whether the infected system is in a sandbox/detonation environment designed to catch malware

- Attempt to contact its command and control (C2) based on specific time instructions
- Discover metadata and other information through timing attacks that reveal the state, position, and capability of the target system

If administrators could deny access to time (local, real, and linear), conducting operations within targeted information systems would be much more difficult—and possibly infeasible—for the adversary. However, it is important to note that haphazardly limiting time queries will likely result in cascading failures and errors. A precise approach is needed to deny access to time.

Keeping Time Confidential

Keep in mind that, because confidentiality is not as entrenched as other forms of time security, applying such security controls will require special effort from your organization and the greater security community.

Determine Your Baseline

Identify the software, applications, systems, and administrative commands in your environment that require access to time. Implement function hooking (interception of function calls) and logging to determine who and what is requesting time. After establishing this baseline, use it to detect abnormal time queries and inform a time-based needs assessment that will tailor additional security controls (for example, Just in Time [JIT]).

Assess Technical Capability

Contact your hardware manufacturers and software vendors to determine what technical controls can be enabled to restrict access to time functions. If there are no such controls, request that new features be implemented to encourage the industry to develop solutions around time confidentiality.

Establish Policy

Denying access to time is a nontraditional security control, but as with more customary controls, enforcement requires establishing strategic policy that details requirements—in this case, limiting access to time and monitoring attempts to access time. Wherever possible, incorporate the concept of time confidentiality in all change management decisions, procurement of new hardware and software, and SOC prioritization. Formally document new policies and ensure that your organization's CISO approves them.

> **CASTLE THEORY THOUGHT EXERCISE**
>
> Consider the scenario in which you are the ruler of a medieval castle with valuable assets within. You receive credible threat intelligence that a shinobi has infiltrated your castle with orders to set it on fire at precisely 3:00 AM. At night, a guard in a tower burns a candle clock and strikes a bell every 120 minutes to keep the other night guards on schedule—a sound you believe the shinobi will also hear.
>
> How can you control access to time to mitigate this threat? Which trusted individuals within your castle require access to time, and to whom can you deny complete access? Using only informational control of time, what actions can you take to thwart the attack or discover the shinobi?

Recommended Security Controls and Mitigations

Where relevant, recommendations are presented with applicable security controls from the NIST 800-53 standard. Each should be evaluated with the concept of time confidentiality in mind.

1. Implement protections that block access to time data in timestamp logs or other information-monitoring logs. Preventing time spillage or timestamp leakage could require physical, environmental, media, and technical controls. [AU-9: Protection of Audit Information]
2. Review your current information architecture with respect to time, including the philosophy, requirements, and tactics necessary to implement access and confidentiality controls around time data in your environment. If stakeholders agree to time restrictions, document them in a security plan with an approved budget, resources, and time dedicated to implementation. [PL-8: Information Security Architecture]
3. Conduct a log review and internal hunt to discover communication occurring over port 123 to any unofficial NTP servers in your environment. Look for NTP communication to external NTP servers and consider blocking access to NTP servers you do not control. [SC-7: Boundary Protection]

Debrief

In this chapter, you learned about some of the tools shinobi used to tell time and what they did with their knowledge of time. We discussed how important time can be to cyber operations and security, noting that current security practices focus primarily on the availability and integrity of time in systems. You were also exposed to a thought exercise that explored how to mitigate a shinobi attack through time manipulation.

In the following chapter, we will discuss how shinobi could turn many things into tools to accomplish tasks. Understanding what the equivalent digital "tools" are may help you detect and safeguard against novel weaponization of such tools or at least hamper their use.

8

TOOLS

Remember, if you use a ninja tool, be sure to use it when the wind is whistling so as to hide any sound and always retrieve it.

No matter how many tools you carry as a shinobi,
remember, above all things, that you should always
have your food on your waist.
—Yoshimori Hyakushu #21

While Hollywood depictions typically show ninjas brandishing throwing stars or a katana, real shinobi developed a vast and eclectic array of tools and weapons, and they were instructed to take great care choosing the right tool for the job.[1] All three shinobi scrolls dedicate substantial space to describing secret tools, many of which were innovative technology for their time. *Bansenshūkai* alone includes five sizeable volumes about tools. It states, among other directives, that the best tools can be used for multiple purposes, are quiet, and are not bulky.[2] *Shōninki* advises shinobi to limit the number of tools they carry, as any piece of equipment has the potential to arouse suspicion if it seems out of place.[3] The scroll also recommends that shinobi seek out and sabotage the tools and weapons of their targets; such instruments were of central importance to a shinobi's capabilities.[4]

Of course, shinobi did not acquire their tools from any big-box shinobi supply store. Instead, according to the guidance of the scrolls, they made effective tools from items that were easily bought, found, or made. This approach had several advantages. Such everyday items could be carried without attracting much suspicion[5] and even act as corroborating props for shinobi disguises. For example, several rulers, including Toyotomi Hideyoshi and Oda Nobunaga, called for sword hunts—mass confiscations of all swords and other weapons from civilians—in an effort to reduce the ability of rebels to attack the ruling army.[6] Under these conditions, any non-samurai who wore a sword or other armaments in public could expect to have their weapons seized. To bypass this tactic, shinobi discreetly modified common farm implements to be used as weapons, as there was no edict against carrying sharp farm tools in public. In the hands of a trained shinobi, everyday farm tools became lethal.

For all their practicality, *Bansenshūkai* asserts that the essential principle of using tools is not simply to wield them but to have an enlightened, Zen-like understanding of their purpose.[7] Shinobi contemplated their tools' usefulness deeply and frequently, constantly training with them and reimagining their uses in the field. As a result, shinobi regularly improved existing tools, invented new ones, and passed this knowledge on to other, allied shinobi.[8]

In this chapter, we will contemplate tools. We'll touch on the dual nature of tools—how the same tool has the capability to do good or bad, depending on its operator. This binary *in-yo,* or *ying-yang,* concept is a useful model to understand how a hacker approaches digital tools. For example, consider how a tool designed to help a user might be used for malicious purposes.

In addition to possessing good-bad potential, each tool can also be repurposed or applied in different ways. Take a moment to think of a dozen or so ways one can use a hammer. Simple thought exercises like this can help deepen your understanding of what exactly a hammer is, how a hammer might be improved, and how a new type of hammer might be invented to accomplish something novel. These same creative skills can be applied to recoding digital and software-based tools. At the highest levels of mastery, this creative repurposing is analogous to the work of a master blacksmith. The blacksmith can forge new tools, machines, and systems that can dramatically change how they think about their own craft; open up new possibilities around what they can build; and enhance their capabilities to develop new weapons, defenses, and tools.

To be clear, the adversarial use of tools is likely a threat we will never fully escape. That said, in this chapter, I will describe the security best practices regarding tools, as well as some enhanced controls that may mitigate attacks.

Living Off the Land

In cybersecurity, *tools* are any instruments that aid the manual or automated operation of a task. If that sounds like a widely inclusive definition, that's because it is. There are physical tools, such as BadUSBs, Wi-Fi sniffers, and lockpicks, and there are software tools, such as platforms, exploits, code, scripts, and executables. An entire computer system itself is a tool. A tool can have a legitimate use but, in the hands of a hacker, become a weapon. Think, for example, of the SSH client an administrator uses to perform remote maintenance on systems, which an attacker can use for reverse SSH tunneling to attack systems and bypass firewalls.

Much like shinobi, cyberadversaries rely heavily on tools to achieve their goals, and they continuously develop, customize, hone, and test their tools against existing technology in the wild. Sophisticated threat groups employ full-time, dedicated tool and capability developers to maintain and improve their tool set. In response, enterprising cyberdefenders work to reverse engineer these custom tools so they can build countermeasures, implement useful security policies and detection signatures, test malicious tool capabilities in sandbox environments, and create application whitelists that identify and block dangerous tools. In some cases, new defenses are so well applied that adversaries cannot download or install their tools to the target system, as the host-based security immediately quarantines the tools, blocks access to them, and alerts security personnel to their presence.

Because host-based security systems can detect and block specialized tools and malware, many adversaries now practice an infiltration tactic called "living off the land." Using this approach, attackers first gather intelligence on the software and tools already in use on the target system. Then, they build their attack using only those applications, since the host system's defenses do not consider those applications harmful. A living-off-the-land attack can use any file on the victim machine's disk, including the task scheduler, web browser, and Windows Management

Instrumentation (WMI) Command-Line Utility, as well as scripting engines such as cmd/bat, JavaScript, Lua, Python, and VBScript. Much as shinobi appropriated common items in the target environment, like farm tools, which they knew would be readily available and blend in, hackers, by co-opting what already exists on the target machine, can turn everyday user and admin tools, applications, and operating system files into tools for their purposes.

One common tool susceptible to exploitation on Windows machines is Microsoft's potent PowerShell framework. Even Microsoft acknowledges that threat actors regularly target PowerShell to infiltrate systems, perform unauthorized actions, and otherwise compromise an organization's systems. In turn, Microsoft offers security and mitigation capabilities, such as Privilege Access Management (PAM) to enforce Just Enough Administration (JEA) in combination with Just in Time (JIT) administration. Unfortunately, JEA/JIT turns PowerShell's ubiquity into an access control nightmare for human IT administrators. How? I'll spare you the more technical details. Just imagine a technician who is called to come troubleshoot a problem, but is only allowed to bring a screwdriver and can only access that screwdriver between 1:00 and 2:00 PM.

Using access control measures to lock down tools works only if an IT team is willing to severely restrict its own effectiveness. Even then, there's an inherent danger when these everyday tools exist on the target system—cybersecurity professionals have observed threat actors freeing tools from their local lock with ease. A fact of cybersecurity is this: as long as these sophisticated tools exist, so does the potential to abuse them.

Securing Tools

The paradox of having tools is that you need them to operate, but so does the adversary. One approach to this challenge is to reduce the number of tools—in terms of quantity, function, access, and availability—to the bare minimum. While this strategy will make it somewhat difficult for you to operate inside your own environment, with adequate security controls, it should make it even *more* difficult for a potential adversary. One downside to this approach is that you are weakening the resiliency and robustness of your capabilities to remotely manage your environment. So, if an adversary compromises essential tools by removing or breaking them, your own protections may sabotage your ability to manage and repair the system. For securing tools, the following steps are a good start:

1. *Determine your baseline.* Conduct role-based employee surveys and perform software inventory audits across all systems in your organization. Document a comprehensive list of users, version numbers, and system locations for every tool in your environment, including all software/applications, scripts, libraries, systems, and roles. This includes OS and system files, such as the following:

sc.exe	*find.exe*	*sdelete.exe*	*runasuser.exe*
net.exe	*curl.exe*	*psexec.exe*	*rdpclip.exe*
powershell.exe	*netstat.exe*	*wce.exe*	*vnc.exe*
ipconfig.exe	*systeminfo.exe*	*winscanx.exe*	*teamviewer.exe*
netsh.exe	*wget.exe*	*wscript.exe*	*nc.exe*
tasklist.exe	*gpresult.exe*	*cscript.exe*	*ammyy.exe*
rar.exe	*whoami.exe*	*robocopy.exe*	*csvde.exe*
wmic.exe	*query.exe*	*certutil.exe*	*lazagne.exe*

2. *Review your findings and assess your needs.* Evaluate every tool to determine which users need it, as well as how, where, and when it is used. For every tool, conduct a risk assessment to determine the potential impact if an adversary gains access. Document how you could restrict a tool's capabilities to increase security while incorporating justifiable compromises for business operations—for example, disabling macros in Microsoft Word and Excel.
3. *Implement restrictions.* Restrict availability, access, and authorization for unnecessarily risky tools. Document any exceptions and plan to revisit the exceptions every quarter to make users request a renewal of their approval. You could even set temporary access that automatically revokes or deletes tools after a period of time. Establish a whitelist of approved tools so that any unrecognized or unauthorized tools are blocked automatically from being delivered to your systems. Consider physically locking all USB, media, Thunderbolt, FireWire, console, and external ports on all systems, with written approval required to unlock and use them.

CASTLE THEORY THOUGHT EXERCISE

Consider the scenario in which you are the ruler of a medieval castle with valuable assets inside. Your estate produces rare, proprietary threads that are necessary for onsite textile construction and repair. They are also sold for considerable sums—income that keeps your domain profitable. You receive credible threat intelligence that a shinobi plans to infiltrate your castle and poison the spindle needle on a spinning wheel, but it is unclear whom they are targeting and what their objective is.

Model threat scenarios in which someone could be pricked by a spindle needle. Then develop mitigations to lower the probability and impact of the prick. For example, you might dull the needles or make people wear protective gloves in the spinning room. Could you reposition the spinning wheel to make it harder for workers to accidentally bump or graze the needle? What access controls could you place on transporting spindle needles within the castle, and what supply chain protections could you implement on new needles coming in? How many ways can you come up with to prevent the poisoned needle from being used for malicious purposes? What other sharp tools might workers substitute for needles, and should you remove access to them? Could you even redesign the spindle wheel to operate without a needle?

Recommended Security Controls and Mitigations

Where relevant, recommendations are presented with applicable security controls from the NIST 800-53 standard. Each should be evaluated with the concept of tools in mind.

1. Evaluate your technical capability to enforce the "principle of least functionality" by disabling, deleting, and restricting access to unnecessary software and system functions in your environment. [CM-7: Least Functionality]
2. Conduct periodic reviews of the functions, tools, and software used for each role and system to determine whether they are necessary or whether they could be removed or disabled. Establish a system to register, track, and manage these tools. [CM-7: Least Functionality | (1) Periodic Review | (3) Registration Compliance]
3. After documenting every tool that a user or system could leverage, restrict users from putting those tools to use for functions

outside the user's role in the organization. [CM-7: Least Functionality | (2) Prevent Program Execution]

4. Implement a whitelist or blacklist (or both) of software, applications, and other tools. [CM-7: Least Functionality | (4) Unauthorized Software/Blacklisting | (5) Authorized Software/Whitelisting]
5. Implement physical and network boundary restrictions on hardware and software tools. For example, restrict sensitive tools to a segregated management-net file server or in portable locked media devices, to be accessed only when needed and in combination with JEA/JIT access controls. [MA-3: Maintenance Tools | (1) Inspect Tools | (3) Prevent Unauthorized Removal | (4) Restricted Tool Use; SC-7: Boundary Protection | (13) Isolation of Security Tools/Mechanisms/Support Components]
6. Evaluate all installed software to determine which imports, APIs, functional calls, and hooks are used by applications known to be safe. Consider using malcode protections to block any tools that use these implementations or others that normal software does not use. Consider your options to restrict, disable, and remove OS functions, modules, components, and libraries that are not used for business operations. [SA-15: Development Process, Standards, and Tools | (5) Attack Surface; SI-3: Malicious Code Protection | (10) Malicious Code Analysis]

Debrief

In this chapter, you learned about tools—how powerful they are and why it's important to keep them safe. You learned about "living off the land" and the complexity of making systems both defensible and functional. You may have also started to ponder the distinctions between tools and malware, as well as how one might program a tool to identify the differences between the two. The thought exercise of the poisoned spindle challenged you to outwit the enemy who's invading an environment you control.

In the following chapter, we will discuss different techniques used by shinobi scouts—smelling, seeing, and hearing—and what we can learn from them, particularly as we apply different types of digital sensors in our cyber environment.

9

SENSORS

Whether day or night, scouts for a far-distance observation should be sent out.

Even if a shinobi does not have impressive physical abilities, remember that the most vital thing is to have acute observation.
—Yoshimori Hyakushu #11

In addition to stationing guards at gates and soldiers at watch posts, *Bansenshūkai* recommends defending a castle by placing scouts surreptitiously along roads, paths, and other approaches. The defending commander should place scouts at staggered intervals around the castle's perimeter.[1] These scouts fulfilled one of three roles:

- Smelling scouts (*kagi*)
- Listening scouts (*monogiki*)
- Outside foot scouts (*togiki*)

Smelling and listening scouts, who used trained dogs and dog handlers, placed themselves in shrouded observation posts—they couldn't see out, but neither could the enemy see in. The scout focused intently on smelling or listening for signs of infiltration. These techniques worked especially well at night, as smelling and listening scouts did not need light to operate.[2]

Outside foot scouts tried to catch infiltrators by conducting sweeps at the edge of enemy territory; hiding on enemy ground and monitoring movement toward their own camp; or using tripwires, noise, or even physical contact to detect intruders. *Bansenshūkai* says that *togiki* scouts should be shinobi themselves, as they must be skilled in stealth and observation, have a preternatural understanding of which direction the enemy will attack from, and be able to successfully detect and engage an enemy ninja.[3]

In addition to human (and animal) scouts, *Bansenshūkai* recommends using active and passive detection techniques to identify enemy infiltrators. Actively, shinobi might lower or swing a *sarubi* (monkey-fire, or "fire on a rope"[4]) into or across a dark area such as a moat, trench, or the bottom of a castle wall to quickly and dynamically illuminate it, from a distance, in a way that fixed lanterns couldn't. Passively, shinobi would build detection systems, for instance, by filling a wide but shallow trench with fine sand, then raking the sand into a complex pattern. Should an enemy bypass exterior defenses, they would leave footprints, alerting guards that the castle had been breached. Footprints in the sand might also tell an observant shinobi which direction the enemy came from and whether they had left the same way—valuable intelligence that could help neutralize an immediate threat and shore up future defenses.[5]

In this chapter, we will look at the different types of security sensors commonly used in networks, comparing and contrasting modern deployment with the ways shinobi historically used sensors. We will highlight sensor placement, as well as sensor countermeasure techniques, learning from the shinobi to enhance our own cybersecurity defenses. We will also propose sensors based on the sensory scouts of ancient times.

Identifying and Detecting Threats with Sensors

In cyber parlance, the term *sensor* encompasses a variety of detection systems and instruments. Most commonly, a sensor is a monitoring device on a tap, T-split, span, or mirror port that copies activity for observation, recording, and analysis. In one such configuration, sensors sniff and capture raw packets (PCAPs) as they cross the wire, then process and analyze them to alert security to suspicious events. Sensors can also be placed "in line," meaning a packet travels through a device that can delay, block, or alter the packet's information, effectively thwarting attacks rather than simply raising a red flag. Secondary sensors, such as Wi-Fi sensors, detect external or other unauthorized signals and connections, while physical security sensors, such as cameras, monitor access to sensitive data centers, server racks, and switch closets. In broader terms, certain software endpoint agents also act as sensors, as they collect events, actions, and activity on a host system and report back to a command and control (C2) system to analyze and raise alerts if necessary.

Organizations often dedicate sensors to certain types of traffic—for example, by configuring email gateway security devices for phishing attempts or spam, intrusion prevention/detection systems for network attacks, firewalls for unauthorized IPs and ports, proxies for suspicious websites, and data loss prevention systems. Sensor-based cybersecurity devices are typically installed at the main egress point of a network, typically at the demilitarized zone (DMZ). Because it is standard to place sensors as far up the network as possible to maximize the amount of traffic they see, if adversaries hide from sensors at the gateway or bypass the main egress to bridge into a network, it's possible for them to operate within the network free from security sensor inspection.

Despite this security liability, most organizations are unlikely to drastically increase the number of sensors in their systems, as purchasing many additional sensors—along with the extra work to license, install, update, maintain, and monitor them all—is financially impractical. Unfortunately, many organizations simply assume that if the main egress sensor does not catch a threat, then more of the same sensor would not be more effective. This is an error in judgment that puts their systems at risk.

Better Sensors

A major problem with sensors is that they almost always require a person to monitor them and act on the information they convey. This problem is compounded by the limitations of security sensors and available analysis platforms. Think of modern security sensors this way: a building has a number of tiny microphones and cameras scattered throughout, but these cameras and microphones are trapped inside little straws—straws that give them narrow fields of capture. Now imagine trying to piece together an active breach while only able to peer through a single straw at a time. Not only that, but each straw is building up thousands of hours of data to store, process, and analyze. This frustrating situation is often alleviated with signatures, algorithms, or machine learning—tools that can help to identify anomalies and malicious activity. However, these automated systems aren't perfect. Often, they create false positives or create such a large flood of legitimate alerts that it can feel the same as not having sensors at all. To remedy these problems, we can take a page from the shinobi: we can identify the paths an enemy is likely to take, and we can hide many types of sensors along those paths to give early warning of attacks. Consider the following guidance as you consider improving the sensors in your organization:

1. *Model your network and identify your weaknesses.* Create a network map and information flow model of your environment—one that describes every system and its purpose, how systems are connected, where information enters and leaves your network, the type of information received, what sensors (if any) inspect information, and the egress points. Identify areas that lack sensors and places you believe are properly monitored. Predict where threat actors will attempt to infiltrate your network. Keep in mind that creating a comprehensive map can take months and requires help across the entire enterprise. Your resulting map might not be perfect, but even a flawed map is better than no map at all.
2. *Conduct red team and pen testing.* Contract a red team to attempt infiltration of your network. Consider a "purple team" approach to the exercise, in which your network defenders (the blue team) observe the red team in real time in the same room and can pause the exercise to ask questions. Query the security sensors before, during, and after the attack to see what they detected or reported, if anything. This information should be highly enlightening. Allow your blue team to consider how different sensor placement could have detected the red team faster and more accurately. Discuss architectural defense changes, sensor tuning, and other solutions that are suggested by the testing.
3. *Detect and block encrypted traffic.* Block all encrypted traffic that cannot be intercepted and inspected by your sensors. Also, take appropriate steps to strip your machines' ability to use unauthorized encryption. Have the red team test your ability to detect encrypted traffic attacks. Most sensors cannot inspect encrypted traffic; therefore, many organizations allow asymmetric encryption, such as elliptic-curve Diffie-Hellman (ECDH), which cannot be broken by root certificates. Allowing unbroken encrypted traffic to leave your organization without going through DLP creates a security gap analogous to when castle guards scrutinize every bare-faced person who enters or leaves through the gate but permit anyone wearing a mask to walk through unchallenged.
4. *Develop "smelling" and "listening" sensors.* Explore opportunities to create sensors that can secretly detect certain types of threat activity. For example, configure an external physical sensor that monitors a system's CPU activity or power consumption and can

detect unauthorized access or use—such as by a cryptocurrency miner—based on whether performance correlates with known commands or logged-in user activity.

5. *Implement passive sensors.* Establish passive interfaces on switches and servers that should never be used. Also, configure sensors to detect and alert locally if an interface is activated, indicating the likely presence of an adversary on your network. Much like a shallow trench filled with sand, such systems can be built to detect lateral movement between network devices where it should not happen.
6. *Install* togiki *sensors.* Place inward-facing sensors outside your network to detect infiltration. For example, with the cooperation of your ISP, configure sensors outside your network boundary to monitor inbound and outbound traffic that your other sensors might not detect. Place sensors in a T-split directly off a device working in conjunction with a host-based sensor, and then diff the devices against each other to determine whether both sensors are reporting the same activity. This approach helps identify compromised endpoint sensors and network interface drivers.

CASTLE THEORY THOUGHT EXERCISE

Consider the scenario in which you are the ruler of a medieval castle with valuable assets inside. You have had three arson events inside your castle in the past week, though a fire watch was on standby and doused the flames before they spread. You believe the arsonist is a shinobi who has learned from your team's responses and will perform a new attack—one that may not even involve fire. Your resources are thin, but your fire watch asks for additional staff and equipment to better respond, your architect wants to reinforce and fireproof sections of the castle, and your head of security requests more guards on the gates to catch the infiltrator.

How would you hide sensors to detect the arsonist or other suspicious actors inside your castle? Could you improve fire watch response time and capability while reducing the number of fire watch members, perhaps by using them as sensors rather than as responders? Where and how might you place human sensors to most effectively detect and alert others to suspicious activity? How would you rotate perimeter guards between sweeping inside and outside the castle, and how would you augment their capabilities to prevent an adversary from identifying when or where the guards are patrolling? What passive sensors could you implement to catch the arsonist?

Recommended Security Controls and Mitigations

Where relevant, recommendations are presented with applicable security controls from the NIST 800-53 standard. Each should be evaluated with the concept of sensors in mind.

1. Implement packet sniffers, full network PCAPs, and other automated sensors to support incident handling, maintenance, and information flow enforcement. [AC-4: Information Flow Enforcement | (14) Security Policy Filter Constraints; IR-4: Incident Handling; MA-3: Maintenance Tools]
2. To safeguard physical access and detect tampering, install sensors on wiring closet locks, cameras to monitor data center and server access, water sensors to detect leaks that can threaten electrical devices, and wiretapping sensors on communication lines. [PE-4: Access Control for Transmission; PE-6: Monitoring Physical Access; PE-15: Water Damage Protection]
3. Run awareness training programs for staff—including non-IT staff—so they can act as human sensors to detect threat activity. Provide a clear, easy, and accessible method for employees to report suspicious activity. [PM-16: Threat Awareness Program]
4. Intercept encrypted communications and allow your sensors to perform deep inspections of unencrypted packets. [AC-4: Information Flow Enforcement: | (4) Content Check Encrypted Information; SC-8: Transmission Confidentiality and Integrity]
5. Implement sensors that can analyze packets and take preventive measures such as blocking or filtering. [SC-5: Denial of Service Protection; SC-7: Boundary Protection | (10) Prevent Exfiltration | (17) Automated Enforcement of Protocol Formats]
6. Prohibit promiscuous sensor activation on non-sensing systems to prevent the release of sensitive information to adversaries who gain unauthorized access. [SC-42: Sensor Capability and Data]
7. Work with your ISP to place Trusted Internet Connection (TIC) sensors outside your network boundary. [AC-17: Remote Access | (3) Managed Access Control Points]
8. Document all internal system connections; their interfaces; the information they process, store, and communicate; and sensor placement between systems. [CA-9: Internal System Connections]
9. Conduct penetration testing and red team exercises to test and validate your sensor placement and capability. [CA-8: Penetration Testing; RA-6: Technical Surveillance Countermeasures Survey]

Debrief

In this chapter, we talked about smelling, hearing, and outside sensory scouts used to detect enemy shinobi in ancient Japan. We also looked at active and passive sensors that castle guards deployed to catch intruders. We then discussed various types of security sensors used today—sensors that help defenders see what's happening on the wires around them. We covered several logistical problems around sensors such as sensor placement, false positives, and sensor management. Lastly, we talked about how to apply ancient shinobi techniques to identify intruders in networked systems.

Next, we will discuss the different types of bridges and ladders shinobi used to bypass castle defenses—a concept that has some importance in regard to sensors. For instance, imagine your castle is protected by a moat and you have placed all of your sensors at the drawbridge. An enemy shinobi who is able to covertly place a bridge of their own without using the drawbridge also effectively bypasses your sensors—making them useless. We'll explore how this bridging concept is almost exactly the same in cybersecurity and how difficult it can be to address.

10

BRIDGES AND LADDERS

There will be no wall or moat that you cannot pass, no matter how high or steep it is, particularly if you use a ninja ladder.

A castle gatehouse is usually most strictly guarded, but the roof is the most convenient place for you to attach a hooked ladder.
—Bansenshūkai, "In-nin II"[1]

The shinobi could move, quietly and unseen, over an enemy's walls and gates, using *ninki* infiltration tools—tools described in both *Bansenshūkai*[2] and *Gunpo Jiyoshu*.[3] Multifaceted ladders and portable bridges like the spiked ladder, cloud ladder, or tool transportation wire[4] enabled shinobi to cross moats, scale walls, and deliver tools to other shinobi safely and stealthily. Sometimes these ladders were "proper," or made by shinobi in advance of a mission, and sometimes they were "temporary," or constructed in the field.[5] These were valuable tools, as they provided access to sensitive locations often left unguarded out of overconfidence that they were inaccessible.

The scrolls also explain how to infiltrate an enemy camp by manipulating the enemy's own security measures. *Shōninki* instructs shinobi to imagine how a bird or fish might access a castle[6]—in other words, to realize the unique advantages that being up high or down low provide. For example, scaling a wall affords the opportunity to bridge across other walls and rooftops with great speed, providing better access to the interior of the castle than passing through a gate might. Swimming across a moat could provide underwater access to a common waterway—one that leads into a castle. The *Bansenshūkai* even recommends purposefully attempting to bridge over the guardhouse gate, where the most guards would logically be stationed, because the defenders might assume that attackers would avoid trying to penetrate at this point.[7]

In this chapter, we will discuss how bridging network domains is similar to bridging castle wall perimeters. Just like castle walls, networks are engineered with barriers and segmentations that assume one must pass through a controlled gateway. Bridges allow threats to bypass these gateways, circumventing the security controls established at gateway egress points. What may seem like a straightforward measure to take, like instructing guards to confront anyone building a bridge across the castle moat, can become futile when, say, the castle architect opted to connect the moat's concentric rings for water management reasons. Connected, three moats are no longer three discrete boundaries that an adversary must pass. Instead, they're a bridge of water to be swum straight into the heart of the castle. Learning how to think like a shinobi and seeing barriers as potential ladder-hooking points can help you reassess your own network and preemptively cut off bridging opportunities.

Network Boundary Bridging

To cybersecurity professionals, a *bridge* is a virtual or physical network device that operates at both the physical and data link layers—layers 1 and 2 of the OSI model—to connect two segments of a network so they form a single aggregate network. The term also refers to any device, tool, or method that enables information to cross a "gap," such as an air-gapped network or segmentation boundary. Bridges typically bypass security controls and safeguards, allowing for data exfiltration from the network or the delivery of unauthorized or malicious data to the network. These potentially dire consequences have pushed cybersecurity professionals to develop detection and mitigation methods to prevent bridging, including:

- Disabling network bridging on wireless Ethernet cards
- Disabling systems with two or more active network interfaces

- Implementing network access controls (NACs) and monitoring to detect new devices on a network
- Installing sensors to detect unauthorized Wi-Fi access points
- Restricting certain networks with VLANs or other router technologies
- Using authentication in the Link Layer Discovery Protocol (LLDP)

Despite evolving security controls, unauthorized bridging still happens—and some advanced infiltration techniques, while proven only in academic or laboratory environments, demonstrate great potential for harm. The most recent examples include taking control of system LEDs to blink bits to an optical receiver in a different room or building, using FM frequency signals to communicate with nearby phones (as with the AirHopper and GSMem exploits), controlling and pulsing fans to send bits through acoustics, and artificially overheating and cooling CPUs to slowly send data (as with the BitWhisper exploit). Threat actors may even be able to bridge networks through a system's power cords via the Ethernet over power technique (EOP, not to be confused with power over Ethernet, POE). In other cases, an organization's VoIP phones could have their microphones and speakers activated remotely, allowing adversaries to transfer sound data or spy on conversations.

Of course, some bridging is less cutting-edge. An adversary could climb onto the roof of an office building, splice into accessible network wires, and install a small earth satellite station that provides robust bridge access to a network. Smartphones are routinely plugged into system USB ports to charge their batteries, but a charging phone also connects a computer to an external cellular network that is not inspected by firewalls, data loss prevention (DLP), or other security tools, completely bypassing an organization's defenses and facilitating data theft or code injection on the host network. When bridging via a *sneakernet*, a user loads information onto portable media and walks it to another computer or network location, manually bypassing security controls. There are also concerns that threats could use the hidden management network—typically on the 10.0.0.0/8 net—that connects directly to consoles of routers, firewalls, and other security systems, using these as jump points to bridge different network VLANs and segments and effectively using the network to bypass its own security. In addition, split tunneling poses a risk, as information may be able to leak to and from different networks through a device connected to both networks simultaneously.

Mature organizations work under the assumption that adversaries are continually developing different bridging technologies to bypass defenses in new, unforeseen ways. Indeed, it appears possible that everything within the electromagnetic spectrum—including acoustic, light, seismic, magnetic, thermal, and radio frequencies—can be a viable means to bridge networks and airgaps.

Countering Bridges

Preventing bridging between systems designed to connect to other systems is a hard problem to solve. While there is no perfect solution, it is possible to reduce bridging opportunities and focus isolation efforts on the most important assets. In addition, countermeasures that negate the capability of bridging techniques can be layered to improve the effectiveness of these defenses.

1. *Identify your weaknesses.* Identify the networks and information systems that hold your organization's sensitive, critical, or high-value data. Create a data-flow diagram (DFD) to model how information is stored and moves in the system. Then identify areas where a covert, out-of-channel bridge attack could occur.
2. *Implement bridge countermeasures.* Consider implementing TEMPEST[8] controls, such as Faraday cages or shielded glass, to block air gap bridging through emissions or other signals. To block rogue bridges, ensure that you have identified and authenticated devices before allowing them to connect to your network or another device. Develop appropriate safeguards to mitigate potential bridging threats identified in your threat model.

CASTLE THEORY THOUGHT EXERCISE

Consider the scenario in which you are the ruler of a medieval castle with valuable information, treasure, and people inside. You receive credible threat intelligence that a shinobi has been using special hooked ladders and cloud bridges to move people or things across your castle walls without the knowledge of your gate guards.

Consider the ways in which you could reconfigure your castle walls to detect and/or prevent ladders or bridges from bypassing them. Can you predict where the shinobi will attempt to bridge your defenses? How might you change your guards' inspection protocols and direct them to look for temporary bridging? How would you react to knowing that your perimeter had been breached, and how would you adjust to working under the assumption that your internal environment had been altered and might not be trustworthy?

Recommended Security Controls and Mitigations

Where relevant, recommendations are presented with applicable security controls from the NIST 800-53 standard. Each should be evaluated with the concept of bridges in mind.

1. Implement boundary protections and information flow controls to prevent external devices, systems, and networks from exfiling data or transferring malicious code onto your network. [AC-4: Information Flow Enforcement | (21) Physical/Logical Separation of Information Flows; AC-19: Access Control for Mobile Devices; AC-20: Use of External Information Systems | (3) Non-Organizationally Owned Systems/Components/Devices; SC-7: Boundary Protection]
2. Enforce wireless access protection controls to block or detect unauthorized wireless signals that bridge across your networks in microwave, UHF/VHF, Bluetooth, 802.11x, and other frequencies. [AC-18: Wireless Access; SC-40: Wireless Link Protection]
3. Audit network access and interconnections to identify external networks or systems—such as remote network printers—that could bridge your network to transmit data. [CA-3 System Interconnections; CA-9 Internal System Connections]
4. Establish strong portable media policies to prevent unauthorized bridging. Require identification and authentication of external media and devices before allowing anything to connect to your environment. [IA-3: Device Identification and Authentication; MP-1 Media Protection Policy and Procedures; MP-2: Media Access; MP-5: Media Transport]
5. Test for TEMPEST leakage or other out-of-channel signals coming from your systems. Using the results, decide where to implement protections that inhibit a signal's ability to be used as a bridge. [PE-19: Information Leakage; SC-37: Out-of-Band Channels]

Debrief

In this chapter, we talked about the philosophy of adversarial bridging, and we discussed bridging network segments and traditional best practices. We looked at multiple-bridging techniques—bridges that can cross gaps in ways you may not have thought of before. The thought exercise in this chapter was designed to prompt thinking about building physical safeguards between ladders and walls; in theory, these can be foundational to innovating modern defenses for the inputs/outputs of a system.

In the following chapter, we will discuss locks and the shinobi practice of lockpicking, which was based on a belief that any lock designed by a human can be picked by a human. We also get a glimpse of a shinobi's approach to security when they must rely on a lock they themselves do not trust. We will discuss the application of locks in cybersecurity, as well as what we can learn from the shinobi to improve our approach to locks and lockpicking.

11

LOCKS

There is no padlock that you cannot open. However, this all depends on how skilled you are; therefore, you should always get hands-on practice.

Opening tools are designed to help you open the doors of the enemy house with ease. Therefore, of all the arts, this is the one conducted when you are closest to the enemy.
—Bansenshūkai, Ninki III[1]

In ancient Japan, locks were simpler than the locking devices of today, as the manufacturing capabilities of the time could not produce the intricate pins, tumblers, and other components that contemporary locks use. However, these older locks were elegantly designed, making exemplary use of "prongs, latches, and the natural forces of gravity and tension" to keep people's valuables safe from intruders and thieves.[2]

Shinobi regularly encountered complex locks during their missions—and devised ways to open all of them. The scrolls indicate that no lock, barrier, or other mechanism was safe from a shinobi with well-constructed tools, sufficient training and ingenuity, and an optimistic mindset. Significant portions of all three scrolls are dedicated to documenting how to make and use various picks, shims, and other probing tools used to open locks, doors, and gates (Figure 11-1).[3]

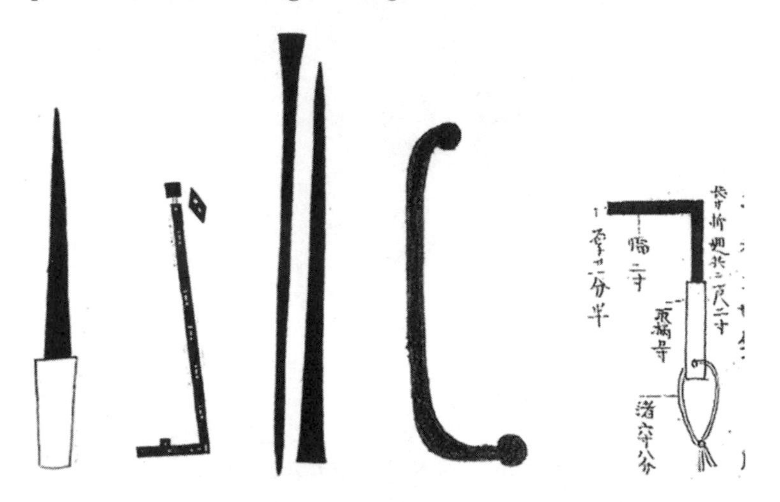

*Figure 11-1: A variety of tools used to open locks, doors, and gates. From left to right, a probing iron, an extendable key, lockpicking shims, a pick for guided padlocks, and a door-opening tool (*Bansenshūkai *and the* Ninpiden*).*

From ring latches to rope, locking bars to hooks and pegs, sophisticated key latches to rudimentary, homemade technology . . . whatever the lock's design, shinobi had methods and tools to bypass it. In fact, shinobi were able to breach any security system or deterrent used at the time.[4] Knowing that locks could not be fully trusted, shinobi themselves developed techniques to take security into their own hands. Some were bluntly simple: when sleeping in lodgings secured by locks they did not trust, shinobi sometimes tied a string from the door or window to the topknot in their hair, ensuring they would wake up if the door latch or lock were opened as they slept.[5]

Today, as in the time of shinobi, people use locks to safeguard their property—and threat actors still use picks to defeat them. The lock, as it always has, serves multiple purposes: it works as a deterrent. It is a visible assurance to an owner that their property is safe. It creates a system of accountability to the key holder(s) if the lock is breached through use of a key. It also serves as a barrier and an alarm, since thieves will take time and make noise as they attempt to bypass it. In this chapter, we will discuss how hackers, much like shinobi, are still picking locks and bypassing security. Furthermore, we'll talk about why physical locks are so important to digital systems and detail the necessary companion precautions.

We will also explore some technological advances in locks and picks, discovering what else the shinobi can teach us about security.

Physical Security

Just as lockpicking is often a gateway hobby into hacking, defeating a lock is a common entry point into cybersecurity. The act of finding flaws in or physically accessing a thing that is supposed to be secure—the visual, tactile, and audible feedback of a lock's opening in your hand after you've beaten its defenses—can be a powerful sensation. It can pique interest in the security field and build confidence in fledgling abilities.

The cybersecurity industry uses locking devices to restrict physical access to buildings, data centers, switching closets, and individual offices.[6] On a more granular level, rack locks limit access to servers, chassis-case locks limit access to a system's physical components, device port locks prevent unauthorized use of USBs or console jacks, tethering locks prevent systems from leaving their location, and power locks keep devices from turning on at all. Locking down physical access to systems is a crucial piece of an organization's cybersecurity strategy. If systems are vulnerable to being tampered with physically, many digital security controls are at risk of being rendered ineffective once the adversary gains physical access. It should be assumed that, if adversaries gain physical access to a machine, they also gain admin-level privileges on the system and acquire its data.

Despite the proliferation of illicit lockpicking tools and techniques, organizations tend to use the same locks year after year, leaving themselves extremely vulnerable to attack. Most information system and building access locks use weak pin tumblers, such as the Yale cylindrical lock—patented in the 1860s and now the world's most common lock due to its low cost and ease of mass production—and tubular locks (or "circle locks"), the most common type of bicycle lock. Criminals construct, sell, and use picking tools that can easily beat these off-the-shelf locks. For example, soda can shims can pry open locks, pen caps can simulate tubular keys, and 3D-printed plastic keys can be easily forged from pictures of the original. For the unskilled criminal, autoelectronic lockpickers can, with the pull of a trigger, do all the work of picking every tumbler lock's pin within seconds.

Large-scale lockpicking countermeasures are few and far between, and some are more concerned with liability than security. For example, certain insurance policies won't cover break-ins and thefts if inferior locks—such as the most common ones sold in the United States—were picked or bypassed during the crime. Some governments issue compliance standards for lock manufacturers, along with restrictions that bar selling substandard locks to citizens. In the cybersecurity realm, select governments safeguard their classified systems and data with a combination of cipher locks or other high-assurance locks and supplemental security controls that mitigate the lock's security flaws.

However, too many doors and systems still use weak lock-and-key defenses—defenses that even a mildly sophisticated threat actor can defeat with ease. Locks and barriers for information systems must be improved to mitigate against common attacks such as shimming, picking, stealing, copying, and forcing.

Improving Locks

Preventing all lockpicking is likely impossible. However, there are many proactive steps you can take to improve the resiliency of your locks. Improving locks will also improve your cybersecurity posture by mitigating unauthorized physical access attacks to your systems.

- *Upgrade your locks.* Evaluate the more advanced locking systems, such as European dimple locks, to determine which ones are compatible with your business requirements and budget. Seek approval from your stakeholders and physical security team and then upgrade all of your locks to models that are more resilient to attack.
- *Think outside the lock.* Consider nontraditional locking solutions for your organization, such as multiple-stage locks. When a first-stage unlock mechanism controls access to a second-stage lock, intruders cannot quickly and easily open both locks at once or in quick succession.

  For instance, to close off an entryway, use two independent locking systems that complement each other. The first stage could be a digital 4-digit PIN lock that would temporarily unfreeze the pins in the second-stage lock, a cylinder lock. While the pins are frozen in the second-stage lock, they are impossible to pick, but a key could be inserted in preparation for activation by the first-stage lock. Once the pins are temporarily unfrozen, the physical key can be turned, and the entryway can be unlocked. However, this window of opportunity opens for only three seconds. After that, the digital lock resets and refreezes the pins. To be successful, the intruder would need to first learn the PIN and then be able to pick the door lock in under three seconds, a feat that may not be humanly possible.
- *Add reinforcements.* Consider reinforcing the thing the lock is securing. You might protect the hinges from tampering or install

strike plates, door/frame reinforcements, door handle shields, or floor guards.

- *Petition the lock industry.* Urge the lock industry to innovate and incorporate new designs into products used to protect information systems. Until there is sufficient consumer pressure to upgrade their outdated products, manufacturers will continue to sell the same familiar, vulnerable equipment.

CASTLE THEORY THOUGHT EXERCISE

Consider the scenario in which you are the ruler of a medieval castle with valuable assets inside. You know all your valuables are kept under lock and key—in chests and vaults, behind doors and gates—and you know a shinobi is capable of bypassing all these locks.

How could you bolster the security of your castle's locks? Would you know if your locks had been opened or bypassed? How might you block a shinobi's access to your locks? How could you configure false locks to trick a shinobi and alert you to an infiltration attempt?

Recommended Security Controls and Mitigations

Where relevant, the recommendations are presented with applicable security controls from the NIST 800-53 standard. Each should be evaluated with the concept of locks in mind.

1. Secure paper files, magnetic tape, hard drives, flash drives, disks, and other physical media in locked, controlled containers. [MP-4: Media Storage; MP-5: Media Transport]
2. Use secure keys or other locking devices to enforce physical access controls and authorization to systems and environments. [PE-3: Physical Access Control | (1) Information System Access | (2) Facility/Information System Boundaries | (4) Lockable Casings | (5) Tamper Protection; PE-4: Access Control for Transmission Medium; PE-5: Access Control for Output Devices]

Debrief

In this chapter, we talked about locks and their purposes. We noted that adversaries, no matter the era, will develop tools and techniques to bypass locks. We touched on the common lock technologies used to protect access to systems and why it's important to upgrade them. It's especially important to remember that, if an adversary gains physical access to your system, you should assume they can compromise it—hence the importance of physically preventing access to those systems with locks.

In the next chapter, we will discuss an advanced tactic shinobi used when the target was very securely locked down—one that effectively tricked their adversary into giving away the key. In a way, an organization's defenses aren't that different. Even if you have the best lock, if you give the key to an intruder, it won't help you.

12

MOON ON THE WATER

After making an agreement with your lord, you should lure the enemy out with bait to infiltrate their defenses.

In this technique, you should lure the enemy with tempting bait, like fishing in the sea or a river, so as to make an enemy who will not normally come out in fact leave its defenses.
—Bansenshūkai, Yo-nin II[1]

With an image straight out of a haiku, *Bansenshūkai* calls an open-disguise infiltration technique *suigetsu no jutsu*—the art of the "moon on the water."[2] While the technique had many uses, shinobi used it primarily to target heavily fortified enemy camps—the kind that restricted people from leaving, entering, or even approaching. Instead of penetrating the camp's defenses by force, shinobi would lure out their target, effectively tricking them into giving away ingress protocols such as insignias and other identifying marks, passwords, code words, and challenge-response signals. This technique also let shinobi tail targets as they returned to camp, lure defenders from their guard posts and infiltrate without resistance, or interact directly with targets and infiltrate through deception or offensive measures.

For targets especially reluctant to leave their heavily fortified defenses, the scroll instructs shinobi to seek help from their commanders to conduct advanced deceptions.[3] For example, a commander could move forces into vulnerable positions, enticing the enemy to attack and thereby depleting the enemy's defenses enough for shinobi to infiltrate. Alternatively, the shinobi would overpower the enemy when they returned, battle weary. The commander might even stage something more elaborate, like the beginning of a full-on, long-term castle siege. Then, shinobi might send a soldier posing as an allied general's messenger to convince the enemy to leave their castle, join in a counteroffensive, and break the siege. To complete the ruse, the shinobi commander would send a small force to masquerade as allied reinforcements, both luring the target from their encampment and allowing shinobi to infiltrate while the gates were open.

According to the scroll, after shinobi successfully infiltrated the target using *suigetsu no jutsu*, they had to keep these thoughts in mind:

- Remain calm. Do not appear lost.
- Mimic the people in the castle.
- Prioritize collecting code words, passwords, challenge responses, and insignias.
- Signal to allies as soon as possible.[4]

In this chapter, we will explore the ways this ancient technique could be deployed by a cyber threat actor and compare it to commonly used social engineering tactics. We'll introduce a way to think abstractly about network communication signals as entering and/or leaving perimeters—despite the computer system's not physically moving—and detail concepts for countering the moon on the water technique and social engineering attacks in general. Lastly, we'll attempt a thought exercise scenario that mimics the conundrum ancient Japanese generals must have faced when targeted by moon on the water.

Social Engineering

The shinobi moon on the water attack bears a striking similarity to today's *social engineering* attacks, which exploit a human target's decision-making processes and cognitive biases to manipulate them into revealing sensitive information or performing self-defeating actions. In cybersecurity, most social engineering tactics are used by adversaries operating inside enemy territory to exploit the target's trust. Examples of typical social engineering attacks include:

Phishing The adversary sends an email that convinces its recipients to open a dangerous document or visit a malicious hyperlink, resulting in malware infection, ransomware execution, data theft, or other attacks.

Pretexting The adversary calls or emails with invented scenarios designed to convince a target to reveal sensitive information or perform malicious actions.

Baiting The adversary strategically plants malicious portable media, such as a USB drive, in a physical location to entice the target to pick it up and connect it to internal systems, creating an opening for system compromise.

Social engineering is a particularly challenging security problem because it exploits human nature in ways that technological controls cannot always defend against. As targets and victims become more aware of social engineering threats, many organizations lean on focused technical controls, security protocols, and user education to protect their valuable assets. Employees are trained in how to properly handle and care for sensitive information and systems, while security teams document procedures to verify the identity of unknown or unsolicited visitors and require physical escorts for non-employees on company grounds. Red teams conduct internal phishing and tailgating tests, among other exercises, to gauge employee awareness of and instill resistance to social engineering tactics. Administrators implement technical controls to block malicious documents and hyperlinks, employ data loss prevention (DLP) software, prevent unauthorized system changes, blacklist unregistered systems and external media, and use caller ID.

While these are all good and necessary security measures, the way people work has changed. And thinking around social engineering attacks has not yet evolved to fully consider defending against moon on the water–style attacks—the kind that attempt to lure the target outside its own defenses.

Today, things like bring your own device (BYOD) policies, full-time remote work, and multitenant clouds make workers and organizations more flexible. However, they also weaken traditionally strong perimeter security architectures and expose employees to new social engineering threats. For example, in most cases, stateful firewall rules do not permit external (internet) communication to pass through the firewall to an internal host. Instead, the firewall requires the internal (intranet) system to initiate contact before it allows responses from the external system to pass through to the internal host. So, while the internal host does not physically leave the organization's defenses, doing so virtually—say, by visiting a malicious website—could allow threat actors to infiltrate within the responding communications. Essentially, this is digital tailgating.

In addition to directly compromising traditional security architectures, threat actors could use a number of moon on the water–style techniques to infiltrate heavily fortified organizations. Consider the following scenarios:

- An adversary triggers a fire alarm within a secure facility, causing employees to exit en masse. While firefighters clear the building, the adversary blends into the crowd of employees to steal or document badges, keys, tokens, faces, fingerprints, and more. To ease the flow of employees returning to work, the facility temporarily turns off badge readers, turnstiles, or other physical access controls, or security is so overwhelmed by the flood of people that they don't notice tailgating.
- An adversary uses a food truck to lure employees from a secure facility. Then they leverage their own status as a non-initiator to perform quid pro quo social engineering on a target, eventually developing a rapport and convincing the target to perform actions they would not in a traditional social engineering scenario.
- An adversary compromises the Wi-Fi network at a café across the street from a business conference to steal the credentials of a target organization's employees. By entering the café with their devices, those employees have left their organization's defenses and unknowingly exposed themselves to an environment controlled by the adversary.
- An adversary conducts large-scale disruptive, denial, or destructive attacks against targeted people, systems, and data, prompting them to move to a less secure disaster recovery operation site that is easier to infiltrate than the organization's permanent headquarters.

Note that while these attacks might not necessarily achieve an adversary's end goal, they could provide means or information that, in conjunction with other exploits, accomplishes malicious objectives.

Defenses Against Social Engineering

Most organizations perform social engineering awareness training and routinely phish test internal staff. While this strategy improves resiliency to such attacks, a significant percentage of personnel always fail. Unfortunately, most organizations leave staff vulnerable to social engineering. We need to do more to give employees the tools they need to guard against such deceptions.

1. *Establish safeguards.* Implement standard trust frameworks for employees to reduce the risk of compromise by social engineering. Identify high-value targets in your environment, and then establish security protocols, policies, and procedures for the appropriate control and handling of sensitive information on those systems (expand these to all systems over time). Conduct training, awareness, and test exercises within your organization to raise the level of employee awareness around social engineering, along with iterative threat modeling to review and improve related security controls.
2. *Implement "slow thinking."* Distribute and discuss Daniel Kahneman's book *Thinking, Fast and Slow*[5] with your security team. The book describes two systems of thought: the quicker, more impulsive "System 1" and the slower, more logical "System 2." Develop solutions that force your employees to slow down and think in System 2 terms, thereby avoiding the cognitive biases and shortcuts social engineers most often exploit. Possible examples include:
    - Configuring your phone-switching system to require an employee who receives an external call to punch in the even digits of the caller's phone number before the system can connect.
    - Configuring your mail client so that employees must type the "from" email address backward before they can open external email attachments.
    - Requiring users visiting non-whitelisted URLs to correctly enter the number of characters in the domain before the browser performs a DNS query.

    All these measures will slow down business operations, but they also help mitigate social engineering attacks.

CASTLE THEORY THOUGHT EXERCISE

Consider the scenario in which you are the ruler of a medieval castle with valuable assets inside. Your castle has been besieged, and you aren't sure

(continued)

whether you have enough food to keep your people fed. You receive a letter from an allied general who says he will send you food and other provisions if you can divert the attention of the enemy troops surrounding your castle at a specific date and time. The letter asks that you send your second-in-command to the allied general's camp nearby to help plan a counteroffensive against the siege.

How do you determine whether the letter is a ruse sent by the enemy? Can you independently verify the letter's authenticity? Assuming the letter is legitimate, how would you lure away the attacking army? Finally, what precautions would you take to receive the supplies while preventing infiltration of your own castle during the exchange?

Recommended Security Controls and Mitigations

Where relevant, recommendations are presented with applicable security controls from the NIST 800-53 standard. Each should be evaluated with the concept of moon on the water in mind.

1. Because security systems and controls can protect information only within established boundaries, implement safeguards that stop information and systems from passing beyond those boundaries and falling into the hands of social engineers. [AC-3: Access Enforcement | (9) Controlled Release; PE-3: Physical Access Control | (2) Facility/Information System Boundaries; SC-7: Boundary Protection]
2. Control your information flow so that even when data goes beyond the normal protective boundaries, it is not allowed to travel to or between unauthorized information systems. [AC-4: Information Flow Enforcement; PL-8: Information Security Architecture; SC-8: Transmission Confidentiality and Integrity]
3. For all non-local (that is, through a network) system maintenance, establish approval protocols, require strong authenticators and documented policies, and implement monitoring. [MA-4: Nonlocal Maintenance]
4. Establish protections for data outside controlled areas and restrict data-handling activities to authorized persons. [MP-5: Media Transport | (1) Protection Outside Controlled Areas]

Debrief

In this chapter, we described the advanced shinobi technique of moon on the water. We looked at various scenarios in which the moon on the water technique could be modernized to target businesses. We explored the challenges that social engineering presents and the various forms it can take. We reviewed existing security practices designed to handle social engineering and examined new defense concepts. And we lifted a thought exercise from the shinobi scrolls to demonstrate how fragile our trust model is and how hard it can be to safeguard against social engineering.

In the next chapter, we will discuss insider threats—one of the most fascinating topics in security. The shinobi scrolls provide detailed instructions on how to identify people who could be recruited as insiders with the help of some social engineering techniques—and they suggest a way to defend against insider threats that is contrary to modern best practices.

13

WORM AGENT

Make a minomushi, or worm agent (aka insider threat), out of an enemy.

A minomushi *is someone who serves the enemy but is made a ninja working for your side. Thus the agent is exactly like a worm in the enemy's stomach, which eats its belly from the inside out.*
—Bansenshūkai, Yo-nin I[1]

Never short on evocative imagery, *Bansenshūkai* describes an open-disguise infiltration technique called "the art of a worm in your stomach" (or "worm agent"), which calls for shinobi to recruit enemy insiders to perform tasks on their behalf. Such recruitment took high emotional intelligence. Shinobi had to choose an appropriate target; engineer opportunities to approach the target; and discreetly parse what the target thought about their employer, personal worth, and secret ambitions.[2] The scroll warns that candidate selection must be undertaken with extreme care, because attempting to recruit the wrong person to become a worm agent—or *minomushi*—could seriously harm a shinobi's mission. To maximize their odds of successful recruitment, shinobi developed eight archetypes of likely worm agents:[3]

- Individuals who have been unfairly or excessively punished by their current employer for prior offenses and who harbor deep-seated bitterness as a result.
- People who, despite being born to privilege or having impressive abilities, are employed beneath their station, have been passed over for promotion, and resent being underutilized.
- Habitual overachievers who consistently deliver good results for their employers but are rewarded with token titles, small bonuses, or insufficient raises—or with nothing at all. Their contributions minimized, they believe they might have had a more fruitful career had they been hired by another employer. They further believe their organization makes stupid decisions because leadership values sycophants and politicians over loyal employees with real accomplishments.
- Smart and talented workers who do not get along with leadership. Because these people tend to garner disapproval easily and are considered annoyances, their employers give them low-level positions, lay the groundwork for constructive dismissal, and generally make them feel unwelcome.
- Experts in their field whose employers exploit their circumstances, such as loyalty oaths or family obligations, to keep them in lower positions.
- Individuals whose job functions are in direct opposition to their personal identity, family needs, or beliefs, leading them to regret the work they do.
- Greedy and conniving people who lack loyalty or a moral compass.
- "Black sheep" employees who have a bad reputation due to past misdeeds and feel frustrated about their diminished status.

After a shinobi selected a potential *minomushi*, they created a plan to become acquainted and build a relationship with the candidate. *Bansenshūkai* instructs shinobi to present themselves as rich and curry the target's favor with money; use friendly banter to discern their likes, beliefs, and sense of humor; and use light banter to surreptitiously discover their inner thoughts. If the target's character aligned with a worm agent archetype, then the shinobi attempted to exploit those *minomushi* traits by promising wealth, recognition, and help with achieving their secret ambitions—or, more directly, alcohol and sex—in exchange for betraying their employer.[4]

Before exploiting the newly turned *minomushi*, shinobi were advised to obtain an oath of betrayal, collect collateral assets to guarantee the worm agent's loyalty, and establish signals and other operational security (OPSEC).[5]

In this chapter, we will review insider threats. We will compare and contrast the disgruntled worker with the recruited insider threat. We will also touch on the detection and deterrent methods that organizations use to deal with insider threats, as well as a new, tailored approach—inspired by the shinobi scrolls—to proactively prevent at-risk employees from becoming insider threats. Lastly, a thought exercise will ask you to imagine which former and/or current employees could become insider threats and to examine how you have interacted with them.

Insider Threats

An *insider threat* is an employee, user, or other internal resource whose actions could harm an organization—whether intentionally or not. Because they did not intend to perform malicious actions, a hapless employee who opens a phishing email and infects their workstation with malware is an unwitting insider threat. On the other hand, a disgruntled worker who purposefully releases a virus into the organization, whether for personal reasons or on behalf of an adversary, is an intentional insider threat. Because insider threats are legitimate, authorized users with authentication, privileges, and access to information systems and data, they are some of cybersecurity's most difficult problems to mitigate.

Many organizations rely on technical controls and threat hunters for early detection of insider threats. Technical detection techniques—things like behavior heuristics—can help identify potential insider threats. Vigilant cyberdefenders and hunters may investigate users who take uncharacteristic or inappropriate actions, including downloading all files to external portable media, performing searches for sensitive or proprietary data unrelated to their job, logging in to perform nonpriority work on weekends or holidays, accessing honeypot systems and files clearly labeled as restricted access, or downloading and using hacker-like tools to perform actions outside their job functions.

But technical controls are only part of a solid defense strategy, even for mature organizations. By checking references; performing background checks, including of criminal and financial history; and screening for drug use, the employer can verify that employees are not plainly vulnerable to undue influence. The human resources function plays a key role in identifying potential insider threats. Some human resources departments conduct annual employee surveys to identify potential issues, and others terminate at-risk employees proactively or recommend rescinding certain access privileges based on troublesome findings. Unfortunately, it is common for organizations to exercise minimal precautions. Most trust their employees, others ignore the issue, and still others accept the risk of insider threats so business operations can run smoothly.

Entities that fight insider threats more aggressively, such as organizations in the defense industry and the intelligence community, implement advanced detection and prevention measures such as polygraphs, routine clearance checks, counterintelligence programs, compartmentalization, and severe legal penalties—not to mention cutting-edge technical controls. However, even these controls cannot guarantee that the malicious actions of all insider threats—especially those assisted by sophisticated adversaries—will be detected and prevented. They also present unique implementation and operational challenges.

A New Approach to Insider Threats

Organizations that focus their efforts on scrutinizing employees and attempting to catch them in the act are waiting too long to address the threat. A more proactive approach is to foster a work environment that doesn't create the conditions in which insider threats thrive. Some of the following suggestions are tailored to remediating specific insider threat archetypes.

1. *Develop detection and mitigation techniques.* Examine the products and technical controls your organization uses to identify and mitigate internal threats. Run staff training and awareness sessions, review security incident reports, and perform red team exercises such as phishing tests to identify repeat unintentional insider threats. Then train, warn, and mitigate these individuals by implementing additional security controls on their accounts, systems, privileges, and access. For example, your security team could restrict staff members' ability and opportunity to perform insider threat actions with strict controls and policies. Some examples include:
    - Enforce a policy that macros cannot be enabled or executed on systems.

- Configure all emails to arrive in plaintext with hyperlinks disabled.
- Quarantine all external email attachments by default.
- Disable web browsing, or make it available only through an isolated internet system that is not connected to your organization's intranet.
- Disable USB ports and external media drives on certain systems.

Monitoring intentional insider threats requires both advanced detection techniques and technologies capable of deception and secrecy. Select these based on appropriate organizational threat modeling and risk assessments.

2. *Implement human resource–based anti-*minomushi *policies.* After the previous technical controls and detection techniques have been implemented and tested, address personnel controls. Ensure that human resources maintains records on current employees, previous employees, and candidates that include indicators of *minomushi* profiles. Ask pointed questions during candidate screening, performance reviews, and exit interviews to capture these diagnostics.
3. *Take special care to prevent the circumstances that create* minomushi *employees.* Your human resources team should consider the following organization-wide policies, presented in order of the eight *minomushi* archetypes:

   - Review employee disciplinary protocols to prevent unfair or excessive punishment—real or perceived—of employees. Require that employees and applicants disclose whether they have family members who have worked for your organization. Encourage human resources to gauge whether employees think the disciplinary actions against them are unfair or excessive, and then work together to find solutions that will mitigate employee animosity.
   - Regularly distribute employee surveys to gauge morale and identify underutilized talent in lower-ranking employees. Conduct transparent interviews with employees and management to determine whether: an employee is ready for a promotion, has gone unrecognized for recent achievements, or needs to grow a specific skill set; the company has a role to promote them into or budget to offer them a raise; or certain

employees perceive themselves to be better or more valuable than their colleagues—and whether a reality check is necessary. Working with management, consider how to alleviate employee bitterness and how to correct perceptions that the organization is not a meritocracy.

- As part of performance reviews, solicit feedback from colleagues to identify managers whom lower-ranking employees consider most valuable, as well as which employees believe they have not received appropriate recognition. Address these grievances with rewards and/or visibility into the company's leadership decisions.
- Encourage leadership to personally coach smart but socially awkward workers, discretely letting them know how they are perceived, with the goal of helping these employees feel more socially accepted and less isolated.
- Review and eliminate company policies that hold back top talent. These may include noncompete agreements, unfair appropriation of employees' intellectual property, and insufficient performance bonuses or retention incentives. While designed to protect the company, these policies may have the opposite effect.
- Conduct open source profiling of current employees and applicants to determine whether they have publicly expressed strong feelings about or have a conflict of interest in the mission of your organization. If so, reassign those employees to positions where they will feel more alignment between their personal values and the work they do or ease their departure from the organization.
- Develop character-profiling techniques to look for indicators that employees and applicants may be susceptible to bribery. Consider reducing system access and privilege levels for these employees, thereby reducing their usefulness to an adversary.

Work closely with employees at high risk for *minomushi* conditions. Give them extra resources, time, and motivation to move past whatever grudges they may hold, seize opportunities for personal growth, and develop self-respect. Minimize or halt organizational actions that reinforce bad memories or continue to punish an employee for past misdeeds.

CASTLE THEORY THOUGHT EXERCISE

Consider the scenario in which you are the ruler of a medieval castle with valuable information, treasure, and people inside. You receive credible threat intelligence that a shinobi plans to recruit someone within your castle to use their trust and access against you. You receive a list of eight different types of people likely to be recruited. It's unclear who specifically is being targeted or what the shinobi's objectives are.

Whom would you first suspect as an insider threat? Why is that person in a vulnerable state, and how could you remediate the situation? How would you detect the recruitment of one of your subjects or catch the recruiter in the act? How might you place guards to prevent insider threat actions? How could you train your subjects to report insider threats without causing everyone to turn on each other? How long should you maintain this insider threat program?

To avoid the political pitfalls of conducting this as a group exercise at your current workplace, consider building and using a list of former employees. If you can perform this exercise discretely with a small group of stakeholders, consider both former and current employees.

Recommended Security Controls and Mitigations

Where relevant, recommendations are presented with applicable security controls from the NIST 800-53 standard. Each should be evaluated with the concept of recruited insider threats in mind. (For more information, see PM-12: Insider Threat Program.)

1. Have the SOC work privately with human resources to correlate information on potential insider threats who display *minomushi* characteristics. The SOC should more closely monitor, audit, and restrict these high-risk individuals. It can also work with human resources to establish insider threat honeypots—for example, files in network shares that say "RESTRICTED DO NOT OPEN"—that identify employees who perform actions consistent with insider threats. [AC-2: Account Management | (13) Disable Accounts for High-Risk Individuals; AU-6: Audit Review, Analysis, and Reporting | (9) Correlation with Information from Nontechnical Sources; SC-26: Honeypots]
2. Use your own account to perform insider threat actions (without red team capabilities) on files and systems you know will not harm

your organization. Actions could include modifying or deleting data, inserting fake data, or stealing data. Document which systems and data your account can access, then use a privileged account such as admin or root to conduct malicious privileged actions. For example, you could create a new admin user with an employee name that does not exist. Ask whether your SOC can discover what data you stole, deleted, or modified within a specific date range to test whether your SOC can properly audit the privileged actions you performed. [AC-6: Leave Privilege | (9) Auditing Use of Privileged Functions; CA-2: Security Assessments | (2) Specialized Assessments]

3. Train your employees to recognize *minomushi* characteristics and insider threat behavior. Enable employees to easily and anonymously report potential *minomushi* conditions with respect to suspected insider threats, similar to how they report phishing scams. Conduct insider threat awareness exercises as part of regular security training. [AT-2: Security Awareness | (2) Insider Threat]

Debrief

In this chapter, we reviewed the shinobi technique of recruiting vulnerable people inside a target organization to perform malicious actions. We detailed the eight insider threat candidate archetypes and discussed the various types of insider threat detection and protection programs currently used by organizations. We described a new defensive approach based on information from the shinobi scrolls—one that uses empathy toward the disgruntled employee. The thought exercise in this chapter challenges participants to evaluate not only potential insiders but also their own actions toward coworkers; it encourages them to think about taking a more cooperative approach to potential insider threats.

In the next chapter, we will discuss long-term insiders: employees recruited by an adversary before they joined your organization. And, since long-term insiders intentionally hide any resentment or malice toward the organization, detecting them is even more problematic.

14

GHOST ON THE MOON

According to Japanese legend, if you knew how to seek the ghost who tends trees on the moon, he could invite you to the moon to eat the leaves of his tree, making you invisible.

In normal times, before the need arises, you should find someone as an undercover agent who will become the betrayer, an enemy you plant and thus make a ninja of him and have him within the enemy castle, camp or vassalage, exactly as the ghost in the legend, Katsuraotoko, is stationed on the moon.
—Bansenshūkai, Yo-nin I[1]

As part of its array of sophisticated infiltration techniques, the *Bansenshūkai* describes a long-term open-disguise tactic called "ghost on the moon." This tactic was designed to acquire privileged information and access through a planted secret agent. First, a shinobi recruits a person who is trustworthy, smart, wise, courageous, and loyal. Or, if the recruit is not loyal to begin with, the scroll suggests taking their family members hostage for the duration of the mission to make them "loyal." Then, the shinobi plants the agent in a foreign province or castle. There, they will spend years working earnestly with the target to build up their reputation, connections, knowledge, and access. Ideally, the plant will be working closely with enemy leadership. The mole must always maintain plausible, reliable, and conspicuous means of contact with the shinobi. If this enemy stronghold ever becomes a target for attack, the shinobi handler can call on the undercover agent for high-confidence intelligence, insider assistance, sabotage, and offensive actions against the enemy, including assassination.[2] And while the ghost on the moon gambit took years to pay off, to patient and tactful shinobi, the reward was worth the time investment.

In this chapter, we will look at the ghost on the moon as a type of insider threat. It can help to think of hardware implants, by way of analogy, as trying to find ghosts on the moon with a telescope. For that reason, we'll cover the subject of implants, supply chain security, and covert hardware backdoors. We will also compare the characteristics of a ghost on the moon plant with ideal hardware implants. We'll touch on supply chain risk management and threat-hunting strategies, with the caveat that underlying issues make this threat nearly impossible to fully defend against.

Implants

Corporate espionage and nation-state spy activities historically have relied on strategically placed agents to accomplish specific long-term missions. Today, technology offers newer and cheaper ways to get the results that have traditionally been possible only with human actors. For example, suppose your organization bought and installed a foreign-manufactured router on its network years ago, and it has functioned perfectly. But, unbeknownst to your security team, an adversary has just activated a hidden implant installed at the factory, providing direct, unfiltered backdoor access to your most sensitive systems and data.

The cybersecurity industry classifies this kind of attack as a *supply chain attack*. Here, *supply chain* refers to the products and services associated with an organization's business activities or systems; examples include hardware, software, and cloud hosting. In the previous example, the router performs the necessary business activity of moving digital information over the network to conduct ecommerce.

While heuristics or threat hunting can detect abnormal router behavior, there is no foolproof way to defend against covert implants. Some organizations may use quality assurance representatives to monitor manufacturing, but they cannot ensure that every system is built correctly.

However, several cybersecurity best practices can mitigate a router-based supply chain attack. A proactive organization could:

1. Perform a threat analysis of all router manufacturers and then use the results to acquire a router less likely to ship with compromised hardware or software
2. Employ a trusted, secure shipping service and procure chain of custody for the router to prevent malicious interception
3. Conduct forensic inspection of the router upon delivery to validate that it has not been compromised or altered from the expected specifications
4. Secure the router with tamper protections and detection technologies to identify and mitigate unauthorized alterations

Note that these steps are not limited to routers. Organizations can take these precautions on every service, device, system, component, and software application in their supply chain.

Covert implants are as valuable to modern nation-states as they were to shinobi, because the need to discover and defend against them poses difficult, long-term organizational challenges. Cybersecurity professionals continually test new concepts to address those challenges. For example, an organization can restrict trust and access to all systems under the assumption that they have already been compromised. However, the significant impact they have on business operations renders many of these concepts a practical impossibility.

Protections from Implants

Organizations attempting to weigh or x-ray every system to find something out of place will likely find themselves lost in the process of trying to manage their supply chain. What's more, advanced threat actors capable of supply chain compromises are likely to embed malicious functions in the default design of the system. In this way, only *they* know the secret to enabling the implant, and it exists in every system. And while an organization's inspection process may be able to see a threat, it might not understand what it's looking at. This is the scope of this problem—it's like trying to find a ghost on the moon. That said, guidance for protecting your organization from these implants is as follows:

1. *Identify supply chain attack conditions.* Create a list of components in your supply chain that have ghost on the moon potential. Include elements that:
    - Are considered high trust

- Can communicate
- Can provide lateral or direct access to sensitive information or systems
- Are not easily inspected
- Are not regularly replaced or updated

Specifically, look at software and hardware that communicates with external systems or exerts control over systems that can perform signal or communication functions (such as firmware on routers, network interface cards [NICs], and VPN concentrators). An implant can also exist as a hardware device, such as an extremely thin metal interface placed inside the PCI interface socket to act as a man-in-the-middle against the NIC, altering the data flow, integrity, confidentiality, and availability of network communications for that interface.

Imagine what your antivirus, hypervisor, vulnerability scanner, or forensic analyst cannot inspect or test in your environment. A key feature of ghost on the moon supply chain candidates is their ability to persist in the target's environment, which likely requires targeting components that do not break or wear down regularly, are not easily replaced or upgraded with cheaper versions over time, are too important to turn off or dispose of, and are difficult to modify and update (such as firmware, BIOS, UEFI, and MINIX). Autonomy and stealth requirements for this class of supply chain implant mean the implant needs to avoid inspection, scans, and other types of integrity testing while having access to some form of processor instruction or execution.

2. *Implement supply chain protections.* Implement supply chain safeguards and protections as needed. A ghost on the moon supply chain attack is one of the most challenging to detect, prevent, or mitigate. Thus, many organizations simply accept or ignore this risk. It can be useful to start with first principles—fundamental truths about security and the purpose of your business—and then use these truths as a rubric to evaluate the threat your organization faces. Review "A Contemporary Look at Saltzer and Schroeder's 1975 Design Principles"[3] or other core security works to determine appropriate mitigations for this threat. It could also be helpful to abstract the problems to higher-level concepts, where they become familiar and understood, and then attempt to solve them. Consider the following Castle Theory Thought Exercise.

CASTLE THEORY THOUGHT EXERCISE

Consider the scenario in which you are the ruler of a medieval castle with valuable assets inside. You receive credible threat intelligence that a scribe in your employ is an enemy "ghost on the moon" plant. This agent has spent the past 10 years learning to copy your handwriting style, vernacular, and sealing techniques, and they have memorized the names and addresses of all your important contacts. The plant has the means to modify your outgoing orders, such as by directing your standing army to travel far from key defense locations. It is not clear which scribe is the plant or whether the scribe has already been activated by an enemy shinobi. Scribes are a scarce resource in your kingdom—acquiring and training them is costly and time intensive—and they are critical to your operations.

How do you detect which scribe is an enemy plant, both pre- and post-activation? Consider what safeguards could prevent the scribe from sending altered orders in your name. What authentication protocols could you implement to prevent message spoofing? What integrity measures might you take to prevent message tampering? What nonrepudiation controls would deny false messages sent in your name? How could you ensure that future scribes are not compromised enemy plants? Finally, consider all these questions in a scenario in which multiple scribes are enemy plants.

Recommended Security Controls and Mitigations

Where relevant, recommendations are presented with applicable security controls from the NIST 800-53 standard. Each should be evaluated with the concept of ghost on the moon in mind.

1. Consider introducing heterogeneity into the supply chain by isolating, segmenting, and layering a diverse set of supply chain components. Supply chain diversity greatly reduces the potential impact of a compromised component. [SC-29: Heterogeneity]
2. Analyze your organization's procurement process to identify areas in which you can reduce the risk of a supply chain attack. Use techniques such as blind buying, trusted shipping, restricting purchases from certain companies or countries, amending purchasing contract language, and randomizing or minimizing acquisition time. [SA-12: Supply Chain Protection | (1) Acquisition Strategies/Tools/Methods]
3. Consider delaying non-security updates or acquisition of new, untested software, hardware, and services for as long as possible.

Implement advanced countermeasures to limit a sophisticated actor's opportunity to target your organization. [SA-12: Supply Chain Protection | (5) Limitation of Harm]

4. Purchase or assess multiple instances of the same hardware, software, component, or service through different vendors to identify alterations or non-genuine elements. [SA-12: Supply Chain Protection | (10) Validate as Genuine and Not Altered; SA-19: Component Authenticity; SI-7: Software, Firmware, and Information Integrity | (12) Integrity Verification]
5. Install independent, out-of-band monitoring mechanisms and sanity tests to verify that high-trust components suspected of supply chain attack are not performing covert communications or altering data streams. [SI-4: Information System Monitoring | (11) Analyze Communications Traffic Anomalies | (17) Integrated Situational Awareness | (18) Analyze Traffic/Covert Exfiltration]

Debrief

In this chapter, we reviewed the shinobi technique of hiring trusted allies to work inside an organization and position themselves to be as useful to the shinobi as possible. We compared this type of plant to hardware implants and discussed the theory behind what devices and systems would be suitable for hardware implants. We talked about supply chain attacks, along with ways to potentially detect them. The thought exercise challenged you to detect a compromised scribe who has privileged access to communications; the scribe represents a router, VPN, or other layer 3 device meant to be transparent to the communicators, highlighting how difficult it can be to determine when such a device is compromised.

In the next chapter, we will discuss the shinobi's backup plan if you do happen to catch them or their plant. The shinobi would often plant false evidence ahead of time, long before their covert mission, enabling them to shift blame if caught. When successful, this tactic tricks the victim into believing an ally betrayed them, and this deception itself harms the target.

15

THE ART OF THE FIREFLIES

The art of fireflies should be performed only after you know everything about the enemy in great detail so that you can construct your deception in accordance with the target's mindset.

Before you carry out surveillance or a covert shinobi activity, you should leave a note for your future reputation.
—Yoshimori Hyakushu #54

The *Bansenshūkai* describes an open-disguise infiltration technique for shinobi called "the art of fireflies" (*hotarubi no jutsu*).[1] I like to think that this technique was named based on how the flash of light from a firefly lingers in your night vision after the fly has moved, causing you to grasp at empty space. *Shōninki* describes the same technique as "the art of camouflage" (*koto wo magirakasu no narai*).[2] Using this technique, shinobi plant physical evidence that baits an enemy into taking some desired action, including misattributing whom the shinobi works for, making false assumptions about the shinobi's motives, and reacting rashly to the attempted attack, exposing themselves to further offensive actions.

A forged letter with incriminating details or misleading evidence about the enemy was the most common *hotarubi no jutsu* technique, with several variations. The scrolls describe shinobi sewing a letter into their collar so that it would be found quickly if they were caught or searched.[3] Or, a shinobi might recruit a willing but inept person to be a "ninja," give them a letter detailing the exact opposite of the shinobi's true plans, and send them on a mission into the adversary's environment, knowing that this "doomed agent" would certainly be captured. Importantly, the recruit themselves would not be aware of this part of the plan. Upon searching the recruit, guards would find the forged letter, which implicated a high-value target—such as the adversary's most capable commander—in a treasonous plot. The "ninja" would likely break under torture and attest to the authenticity of the message, further damning the target.[4] This all served to deceive the enemy into attacking or disposing of their own allies.

In an even more elaborate variation, prior to the mission, the shinobi would carefully plant evidence that supported the letter's false story and place the forged letter in an incriminating location, such as the quarters of the enemy commander's trusted adviser. The forged letter then became a safeguard. If the shinobi were caught, they would withstand torture until they could determine the enemy's objectives, and then reveal their secret knowledge of the letter. The enemy would then find the letter and the connected evidence. Having built credibility, the shinobi would then pledge to become a double agent or share secrets about their employer in exchange for not being executed.[5] This technique left the enemy confused about the shinobi's motives, concerned about potential betrayal, and in doubt about who the real adversary was.

In this chapter, we will review the challenges associated with attributing threats to a specific adversary and/or source. We'll cover attribution investigations using threat analytics, observable evidence, and behavior-based intelligence assessments. We'll also discuss the problem of sophisticated adversaries who are aware of these attribution methods and thus take countermeasures. The more emphasis a defender places on attribution, the more difficult and risky cyber threat actors can make pursuing leads, so we'll also discuss ways to address this increased risk.

Attribution

Attribution, in a cybersecurity context, refers to an assessment of observable evidence that can be used to identify actors in cyberspace. The evidence can take many forms. A threat actor's behavior, tools, techniques, tactics, procedures, capabilities, motives, opportunities, and intent, among other information, all provide valuable context and drive responses to security events.

For example, suppose your home alarm went off, indicating a window had been broken. Your response would vary drastically based on your level of attribution knowledge: a firefighter entering your home to extinguish a blaze would evoke a different response than a robber breaking in to steal your belongings, or an errant golf ball crashing through the window. Of course, attribution isn't always simple to attain. A thief can exercise some control over observable evidence by wearing gloves and a mask. They could even wear a firefighter outfit to disguise their identity and deceive homeowners into acquiescing to their entry. A thief could plant, destroy, or avoid creating evidence of the crime during or after the act, impeding the subsequent work of forensic investigators. A truly sophisticated criminal might even frame another criminal using spoofed fingerprint pads; stolen hair, blood, or clothing samples; a realistic 3D-printed mask; or a weapon acquired from the unsuspecting patsy. If the framed individual has no alibi, or the crime is committed against a target consistent with their motivations, then authorities would have every reason to suspect or arrest the patsy.

Cybersecurity professionals face these types of attribution problems and then some. Attribution is particularly difficult due to the inherent anonymity of the cyber environment. Even after executing the difficult task of tracking an attack or event to a source computer and physical address, cybersecurity professionals can find it exceedingly hard to verify the identity of the human attacker. Attempts to trace the threat actor's origin on the compromised machine often lead to tunnels, VPNs, encryption, and rented infrastructure with no meaningful logs or evidence. Sophisticated threat actors may even compromise and remotely connect to foreign machines, using them as platforms to launch attacks against other systems. Even after detecting the adversary, it may be advisable in certain cases to not immediately block them or remove their access; instead, it may be beneficial to monitor them for a while to determine their goals and identifying characteristics.[6]

In some cases, threat groups deliberately leave behind tools or other observables to push an attribution narrative. The United States, Russia, and North Korea have reportedly altered or copied code segments, strings, infrastructure, and artifacts in their cybertools to cause misattribution.[7] When cybersecurity professionals discover and reverse engineer particularly stealthy malware, they occasionally observe unique, superfluous strings in the malware traces. Perhaps these strings were overlooked—a tradecraft error by the operator or developer. But they could also be "the art of fireflies"—evidence designed to be discovered and used for (mis)attribution.

Note that the same mechanisms that make deception possible also provide powerful means of identification. Memory dumps, disk images, registries, caches, network captures, logs, net flows, file analyses, strings, metadata, and more help identify cyber threat actors. Various intelligence disciplines, such as signal intelligence (SIGINT), cyber intelligence (CYBINT), and open source intelligence (OSINT), also contribute to attribution, while human intelligence (HUMINT) capabilities collect data from specific sources that, once processed and analyzed, helps indicate who may have conducted cyberattacks. These capabilities are typically kept secret, as disclosing their existence would inform targets how to avoid, deny, or deceive these systems, stunting the ability to generate useful intelligence and threat attribution.

Approaches to Handling Attribution

It is reasonable for organizations to want to know the identity and origin of threat actors who compromise their systems and networks. It's understandable that many want to take action, such as hacking back, to discover who these threat actors are. However, threat actors, like the shinobi, will always find ways to conduct covert malicious actions through denial and deception, making attribution uncertain. Furthermore, to take a lesson from history, the need to conduct shinobi attribution only ceased once Japan was unified under peaceful rule and shinobi were no more. The world is unlikely to experience unity in the foreseeable future, so nation-state cyberattacks are likely to continue. Until world peace happens, the following approaches to attribution can help you identify what, if anything, you can do about ongoing cyber conflict:

1. *Shed your cognitive biases.* Reflect on your own cognitive biases and flawed logic. Everybody has holes in their thinking, but we can be mindful of them and work to correct them. Construct your own case studies. Review prior judgments that turned out to be incorrect, identify the mistakes made, and consider how to improve your analytical ability. This important work can be done in small steps (logic puzzles, crosswords, and brainteasers are a great way to improve cognitive function) or big strides. You can study articles and books on psychology that discuss known cognitive biases

and logical fallacies and learn structured analytical techniques to overcome your own.[8]

2. *Build attribution capabilities.* Examine what data sources, systems, knowledge, and controls you can use to influence attribution at your organization. Are you running open, unprotected Wi-Fi that allows unregistered, unauthenticated, and unidentified threat actors to anonymously connect to your network and launch attacks? Are you managing routers that allow spoofed IPs, or do they use reverse-path forwarding (RFP) protection technologies to prevent anonymized attacks from within your network? Are you correctly publishing a sender policy framework to prevent threat actors from spoofing email addresses and assuming your organization's identity?

   While many of these configuration changes incur no direct costs, the time and labor (and opportunity costs) to implement such wide-reaching changes can give management pause. However, consider whether a prior decision to invest in good cameras and lighting helps a storekeeper correctly identify a vandal. Establishing sound logging, documentation, and evidence collection practices improves attribution capabilities, enforces greater technological accountability, and provides end users with better visibility into network threats.

3. . . . *Or forget about attribution.* Work with your organization's stakeholders to determine the scope of attribution efforts necessary to mitigate risk. For organizations with the ability to arrest threat actors or launch counteroffensive attacks, attribution is a necessity. However, most organizations cannot or should not attempt to catch or attack threat actors, learn their identities, or map their capabilities. In reality, attribution to a specific threat actor is not always necessary. Awareness of the threat can be enough to analyze and defend against it.

   For example, suppose two threat actors target your organization's intellectual property. One wants to sell the information on the black market to make money, and the other wants the information to help build weapons systems for their country. It actually doesn't matter. Regardless of the threat actors' purpose and an organization's capability to track them down, defenders must ultimately restrict or deny opportunities to exploit their security flaws. The organization does not necessarily need to assess a threat actor's motivation to avoid the threat.

CASTLE THEORY THOUGHT EXERCISE

Consider the scenario in which you are the ruler of a medieval castle with valuable assets inside. Your guards capture a stranger in the act of digging a tunnel under one of your castle walls. After intense interrogation, the stranger claims they were paid to dig a tunnel to the castle's food storage so bandits could steal the supplies. However, your guards search the prisoner and discover a note with instructions on how to communicate with one of your trusted advisers. The note indicates that this adviser has a plan to spur rebellion against your rule by depriving your villagers of food. The message appears authentic. Your guards cannot identify the intruder or whom they are working for.

Consider how you would conduct attribution to determine who the intruder is, where they're from, what their motivation might be, and whom they might be working for. How could you test the stranger's assertion that their ultimate aim is to steal food—as opposed to, say, destroy the food, provide an infiltration route for a different threat actor, attack castle inhabitants, or even start a rebellion? How could you confirm your adviser's role in enemy schemes? What actions would you take if you did find further evidence for the intruder's attribution scenario? And what would you do if you couldn't prove it?

Recommended Security Controls and Mitigations

Where relevant, recommendations are presented with applicable security controls from the NIST 800-53 standard. Each should be evaluated with the concept of attribution in mind.

1. Map accounts to user identities. Verify the identity of the individual associated with the user account via biometrics, identification, logical or physical evidence, or access controls. [SA-12: Supply Chain Protection | (14) Identity and Traceability]
2. Develop a plan that defines how your organization handles attribution assessments of threat agents. [IR-8: Incident Response]
3. Establish threat awareness programs that collect and share information on the characteristics of threat actors, how to identify them in your environment, evidence of attribution, and other observables. Use specific collection capabilities such as honeypots

for attribution purposes. [PM-16: Threat Awareness Program; SC-26: HoneyPots]

4. Apply security and collection controls. Perform threat modeling to identify threat agents. [SA-8: Security and Privacy Engineering Principles]

Debrief

In this chapter, we reviewed the art of the fireflies—a misattribution technique used by the shinobi. Cyber threat groups are continually evolving in sophistication, and they are likely to incorporate this technique into their operations security procedures, if they haven't already. We noted that several threat groups are believed to be using misattribution techniques already and discussed approaches to handling attribution, and how the future for attribution is bleak.

In the next chapter, we will discuss shinobi tactics for maintaining plausible deniability when defenders interrogated them. The chapter will also discuss advanced shinobi interrogation techniques and tools used when capturing enemy shinobi.

16

LIVE CAPTURE

Use good judgment to determine whether the target is actually inattentive or whether they are employing a ruse to lure ninjas and capture them.

If you find a suspicious individual while you are on night patrol, you should capture him alive by calling on all your resources.

—Yoshimori Hyakushu #74

Though shinobi encountered deadly violence as an everyday part of the job, *Bansenshūkai* recommends that enemies, especially suspected ninjas, be captured alive rather than immediately killed. Searching and interrogating a captured ninja allows shinobi to discover what the attacker has done or is planning to do, determine who the intruder's employer is, and learn valuable secrets and tradecraft, all of which could greatly help guards defend against ninja attacks and help lords to understand strategic threats. In addition, the captured enemy might turn out to be a comrade in disguise, a fact that would not be clear until deep interrogation.[1] The *Ninpiden* calls for the suspected ninja to be bound hand and foot and placed on a leash. The *Ninpiden* also recommends using tools, such as a spiked gag, to prevent the captive from talking, as a skillful ninja could alert allies, persuade their captor to release them, or even bite off their own tongue to commit suicide.[2]

The scrolls acknowledge that capturing an enemy ninja alive is no easy task. One of *Bansenshūkai*'s more direct techniques involves loading a musket with a chili powder–infused cotton ball—a sort of ancient tear gas or pepper spray. When fired at close range, this projectile would create debilitating irritation in the target's eyes and nose, rendering them more susceptible to capture. The scrolls also describe more oblique tactics, such as *fushi-kamari* ambushes and traps. For example, the tiger fall trap (*mogari* or *koraku*) described in *Bansenshūkai Gunyo-hiki* was originally designed to capture tigers (as the name suggests) but was later modified to capture ninjas. In it, barriers funnel an intruder through a maze of hidden traps. While allies would know a trusted path, a ninja infiltrating alone at night would not, making it likely they would fall into the trap. Other trap methods used *tsuiritei*, or "fake suspended wall sections," which are veneers that look like real walls but are built with wedges and false posts. When a ninja would attempt to scale these fake walls, the walls would collapse, surprising and likely injuring the ninja and thus permitting their easy capture.[3]

Bansenshūkai also suggests defensive measures to guard against capture, suggesting ways to detect and avoid *fushi-kamari* ambushes. Shinobi were advised to scout forests, fields, valleys, trenches, and other settings for unnatural behavior from birds, other animals, and even the grass, all of which could indicate a trap. Dummies and unusual smells also tip the hand of a potential ambush.[4] In enemy territory, shinobi could deploy a number of evasive tactics, including:

Quail hiding (*uzura-gakure*) A shinobi would curl into a ball on the ground and concentrate on being blind, unaware, and unresponsive so the enemy would be unlikely to find them. Even when prodded by a guard with a spear or sword, they would not react.

Raccoon dog retreat (*tanuki-noki*) While fleeing on foot, a shinobi would decide to be "caught" by a faster pursuer. When the gap between them narrowed, the shinobi would drop to the ground without warning and aim their sword at the pursuer's waist, impaling the pursuer before they could react.

Retreat by 100 firecrackers (*hyakurai-ju*) A shinobi would place firecrackers near the target, either setting them on a delayed fuse or arranging for allies to light them. The sound would distract the enemy pursuers.

Fox hiding (*kitsune-gakure*) A shinobi would escape by moving vertically. Instead of trying to flee enemy territory by moving from point A to point B, the shinobi would climb a tall tree or hide in a moat, changing the dimensions of the chase. This tactic often stumped the enemy, who was unlikely to think to look up or down for the target.[5]

Other methods of escape included imitation—mimicking a dog or other animal to deceive pursuers—and false conversation—language that would mislead the enemy, allowing the shinobi to flee.[6] For example, a shinobi who knew they were being followed might pretend not to hear the pursuers and whisper to an imaginary ally so the alert guards would overhear them. If the shinobi said, "Let's quietly move to the lord's bedroom so we may kill him in his sleep," the guards would likely send forces to the lord's bedroom, allowing the shinobi to escape in another direction.

Of course, the best way for shinobi to avoid being captured was to leave behind no evidence that could lead investigators to suspect a breach in the first place. The scrolls stress the importance of conducting missions without trace so that the target has no cause to suspect a shinobi on the premises. Guidance on operating covertly abounds in the scrolls; the writing is artfully vivid in places. *Yoshimori Hyakushu* #53 states, "If you have to steal in as a shinobi when it is snowing, the first thing you must be careful about is your footsteps."[7]

Capturing threats alive is, unfortunately, not always top of mind for many organizations. When some organizations detect a threat on a system, they do the opposite of what is recommended in the shinobi scrolls: they immediately unplug the machine, wipe all data, reformat the drive, and install a fresh version of the operating system. While this wipe-and-forget response eradicates the threat, it also eliminates any opportunity to capture the threat, let alone investigate it or analyze its goals, what it has already accomplished, and how.

In this chapter, we will discuss the importance of being able to capture and interact with cyber threats while they are "alive." We will review existing forensics/capture methods, along with ways threat actors may attempt to evade them. We'll consider ways to capture cyber threats "alive" with tiger traps and honey ambushes—techniques inspired by the ancient shinobi. In addition, we will touch on modern implementations of shinobi evasion tactics (e.g., quail hiding and fox hiding) that have been used by persistent threats. Lastly, we'll cover much of the capture and interrogation guidance from the shinobi scrolls—guidance around how to properly control a threat so it cannot alert its allies or self-destruct.

Live Analysis

In cybersecurity, computer forensic imaging provides necessary threat intelligence. Forensic images are typically made after a security incident (such as a malware infection) or a use violation (such as the download of child pornography onto a device), with imaging done in a way that preserves evidence without disrupting the integrity of the data on the system under investigation. Evidence from a forensic image can help security professionals learn what the threat was and how it exploited vulnerabilities. Then, in time, it can provide the information necessary to develop signatures, safeguards, and proactive blocking measures. For instance, determining that an attacker was after specific intellectual property on one critical system tells defenders to protect that system's data. If forensics determines that the attack succeeded and sensitive data was compromised, the organization can use that knowledge to determine its strategic business response. If the threat failed, the organization can prepare for possible follow-up attacks. Forensic indicators might also provide an understanding of who was responsible for the threat, further dictating the response. An organization's strategy should take into account the severity of the threat—for instance, whether the attacker was a foreign government, a disgruntled employee, or a kid performing harmless notoriety hacking.

Collecting a device's data for analysis involves *live capture* (also known as *live analysis* or *live acquisition*) and *imaging* (also *forensic imaging* or *mirroring*). Organizations use honeypots and other deceptive virtual environments to live capture and even interact with attackers. Such systems are often configured to lure in hackers or be easily accessible to malware so that when the threat infiltrates the system, hidden logging and monitoring controls capture exactly what the threat does and how, along with other observables. Unfortunately, many attackers are aware of these honeypots and perform tests to determine whether they are inside a simulated environment meant to collect intelligence. If their suspicions are confirmed, attackers will behave differently or cease operations, undermining the security team's efforts. Network access control (NAC) devices can also contain live threats by dynamically switching a system to an infected VLAN, where it remains online and "live" while defenders respond.

Forensics are not typically performed on a live capture. Rather, the forensic analyst looks at static, inert, or dead data, which may have lost certain information or the threat's unique details. This is commonly seen in fileless malware, which resides in memory, or in specific malicious configurations or artifacts, such as those in routing table caches. Live analysis is not conducted more often for a number of reasons, including:

- Specialized technology requirements
- Having to bypass organizational policies that require disconnecting, unplugging, quarantining, or blocking compromised systems
- A lack of capable forensic resources that are physically onsite to conduct live analysis
- Lack of employee access to vital systems during an investigation

Perhaps most importantly, if live analysis is mishandled, the threat can become aware of the forensic imaging software on the system and decide to hide, delete itself, perform antiforensic countermeasures, or execute destructive attacks against the system.

To bypass forensic capture techniques, threats deploy in multiple stages. During the initial stage, reconnaissance, the threat looks for the presence of capturing technology, only loading malware and tools after it validates that it can operate safely within the environment. Such precautions are necessary for the threat actor. If a successful capture and forensic analysis occurs, the threat's tools and techniques can be shared with other organizations and defenders, allowing them to learn from the attack, patch against it, or develop countermeasures. Law enforcement may even use forensic capture tactics to track down or provide evidence against threat actors.

Recently, sophisticated actors have moved laterally into computer and network areas that standard forensic imaging, capture, and analysis tools do not or cannot inspect. These actors' innovations include installing hard drive firmware that creates a hidden, encoded filesystem; embedding malware in BIOS storage; leveraging local microchip storage to operate outside normal working memory; and changing low-level modules and code on networking gear such as routers, switches, smart printers, and other devices not traditionally inspected by or even practical for forensic imaging. Certain threats imitate core OS or trusted security components by infiltrating the original manufacturer, who is inherently trusted and not considered for forensic analysis. Others hide by deleting forensic evidence, moving to the memory of a system that does not reset often—such as a domain controller—and then waiting for forensic scrutiny on the systems of interest to subside before returning to the intended target.

Confronting Live Threats

Organizations too often find themselves dealing with an active security incident when the single person trained to use forensic imaging tools is out of the office. It sometimes takes days before the quarantined machine can be shipped to that person for examination, and by then, the attack is no longer a live representation of the current threat. This inability to operate at the same speed as the threat, or faster, leaves defenders relegated to the role of a forensic janitor—the person who collects evidence and cleans up infections after the threat actor has already achieved their objectives. Proactively establishing capabilities, traps, and ambushes to confront the threat is necessary to capture it alive and interrogate it thoroughly.

1. *Establish a forensic capability.* Commit to and invest in establishing a dedicated team with the equipment, experience, certification, and authorization to perform computer forensics. Create forensic kits with write blockers, secure hard drives, and other specialized software and devices. Ensure that all systems used for capture and analysis have appropriate forensic agents so the team can immediately identify, locate, isolate, and perform collection. Ensure that all employees understand how they can help the forensic team identify and locate affected systems and preserve evidence. If it has been more than a month since they conducted a forensic investigation, run refresher training courses or exercises with the forensic team. Most importantly, when a forensic report is done, read it to discover root causes of security incidents and take proactive measures to remediate the vulnerabilities exploited.
2. *Conduct honey ambushes.* Where appropriate, empower your team to ambush threat actors rather than simply following their trail or catching them in a honeypot. Aggressively trapping and ambushing threats requires close partnerships with cloud hosts, ISPs, registrars, VPN service providers, the Internet Crime Complaint Center (IC3), financial services, law enforcement organizations, private security companies, and commercial companies. Support the goal of creating network territory hostile to threat actors, where the combined forces of you and your partners can ambush threat actors, groups, or campaigns to capture evidence, malware, tools, and exploits themselves.
3. *Set tiger traps.* Consider creating tiger fall traps in likely targets in your network, such as a domain controller. A market opportunity exists for a product that serves as an operational production system with honeypot capabilities that trigger if the wrong action is performed. Because threat actors attempting to bypass security controls typically pivot from one system to another or move laterally across systems and networks, it may be possible to establish false or booby-trapped jumpboxes that seem like routes to other

networks but in fact trap the threat. Deploy these traps in such a way that the wrong action causes a system to freeze, lock, or isolate the attack, in turn allowing defenders to examine, interact with, or forensically live capture the threat. Do this by freezing the CPU clock, causing the hard drive to operate in buffer mode only, or using a hypervisor to trap and log the activity. Provide training to ensure that system admins and other IT professionals can remotely traverse a legitimate path without falling into the trap.

CASTLE THEORY THOUGHT EXERCISE

Consider the scenario in which you are the ruler of a medieval castle with valuable assets inside. Your guards recently captured an intruder they believed to be a ninja, quickly killed the suspect, and then set the body on fire. The guards say they took these measures to remove any residual risk the ninja posed. When you ask your guards why they thought the intruder was a ninja, what the intruder carried on their person, what this person was doing in the castle, and how a stranger successfully infiltrated your stronghold, the guards do not know. They seem to expect praise for quickly terminating the threat while suffering minimal harm themselves.

How could you establish better protocols, procedures, and tools for your guards to safely apprehend suspected intruders? How would you have interrogated the ninja—if the intruder was indeed a ninja—had your guards not killed them? What would you have looked for in the ninja's possessions had they not been burned? How do you think the ninja infiltrated your castle, and how could you confirm those suspicions? How would you search your castle to determine whether the ninja performed sabotage, placed traps, or sent a signal before they died? What would you ask the guard who discovered the ninja, and how could their answers help you train other guards? What do you expect to learn from this investigation, and what decisions or actions might you take based on your findings?

Recommended Security Controls and Mitigations

Where relevant, recommendations are presented with applicable security controls from the NIST 800-53 standard. Each should be evaluated with the concept of live capture in mind.

1. Restrict the use of external systems and components within your organization if you do not have the authorization or capability

to perform forensic investigations on them. [AC-20: Use of External System | (3) Non-Organizationally Owned Systems and Components]

2. Using external sensors and SIEMs that cannot be easily accessed, implement automated mechanisms to fully collect live data, PCAPs, syslog, and other data needed for forensic analysis. [AU-2: Audit Events; AU-5: Response to Audit Processing Failures | (2) Real-Time Alerts; IR-4: Incident Handling | (1) Automated Incident Handling Processes; SA-9: External System Services | (5) Processing, Storage, and Service Location; SC-7: Boundary Protection | (13) Isolation of Security Tools, Mechanisms, and Support Components]
3. If you decide to implement non-persistence as a countermeasure against threats—such as by regularly reimaging or rebuilding all your systems to destroy any unauthorized access—consider performing a forensic capture before reimaging or teardown to preserve evidence of threats. [AU-11: Audit Record Retention | (1) Long-Term Retrieval Capability; MP-6: Media Sanitization | (8) Remote Purging or Wiping of Information; SI-14: Non-Persistence; SI-18: Information Disposal]
4. Implement, document, and enforce baseline system configurations in your organization so forensic analysts can more easily determine what information could have been altered by a threat. [CM-2: Baseline Configuration | (7) Configure Systems and Components for High-Risk Areas; SC-34: Non-Modifiable Executable Programs]
5. Provide training and simulated exercises for your forensic staff to facilitate effective responses in the event of a security incident. [IR-2: Incident Response Training | (1) Simulated Events]
6. Establish a forensic analysis team with the capability and authorization to conduct real-time forensic collection and investigation. [IR-10: Integrated Information Security Analysis Team]
7. Use safeguards to validate that forensic systems, software, and hardware have not been tampered with. [SA-12: Supply Chain Risk Management | (10) Validate as Genuine and Not Altered | (14) Identity and Traceability]

Debrief

In this chapter, we reviewed the shinobi techniques of capturing and interrogating enemy shinobi, as well as tactics used to evade capture. We touched on how collecting more forensic evidence gives the threat actor more opportunities to feed investigators false data points—and why it can be better to interact with live threats. We discussed best practices around forensic capabilities to gain visibility into threats, along with advanced techniques, such as ambushes and traps, for confronting threats.

In the next chapter, we will discuss the most destructive mode of attack in the shinobi's arsenal: attacking with fire.

17

FIRE ATTACK

First, it is easy to set fires; second, it is not easy for the enemy to put out the fire; and third, if your allies are coming to attack the castle at the same time, the enemy will lose any advantage as the fortifications will be understaffed.

If you are going to set fire to the enemy's castle or camp, you need to prearrange the ignition time with your allies.
—Yoshimori Hyakushu #83

One of the most impactful things a shinobi could do after infiltrating a castle or fortification was start a fire—ideally in or around gunpowder storehouses, wood stores, food or supply depots, or bridges. A well-set fire spread quickly while staying out of sight; could not be contained or extinguished easily; and became an immediate danger to the castle's integrity, supplies, and inhabitants. Castle defenders were forced to choose between putting out the flames and fighting the enemy army signaled to attack by the arsonist. Attempting to fight both battles at once weakened a target's ability to do either. Those who fought the fire were easily overtaken by the advancing soldiers, while those who ignored the fire to take up arms ultimately lost the battle no matter how well they fought.[1]

The scrolls talk at length about fire attacks, including the various tools, tactics, and skills used to execute them. Before an attack, shinobi studied a castle's inhabitants to determine when they slept or when key positions went unguarded. They then worked with other invaders to coordinate timing. Shinobi engineered numerous custom tools for these attacks, such as fire arrows, covert fire-holding cylinders, land mines, bombs, and throwable torches.[2] Among the most visually dynamic weapons were "heat horses"—horses with special torches tied to their saddles and set loose to run wildly inside fortifications, spreading fire chaotically, distracting guards and inhabitants, and proving difficult to contain. Amid the confusion, shinobi communicated with forces concealed outside the castle to cue the attack once the fire had sufficiently spread.[3]

While medieval armies had the capability to initiate a fire attack from afar—by deploying archers to shoot fire arrows, for example—*Bansenshūkai* recommends that commanders employ shinobi to set the fire instead. Compared to external attacks, fires set by shinobi would not be spotted and extinguished as quickly. Also, the shinobi could set them near combustible or strategically valuable items, and an agent could feed them until they grew.[4]

The success of fire attacks made them ubiquitous in feudal Japan, so many castles began implementing targeted countermeasures. These included fireproofing fortifications with *dozo-zukuri* ("fireproofing with plaster") or fire-resistant lacquer,[5] building with fireproof or fire-resistant materials such as clay or rock, using fire-resistant roof tiles, establishing fire watch teams, and creating firebreaks by designating inconsequential buildings (i.e., buildings that could be sacrificed to prevent fire from spreading to critical infrastructure).[6] Guards were also warned that fires might be purposeful distractions to facilitate theft, attack, or other actions[7] (advice later mirrored in the *Gunpo Jiyoshu* manual[8]).

It is important to remember that shinobi did not have automatic lighters and that defenders kept a constant lookout for arsonists (much like modern organizations that maintain antivirus and threat detection everywhere). Shinobi engineered ingenious methods to deliver fire covertly, weaponize it, and exploit combustible targets. When imagining how cyberattacks could be delivered and weaponized against targets, keep shinobi ingenuity with fire attacks in mind.

In this chapter, we will review how, in the context of cyberwar, shinobi fire attacks are surprisingly similar to modern hybrid tactics. Fire is a great analogy for wormable/self-propagating cyberattacks, as it spreads to everything it can touch. We will review examples of destructive cyberattacks, as well as how modern adversaries time and coordinate them. We will touch on the various defenses that organizations use to prevent, mitigate, contain, and recover from cyberattacks. Takeaways from this chapter can be applied to firewalls, as well as new, more advanced network defense strategies.

Destructive Cyber Attacks

Not long after computers were able to connect and communicate with each other, self-propagating viruses and worms were born. Destructive attacks have only gotten more prolific with time. Now, a destructive attack on one organization's network can quickly spread like fire, destroying systems and data across the internet. Considering the growing interconnectedness of systems in cyberspace as well as inherent security flaws, a network or machine connected to the internet without patches or other safeguards is basically kindling just waiting to be lit.

In the early 2000s, the industry saw its first ransomware attacks. In these attacks, malware encrypts a system or network's data (and deletes the backups) until the target pays to unencrypt them. These viruses quickly spread from systems to network storage to the cloud, holding data hostage or, in the case of nonpayment, destroying it through encryption. Like ninja fire attacks, ransomware is often used to distract from bigger gambits. For example, adversaries (believed to be North Korean) deployed the FEIB Hermes ransomware attack to divert cyber defenders' attention while the attackers executed the SWIFT financial attack, which netted them millions of dollars.[9]

Next came wiper malware attacks, in which the adversary plants "time bomb" viruses in multiple systems to delete all system data and wipe backups at a specified, opportune time. One example is the Shamoon virus, which is believed to have been conducted by Iranian threat actors against Saudi Arabia and was launched at the start of a weekend holiday to destroy data and disable industrial oil systems.[10]

Recently, attackers have deployed sabotage malware against industrial control systems, giving the attackers the capability to read sensors or control mechanical switches, solenoid, or other physical actuators that operate blast furnaces,[11] electrical grids,[12] anti–air defense systems,[13] and nuclear centrifuges.[14] Such an attack could disable these critical systems or cause them to malfunction, potentially leading to explosions, other physical destruction, or simultaneous kinetic attacks.

Administrative efforts to prevent the spread of attacks include reducing the attack surface by hardening systems so that when systems are attacked, fine-tuned security controls limit the damage. Also useful is resiliency, in which multiple backups of systems and data in other locations and networks give organizations a fallback when a cyberattack successfully compromises the primary systems. (Sometimes these backups are even analog or manual systems.)

More technical defense solutions include placing firewalls on the perimeter of the network. However, if an attacker bypasses them, infiltrates the network, and starts a self-propagating destructive attack, a firewall may let the attack get outside of its network; in other words, firewalls are typically designed to block incoming attacks, not outgoing attacks. Other efforts to detect and stop destructive attacks include antivirus software, intrusion prevention systems (IPS), host intrusion detection systems (HIDS), and Group Policy Objects (GPO). Such technical safeguards might immediately identify a destructive attack, respond to it, and neutralize it, but they are typically signature based and therefore not always effective.

A newer approach is cyber insurance, which is an agreement that protects an organization from the legal and financial fallout of a breach. While such an insurance policy may mitigate an organization's liability in the case of a cyberattack, it does not defend against attacks, just like fire insurance does not defend against flames.

Arguably the best option for defense against destructive attacks includes strict network segregation and isolation (air gapping) to limit resource access and prevent the spread of a self-propagating virus. While this is an exceptionally effective way to block a cyberattack, it is not always feasible given its potentially high impact on business functions. Also, it can be bypassed by sneakernets and insider threats.

Safeguards from (Cyber) Fire Attacks

It is common for organizations to procure fire insurance and to pursue fire prevention and containment strategies. However, for whatever reason, some organizations purchase cyber insurance without implementing safeguards against cyberattacks. It may be that they don't see the same level of risk from cyberattacks as from a real fire where, after all, property and even human life are at stake. But with the growth of the Internet of Things (IoT) and the increasing convergence of the physical world with cyberspace, risks will only increase. Taking the following defensive measures may be immensely helpful to your organization:

1. *Conduct cyber fire drills.* Simulate destructive attacks to test backups, failovers, responsiveness, recovery, and the ability to

"evacuate" data or systems in a timely fashion. This exercise differs from disaster recovery or backup tests in that, rather than an imagined threat scenario, an active simulated threat is interacting with the network. (Take measures such as encrypting data with a known key to ensure that you don't destroy any data during the exercises.)

Netflix runs a perpetual exercise called "Chaos Monkey" that randomly disconnects servers, breaks configurations, and turns off services. The organization is therefore constantly testing that it can smoothly and immediately load balance or fail over to backups without issue. In the event of a real problem, the security team has already designed and tested workable solutions. Netflix has released Chaos Monkey to the public for free, so any organization can use it to improve the ability to detect, resist, respond to, and recover from destructive attacks.[15]

2. *(Cyber) fireproof systems.* Dedicate resources to studying how a selected destructive attack spreads, what it destroys, and what makes your systems vulnerable to it. Implement read-only hard drive adapters that conduct operations in the hard drive buffer, keeping the data locked "behind glass" and incapable of being destroyed because nothing can interact with it in its read-only state. Remove the "combustible" software: applications, libraries, functions, and other system components that are known to spread destructive attacks.

   A commercial opportunity exists to develop specialized software, hardware, and devices that cyber fireproof systems. These applications could have a large market impact by making servers or data resistant to destructive attacks, or at least slowing or halting their progress.

3. *Set cyber firetraps.* There is a large market opportunity for creating automated denial and deception "cyber firetraps" that lure adversaries or malicious programs into infinite loops or trigger mechanisms that cause the attack to quarantine, extinguish, or contain itself. One clever, publicly reported defense is to set up folders on network shares with infinitely recursive directories; when malware tries to iterate over folders to find more data, it gets stuck in a never-ending loop.[16] Specialized sensors could be deployed to locate this behavior. They could then either alert incident response teams or trigger a command to kill the process that initiated the infinite directory.

4. *Create dynamic cyber firebreak/cut lines.* Cyberattacks spread so easily because systems are typically powered on and connected to each other. While an attack may not be able to directly compromise a given system, it can spread to other, interconnected systems. This is repeatedly demonstrated by the hundreds of thousands (if not millions) of botnets, worms, and other self-spreading malware in cyberspace.

   While most network segregation and isolation happens through statically designed architecture, IT organizations can implement additional manual and software-based "break" lines. Some organizations have been known to install a master solenoid switch that manually disconnects the organization from the internet. Internal intranet communications continue, but all external network connections immediately disconnect, creating a physical air gap. The need for this capability might seem extreme or unlikely, but in the event of a global "cyber fire," the organization has the option to quickly and easily break away from the threat without using a fire axe to sever cables.

   A twist on this implementation would see every system, room, floor, and building with its own master switch, allowing security staff to make quick decisions that thwart destructive attacks. Upon hearing of an attack from leadership, staff could quickly download any critical work documents and then flip their switch, segregating their computer from the network and preventing the spread of the attack.

CASTLE THEORY THOUGHT EXERCISE

Consider the scenario in which you are the ruler of a medieval castle with valuable assets inside. You spend large parts of your fortune fireproofing your castle. You build it from stone, fortify it with all the newest fire defense technologies, and train your guards in how to respond to a fire.

In what ways are you still vulnerable to fire attack? For instance, how might you protect or move your gunpowder stores? Could you isolate them while satisfying your military advisers, who say that your army cannot defend the castle without ready access to gunpowder? How would you fireproof your food stores without ruining the food? How might you sanitize or filter goods moving through your castle to prevent the circulation of combustible materials? Where would you create firebreaks in your camps, barracks, and other areas of the castle? What firetraps could you design to contain or extinguish a spreading fire or to catch the arsonist? Can you design a fire drill exercise that uses real fire to train your soldiers, but without exposing your castle to risk?

Recommended Security Controls and Mitigations

Where relevant, recommendations are presented with applicable security controls from the NIST 800-53 standard. Each should be evaluated with the concept of fire attacks in mind.

1. Monitor for indicators of destructive actions within your organization. Prevent tampering of system-monitoring logs, audit events, and sensor data by forwarding data to segmented event collectors. [AU-6: Audit Review, Analysis, and Reporting | (7) Permitted Actions; AU-9: Protection of Audit Information; SI-4: System Monitoring]
2. Implement network, system, and process segregation/isolation to reduce the ability of destructive attacks to spread across your network. [CA-3: System Interconnections; SC-3: Security Function Isolation; SC-7: Boundary Protection | (21) Isolation of System Components; SC-11: Trusted Path | (1) Logical Isolation; SC-39: Process Isolation]
3. Conduct backup tests and resiliency exercises to determine whether recovery mechanisms and fail-safes work as expected. [CP-9: System Backup | (1) Testing for Reliability and Integrity | (2) Test Restoration Using Sampling; CP-10: System Recovery and Reconstitution | (1) Contingency Plan Testing]
4. Require dual authorization from qualified, authorized individuals before allowing commands that delete or destroy data. [CP-9: System Backup | (7) Dual Authorization]
5. Implement measures to maintain your organization's security in the event of a destructive attack that causes security systems to fail. For instance, configure firewalls that go offline to block everything rather than allow everything, or configure systems to go into "safe mode" when an attack is detected. [CP-12: Safe Mode; SC-24: Fail in Known State]
6. Maintain media transport mechanisms that are safeguarded against destructive attacks. For example, ensure that a hard drive

containing sensitive data is kept offline, disconnected, and stored in a secure place where a physically destructive attack, such as a real fire, could not compromise it. [MP-5: Media Transport; PE-18: Location of System Components; SC-28: Protection of Information at Rest]

7. Before connecting portable media or devices to your organization's systems or networks, test and scan them for evidence of malicious software. [MP-6: Media Sanitization; SC-41: Port and I/O Device Access]
8. Conduct risk assessments to determine which data and systems, if compromised, would most harm your organization. Take advanced precautions with and install special safeguards on those systems and data. [RA-3: Risk Assessment; SA-20: Customized Development of Critical Components]
9. Build defenses such as malicious code protections and detonation chambers to look for evidence of destructive attack capabilities. [SC-44: Detonation Chambers; SI-3: Malicious Code Protection]

Debrief

In this chapter, we reviewed fire attacks and the various techniques shinobi used to secretly carry flames and weaponize fire. We looked at several high-profile cyberattacks, along with ways to defend against them. We also looked more generally at ways in which cyber threats act like the digital twin of fire attacks.

In the next chapter, we will discuss in detail how shinobi would communicate and coordinate with external allies to start a fire attack. Shinobi accomplished covert command and control (C2) communication in a multitude of clever ways—ways that parallel methods some malware uses to perform C2 communication.

18

COVERT COMMUNICATION

When a shinobi is going to communicate with the general after he has gotten into the enemy's castle, the shinobi needs to let his allies know where he is. It is essential to arrange for the time and place to do this.

For success on a night attack, send shinobi in advance to know the details of the enemy's position before you give your orders.
—Yoshimori Hyakushu #12

Because shinobi were first and foremost experts in espionage, they had to safely relay secret messages containing scouting reports, attack plans, and other critical information to help their lords and allies make informed tactical and strategic decisions. Similarly, lords, generals, and other shinobi needed to covertly tell an infiltrated shinobi when to set a fire or execute other tactics. These messages had to be easily deciphered by the recipient shinobi but indiscernible to everyone else.

The *Bansenshūkai*, *Ninpiden*, and *Gunpo Jiyoshu* scrolls all describe secret methods shinobi used to communicate with other shinobi, friendly armies, or their employers after infiltrating enemy territory. Some are brutally simple. The *Bansenshūkai* describes hiding a message in the belly of a fish or even inside a person (use your imagination) who can easily travel across borders without suspicion. Common choices were monks and beggars. Obfuscation techniques discussed in the same scroll include cutting a message into several pieces and sending each piece by a different courier, to be reassembled by the recipient, as well as making inks from tangerine juice, rusty water, sake, or castor oil that dry invisibly on paper but are revealed with fire. Shinobi even developed the *shinobi iroha*—a custom alphabet indecipherable to non-shinobi—and used fragmented words or characters to create contextual ambiguity that only the shinobi meant to receive the message would understand.[1]

A popular—and direct—method of sending secret messages was *yabumi*, wherein what appears to be a normal arrow actually has a secret scroll rolled around the bamboo shaft, along with marks on the fletching to identify the recipient. Given the logistical realities of feudal Japan, shinobi could not always guarantee that they could fire a *yabumi* arrow at a prearranged time and place, so they developed an arrow "handshake" that, to an outsider, might have looked like a skirmish. If one side saw a specific number of arrows shot rapidly at the same spot, they returned fire with a specific number of arrows aimed to land in front of the shooter. This signal and countersignal established a friendly connection. The shinobi could then shoot the *yabumi* arrow, which would be picked up and delivered to the intended target.[2] This method of communication became so common that the *Gunpo Jiyoshu* manual warns that the enemy may send deceptive letters by arrow; thus, the recipient should closely examine *yabumi* messages using some of the linguistic techniques described earlier in this book.[3]

For long-distance signaling or when sending a scroll wasn't feasible, shinobi devised flag, fire, smoke, and lamp signals (*hikyakubi*). When even these were not possible, they employed secret drums, gongs, and conches. A loud, unique blast of the signaling device told the shinobi inside enemy lines to prepare to receive a secret communication. The exact signal pattern was agreed upon one to six days before infiltration to avoid confusion. After the initial *hikyakubi* signal, the message was delivered through drum, gong, or conch signals.[4]

In this chapter, we will look at how the covert communication methods of the shinobi closely resemble modern malware command and control communication. We will discuss why command and control communications are needed and their role in threat activity. We'll touch on various techniques that modern adversaries have used to covertly conduct this communication. We will also explore various defenses against this technique and the challenges of using it. Lastly, we'll list a large collection of security best practices to defend against command and control communications. The fact that the shinobi scrolls offer no guidance around how to stop covert communication suggests there may not be a good solution for it.

Command and Control Communication

It is typically not feasible for malware to be wholly independent and autonomous. If it were, the malware would be exceedingly large, complex, suspicious, and visible to defenders. Rather, most malware needs tactical guidance from its controllers during a threat campaign, so threat actors use a technique called *command and control* (abbreviated as C2, CnC, or C&C) to communicate with malware, backdoors, implants, and compromised systems under their control in target networks. Operators use C2 communication to send commands to a compromised system, prompting it to execute actions such as downloading data, updating its configuration, or even deleting itself. The C2 implant can also initiate communication by sending statistics or valuable files, asking for new commands, or beaconing back to report that the system is online, along with its location and current status. Cyber threat actors often establish C2 infrastructure such as domain names, IPs, and websites one to six weeks prior to infiltration.

C2 functionality is widely known, and many firewalls, IDS/IPS, and other security devices and controls can prevent adversaries from communicating directly to target systems or vice versa. To bypass these controls, threat actors continually develop more advanced C2 techniques, tactics, and procedures (TTPs). For example, C2 data can be embedded in the payload of a ping or in commands hidden in pictures hosted on public websites. Adversaries have used C2 in Twitter feeds and comments on trusted sites. They have also used C2 to establish proxies and email relays on compromised systems; they then communicate over known protocols and safe sites that are not blocked by security controls and devices. Phones plugged into compromised systems can be infected with malware that, upon USB connection, "calls" the C2 via cell phone towers, bypassing firewalls and other network defenses and facilitating communication between the infected host and the C2 while the phone's battery charges. Some C2 communication methods use blinking LEDs (like a signal fire), vary CPU temperature (like a smoke signal), use the sounds of hard drives or PC speakers (like signal drums), and leverage electromagnetic spectrum waves to bypass the air gap to a nearby machine.

Threat actors layer C2 communications with obfuscation, encryption, and other confidentiality techniques to maintain contact with a compromised system without disclosing evidence of the commands to the victims. Adversaries may avoid detection by:

- Limiting the amount of data that is communicated on a daily basis so the daily amount never seems anomalous (for example, 100MB max per day to mask downloading 1.5TB over two weeks)
- Sending or receiving beacons only during active user time to blend in with legitimate user traffic (for example, not beaconing very often in the small hours of the morning on a Sunday or holiday)
- Rotating to new, random, or dynamic C2 points to avoid statistical anomalies
- Regularly generating pseudo-legitimate traffic to avoid scrutiny from behavior analysis
- Disabling or deleting activity logs to hide from forensics

Advanced C2 TTPs can be particularly sinister, virtually undetectable, and hard to block. Consider the example of a Windows IT admin who has implemented such strict firewall controls that the only site they can visit is *technet.microsoft.com*, the official Microsoft web portal for IT professionals. Only the HTTPS protocol is allowed, antivirus is current and running, and the operating system is fully patched. No external programs such as email, Skype, or iTunes are running, with the exception of the Microsoft TechNet website, which the admin needs to do their job. That may sound secure, but consider that Chinese APT17 (also called Deputy Dog or Aurora Panda) encoded hidden IP addresses in comments posted on Microsoft TechNet pages—comments that communicated with a BLACKCOFFEE remote access trojan on a compromised system.[5] If anyone had inspected proxy traffic, behavior analysis, anomaly heuristics, IDS signatures, antivirus, or firewall alerts, nothing notable would have indicated that malicious communications were happening.

Advanced defense efforts to counter sophisticated C2s typically involve air gapping the systems, but new C2 communication techniques have been developed in recent years. One example is using a USB loaded with rootkits or compromised firmware and malware that, once plugged into a system, initiate communications with the implant on the compromised system, collect the packaged data, and discreetly upload it for exfiltration to an external C2.

Controlling Coms

It is common for organizations to subscribe to multiple threat indicator feeds. These feeds continually supply the organization with malicious URLs, IPs, and domains that have been observed working as C2s. The organization will then alert and/or block those threats in their firewalls and security devices. This is a good starting point for defending against C2s, but there is an endless supply of new URLs, IPs, and domains, allowing threat actors to take up new identities and evade the threat indicator feeds. Both old and new approaches are needed to address C2s, some of which are suggested below.

1. *Follow best practices.* While it may be impractical or even impossible to prevent all C2 communications, you can block basic or moderately advanced C2s by implementing cybersecurity best practices: know your network, set boundary and flow controls, establish whitelists, and authorize hunt teams to proactively block or intercept C2 communications. Do not take shortcuts on best practices. Rather, commit to doing solid security work. Document, test, and validate your best practices and consult with independent third-party assessors for additional measures and validation. Invest in improving security while maintaining and bettering your existing best-practice infrastructure.

2. *Implement segmentation with "remote viewing" controls.* Network segmentation and isolation means establishing multiple networks and machines, such as an intranet machine and an unclassified internet machine that are segmented from each other. Segmentation should prevent C2 communication from bridging across boundaries. Unfortunately, it's common for users to briefly plug their intranet machine into the internet to download documents or libraries or commit some other breach of security protocol. One approach to such issues is to configure the intranet machine so it remotely views another isolated machine that is connected to the internet. The isolated internet box is not physically or directly accessible by users; they may issue commands and view the screen, but they do not receive the actual raw information from the isolated internet box in their remote viewing box. The remote viewing box is effectively a TV monitor displaying another computer in a different room. As such, C2 communication, malware, and exploits cannot jump through the video signal to cause harm.

CASTLE THEORY THOUGHT EXERCISE

Consider the scenario in which you are the ruler of a medieval castle with valuable assets inside. Every week, your scribes produce new scrolls that outline state secrets, new research and discoveries, financial data, and other sensitive information. It is imperative that these scrolls not end up in enemy hands. However, there are rumors that someone is making copies of important scrolls in your private library, and recent enemy actions seem to confirm these reports. None of the scribes or archivists are suspected of copying and exfiltrating the scrolls, so you are not looking for an insider threat.

What access restrictions or physical protections could you place on the scrolls to prevent their exfiltration or reproduction? How could you monitor for the theft or removal of these scrolls while still permitting the normal transit of goods and people to and from your castle? Could you store your scrolls in such a way that the enemy would not know which scrolls have the most value? What other ways might a threat actor obtain access to the scrolls—or steal the information without access—and how would you defend against them?

Recommended Security Controls and Mitigations

Where relevant, recommendations are presented with applicable security controls from the NIST 800-53 standard. Each should be evaluated with the concept of C2s in mind.

1. Implement safeguards on systems, network boundaries, and network egress points that look for signs of data exfiltration on your network. This could mean blocking encrypted tunnels that your sensors cannot intercept, along with looking for evidence of unauthorized protocols, data formats, data watermarks, sensitive data labels, and large files or streams exiting your network. [AC-4: Information Flow Enforcement | (4) Content Check Encrypted Information; SC-7: Boundary Protection | (10) Prevent Exfiltration; SI-4: System Monitoring | (10) Visibility of Encrypted Communications]
2. Establish multiple networks with isolation and segmentation between internet and intranet resources. Restrict critical internal systems from connecting to the internet. [AC-4: Information Flow Enforcement | (21) Physical and Logical

Separation of Information Flows; CA-3: System Interconnections | (1) Unclassified National Security System Connections | (2) Classified National Security System Connections | (5) Restrictions on External System Connections; SC-7: Boundary Protection | (1) Physically Separated Subnetworks | (11) Restrict Incoming Communications Traffic | (22) Separate Subnets for Connecting to Different Security Domains]

3. Restrict remote access to any systems with critical information. [AC-17: Remote Access]
4. Implement restrictions and configuration controls to detect and prevent unauthorized wireless communications. [AC-18: Wireless Access | (2) Monitoring Unauthorized Connections; PE-19: Information Leakage; SC-31: Covert Channel Analysis; SC-40: Wireless Link Protection; SI-4: System Monitoring | (15) Wireless to Wireline Communications]
5. Train your security team and employees to identify C2 communications. [AT-3: Role-based Training | (4) Suspicious Communications and Anomalous System Behavior; SI-4: System Monitoring | (11) Analyze Communications Traffic Anomalies | (13) Analyze Traffic and Event Patterns | (18) Analyze Traffic and Covert Exfiltration]
6. Deny any unauthorized software that could be a C2 backdoor or implant from running on your systems. [CM-7: Least Functionality | (5) Authorized Software–Whitelisting]
7. Safeguard direct physical connections to systems that bypass security controls and boundaries; these include switch closets, Ethernet wall jacks, and computer interfaces. [PE-6: Monitoring Physical Access; SC-7: Boundary Protection | (14) Protects Against Unauthorized Physical Connections | (19) Block communication from non-organizationally configured hosts]
8. Require inspection and scanning of removable media that enters or leaves your organization to prevent personnel from manually performing C2 communication through delivery and removal of external media. [PE-16: Delivery and Removal]
9. Implement a whitelist to deny communication to any resource or address that has not been approved for an exception. Many C2 sites are brand-new domains with no history of legitimate use by your organization. [SC-7: Boundary Protection | (5) Deny by Default—Allow by Exception]

Debrief

In this chapter, we reviewed the various communication methods shinobi used to receive and send commands to allies. We described various modern C2 methods, along with their comparative shinobi methods. However, we only scratched the surface, as it's very likely that the most sophisticated C2 techniques have yet to be discovered. Just like the best of the shinobi's covert communication methods were never written down, we may never learn of the genius and creativity behind the most advanced C2 techniques. We discussed several best practices, including whitelisting and encryption inspection, as ways to mitigate an adversary's C2s, but an ideal solution to the problem remains to be found.

In the next chapter, we will discuss shinobi call signs. These were methods of communicating with allies inside enemy territory by leaving unique marks or messages. Similar to a dead drop, call signs never leave the boundaries of an environment, so traditional methods of blocking or detecting C2 communication generally do not work against them.

19

CALL SIGNS

When you steal in, the first thing you should do is mark the route, showing allies the exit and how to escape.

After you have slipped into the enemy's area successfully, give more attention to not accidentally fighting yourselves than to the enemy.
—Yoshimori Hyakushu #26

While shinobi are often portrayed in popular culture as lone actors, many shinobi worked in teams. These teams were particularly adept at discretely relaying information to each other in the field. The *Gunpo Jiyoshu* manual describes three call signs, or physical markers, that the shinobi developed to communicate with each other without arousing suspicion. Based on what the markers were and where they were placed, call signs helped shinobi identify a target, marked which path they should take at a fork in the road, provided directions to an enemy stronghold, or coordinated an attack, among other actions. Though call signs were well known within shinobi circles, participating shinobi agreed to custom variations prior to a mission to ensure that targets or even enemy shinobi could not recognize the call signs in the field. The scrolls suggest using markers that are portable, disposable, quick to deploy and retract, and placed at ground level. Most importantly, the markers had to be visually unique yet unremarkable to the uninitiated.

For example, a shinobi might agree to inform their fellow shinobi of their whereabouts by leaving dyed grains of rice in a predetermined, seemingly innocuous location. One shinobi would leave red rice, another green, and so on, so that when a fellow shinobi saw those few colored grains, they would know their ally had already passed through. The beauty of the system was that, while the shinobi could quickly identify these items, ordinary passersby would not notice a few oddly colored grains of rice. Using similar methods, the shinobi could subtly point a piece of broken bamboo to direct an ally toward a chosen footpath, or they could leave a small piece of paper on the ground to identify a dwelling that would be burned down, lessening the chance that team members would find themselves either victims or suspects of arson.[1]

In this chapter, we will explore the ways that call sign techniques could be used in networked environments and why cyber threat actors might use them. We will hypothesize where in the network call signs could be placed and what they might look like. In addition, we will discuss how one could hunt for these call signs in a target network. We will review the challenge of detecting creative call signs and touch on the crux of this challenge: controlling and monitoring your environment for an adversary's actions. You will get a chance, in the thought exercise, to build up mental models and solutions to deal with the challenge of enemy call signs. You will also be exposed to security controls that may prevent threat actors from using call signs in your environment, as well as limit their capabilities.

Operator Tradecraft

During the Democratic National Committee hack of 2016, the Russian military agency GRU (also known as APT28 or FANCYBEAR) and its allied security agency FSB (APT29 or COZYBEAR) were operating on the same network and systems, but they failed to use call signs to communicate with each other. This oversight resulted in duplication of effort and the creation of observables, anomalies, and other indicators of compromise in the victim's network, likely contributing to the failure of both operations.[2] The lack of communication, which probably stemmed from compartmentalization between the two intelligence organizations, gives us a sense of what cyber espionage threat groups could learn from the shinobi.

While the cybersecurity community has not yet observed overlapping threat groups using covert markers, the DNC hack demonstrates the need for such a protocol to exist. It's reasonable to assume that the GRU and FSB performed an after-action report of their DNC hack tradecraft efforts, and they may already have decided to implement a call sign protocol in future operations where target overlap is a concern. If cyber espionage organizations begin to work regularly in insulated but intersecting formations, they will need a way to communicate various information, including simply their presence on systems and networks and details about their targets, when using normal communication channels is not possible.

If these call signs did exist, what would they look like? Effective cyber call signs would most likely:

- Change over time, as shinobi markers did
- Be implemented in tools and malwares that cannot be captured and reverse engineered. Humans using keyboards would be needed to identify them.
- Exist in a location that the overlapping espionage group would surely find, such as the valuable and unique primary domain controller (DC). Given the presence of file security monitors and the operational reality that DCs do not restart very often, a threat group might place the marker in the DC's memory to maximize its persistence and minimize its detectability.

It remains unclear what kind of strings or unique hex bytes could function as markers; in what cache, temporary table, or memory location markers could reside; and how another operator could easily discover them. Note, however, that the cybersecurity industry has observed multiple malware families that leave specific files or registry keys as a signal to future copies of the virus that the infection has already successfully spread to a given machine (and thus that they need not attempt to infect it again).[3] Though this call sign functionality could not be implemented as easily against dynamic human threat actors, defenders could create files and registry keys that falsely signal infection, prompting malware to move on innocuously.

Detecting the Presence of Call Signs

Many organizations struggle to identify which user deleted a file from a shared network drive, let alone to detect covert call signs hidden inside remote parts of a system. Nonetheless, defenders will increasingly need to be able to defend against threats that communicate with each other, inside the defender's environment. To have a chance of catching threat actors, defenders will need training, and they will need to implement detection tools and have host visibility.

1. *Implement advanced memory monitoring.* Identify high-value systems in your network—systems that you believe a threat actor would target or need to access to move onward to a target. Then, explore the existing capabilities of your organization to monitor and restrict memory changes on these systems. Look at products and services offered by vendors as well. Evaluate the amount of effort and time that would be necessary to investigate the source of such memory changes. Finally, determine whether you could confidently identify whether those changes indicated that the target machines had been compromised.
2. *Train your personnel.* Train your security, hunt, and IT teams to consider forensic artifacts in memory as potential indictors of compromise, especially when these are found in high-value targets, rather than dismissing any incongruities they find.

CASTLE THEORY THOUGHT EXERCISE

Consider the scenario in which you are the ruler of a medieval castle with valuable assets inside. You receive reliable intelligence that teams of shinobi are targeting your castle and that they are using call signs to communicate with each other. Their covert signals include placing discreet markers on the ground, including dyed rice, flour, and broken bamboo.

How would you train your guards to be aware of these techniques—and of techniques you have not yet considered? How could you help them manage the false alerts likely to occur when your own people accidentally drop rice on the ground or when animals and wind disturb the environment? What architectural changes could you make to your castle and the grounds to more easily detect secret markers? What countermeasures would destroy, disrupt, or degrade the ability of these markers to communicate or deceive the shinobi who are sending and receiving the signals?

Recommended Security Controls and Mitigations

Where relevant, recommendations are presented with applicable security controls from the NIST 800-53 standard. Each should be evaluated with the concept of call signs in mind.

1. Ensure that prior user information is unavailable to current users who obtain access to the same system or resources. [SC-4: Information in Shared Resources]
2. Identify system communications that could be used for unauthorized information flows. A good example of a potential covert channel comes from control "PE-8: Visitor Access Records." Paper log books or unrestricted digital devices that visitors use to sign in to facilities could be vulnerable to information markers that signal to compartmentalized espionage actors that other teams have visited the location. [SC-31: Covert Channel Analysis]
3. Search for indicators of potential attacks and unauthorized system use and deploy monitoring devices to track information transactions of interest. [SI-4: System Monitoring]
4. Protect system memory from unauthorized changes. [SI-16: Memory Protection]

Debrief

In this chapter, we reviewed the physical markers shinobi teams used to signal to each other inside enemy territory. We learned why these call signs were useful and the characteristics of good call signs according to the scrolls. We then reviewed a cyber espionage operation where a lack of call signs and the resulting uncoordination contributed to revealing threat group activity. We discussed how modern threat groups will likely continue to gain sophistication—a sophistication that may include adopting call sign techniques. We explored what modern digital call signs could look like as well as how we might notice them.

In the following chapter, we will discuss the opposite of shinobi call signs: precautions that shinobi took to leave no trace of their activity inside enemy territory, as the scrolls instructed. Advanced techniques included creating false signals intended to deceive the defender.

20

LIGHT, NOISE, AND LITTER DISCIPLINE

The traditions of the ancient shinobi say you should lock the doors before you have a look at the enemy with fire.

If you have to steal in as a shinobi when it is snowing, the first thing you must be careful about is your footsteps.
—Yoshimori Hyakushu #53

Avoiding unwanted attention was a core discipline of their trade, and shinobi trained diligently on being stealthy. If lanterns emitted light that disturbed animals, footsteps echoed and woke a sleeping target, or food waste alerted a guard to the presence of an intruder, then a shinobi put their mission—if not their life—in jeopardy. As such, the scrolls provide substantial guidance around moving and operating tactically while maintaining light, noise, and litter discipline.

Light discipline includes general tactics. For example, the scrolls recommend that infiltrating shinobi lock a door from the inside before igniting a torch to prevent the light (and any people in the room) from escaping.[1] It also includes specific techniques. *Bansenshūkai* details a number of clever tools for light management, such as the *torinoko* fire egg. This is a bundle of special flammable material with an ember at the center, compressed to the shape and size of an egg. The egg rests in the shinobi's palm such that opening or closing the hand controls the amount of oxygen that reaches the ember, brightening or dimming the light and allowing the carrier to direct the light in specific, narrow directions.[2] With this tool, a shinobi could quickly open their hand to see who was sleeping inside a room, then instantly extinguish the light by making a tight fist. Thus, the fire egg has the same on-demand directional and on/off light control as a modern tactical flashlight.

Silence was critical for shinobi, and the scrolls describe an array of techniques to remain quiet while infiltrating a target. The *Ninpiden* suggests biting down on a strip of paper to dampen the sound of breathing. Similarly, some shinobi moved through close quarters by grabbing the soles of their feet with the palms of their hands, then walking on their hands to mute the sound of footsteps. This technique must have required considerable practice and conditioning to execute successfully. It was also common for shinobi to carry oil or other viscous substances to grease creaky gate hinges or wooden sliding doors—anything that might squeak and alert people to their presence. The scrolls also warn against applying these liquids too liberally, as they could visibly pool, tipping off a guard to the fact that someone had trespassed.[3]

Not all shinobi noise discipline techniques minimized noise. The scrolls also provide guidance for creating a purposeful ruckus. *Shōninki* describes a noise discipline technique called *kutsukae*, or "changing your footwear," which actually involves varying your footsteps rather than putting on different shoes. An infiltrating shinobi can shuffle, skip, fake a limp, take choppy steps, or make audible but distinct footstep noises to deceive anyone listening. Then, when they change to their natural gait, listeners assume they're hearing a different person or erroneously believe that the person they're tracking suddenly stopped.[4] The *Ninpiden* describes clapping wooden blocks together or yelling "Thief!" or "Help!" to simulate an alarm, testing the guards' reaction to noise.[5] *Bansenshūkai* describes a more controlled noise test, in which a shinobi near a target or guard whispers progressively more loudly to determine the target's noise detection threshold. Noise tests help shinobi make specific observations about how the target responds, including:

- How quickly did the target react?
- Was there debate between guards about hearing a noise?
- Did guards emerge quickly and alertly, with weapons in hand?

- Did the noise seem to catch the target off guard?
- Was the target completely oblivious?

These observations not only tell the shinobi how keen the target's awareness and hearing are but also reveal the target's skill and preparation in responding to events—information the shinobi can use to tailor the infiltration.[6]

In terms of physical evidence, shinobi used "leave no trace" long before it was an environmental mantra. A tool called *nagabukuro* (or "long bag") helps with both sound and litter containment. When shinobi scaled a high wall and needed to cut a hole to crawl through, they hung the large, thick, leather *nagabukuro* bag lined with fur or felt beneath them to catch debris falling from the wall and muffle the sound. The shinobi could then lower the scraps quietly to a discreet place on the ground below. This was much better option than letting debris crash to the ground or splash into a moat.[7]

In this chapter, we abstract the light, noise, and litter of shinobi infiltrators into their cyber threat equivalents. We will review some tools and techniques that threat groups have used to minimize the evidence they leave behind, as well as some procedural tradecraft disciplines. We'll discuss the topic of detecting "low and slow" threats, along with modifying your environment so it works to your advantage. The thought exercise will look at a technique used by shinobi to mask their footsteps that could in theory be applied to modern digital systems. At the end of the chapter, we'll cover detection discipline as a way to counter a sophisticated adversary—one who is mindful of the observables they may leave (or not leave) in your network.

Cyber Light, Noise, and Litter

The digital world does not always behave in the same ways as the physical world. It can be challenging to understand and continuously hunt for the cyber equivalents of light, noise, and litter. Because defenders lack the time, resources, and capability to monitor and hunt within digital systems under their control, an adversary's light, noise, and/or litter trail too often goes undocumented. As a result, threat actors may have an easier time performing cyber infiltration than physical infiltration.

Many scanning and exploitation tools and frameworks, such as Nmap,[8] have throttling modes or other "low-and-slow" methods that attempt to exercise discipline on the size of packets or payloads, packet frequency, and bandwidth usage on a target network. Adversaries have developed extremely small malicious files (for instance, the China Chopper can be less than 4KB[9]) that exploit defenders' assumption that a file with such a slight footprint won't cause harm. Malware can be configured to minimize the amount of noise it makes by beaconing command and control (C2) posts infrequently, or it can minimize the noise in process logs or memory by purposefully going to sleep or executing a no-operation (NOP) for long periods. To avoid leaving digital litter that could reveal its presence, certain malware does not drop any files to disk. Adversaries and malware on neighboring network infrastructure can choose to passively collect information, leading to a slow but fruitful understanding of the environment inside the target. Notably, many of these threats also choose to accept the risk of cyber light, noise, and/or litter that results from running their campaigns.

It is reasonable to assume that sufficiently advanced adversaries have procedures to limit cyber light, noise, and litter, such as:

- Limiting communication with a target to less than 100MB per day
- Ensuring that malware artifacts, files, and strings are not easily identified as litter that could reveal their own presence or be attributed to the malware
- "Silencing" logs, alerts, tripwires, and other sensors so security is not alerted to the intruder's presence

It seems that most current security devices and systems are designed to trigger in response to the exact signature of a known threat, such as a specific IP, event log, or byte pattern. Even with specialized software that shows analysts threat activity in real time, such as Wireshark,[10] it takes significant effort to collect, process, and study this information. Contrast this workflow with that of hearing footsteps and reacting. Because humans cannot perceive the digital realm with our senses in the same way that we perceive the physical environment, security measures are basically guards with visual and hearing impairments waiting for a prompt to take action against a threat across the room.

Detection Discipline

Unfortunately, there is no ideal solution for catching someone skilled in the ways of not being caught. Some threat actors have such an advantage over defenders in this realm that they can gain unauthorized access to the security team's incident ticket tool and monitor it for any new investigations that reference their own threat activity. However, there are improvements to be made, training to be had, countermeasures to deploy, and tricks defenders can try to trip up or catch the threat in a tradecraft error.

1. *Practice awareness.* As part of training for threat hunting, incident response, and security analysis, teach your security team to look for indications of an adversary's light, noise, or litter.
2. *Install squeaky gates.* Consider implementing deceptive attack sensing and warning (AS&W) indicators, such as security events that go off every minute on domain controllers or other sensitive systems or networking devices. For example, you might implement a warning that says "[Security Event Log Alert]: Windows failed to activate Windows Defender/Verify this version of Windows." This may deceive an infiltrating adversary into thinking you're not paying attention to your alerts, prompting the adversary to "turn off" or "redirect" security logs away from your sensors or analysts. The sudden absence of the false alert will inform your defenders of the adversary's presence (or, in the case of a legitimate crash, of the need to reboot the system or have IT investigate the outage).
3. *Break out the wooden clappers.* Consider how an advanced adversary could purposefully trigger alerts or cause noticeable network noise from a protected or hidden location in your environment (that is, attacking known honeypots) to observe your security team's ability to detect and respond. This is the cyber equivalent of a ninja running through your house at night slamming two pieces of wood together to test your response. It's reasonable to assume that some adversaries may assess your security in this way so they can determine whether they can use zero days or other covert techniques without fear of discovery.

CASTLE THEORY THOUGHT EXERCISE

Consider the scenario in which you are the ruler of a medieval castle with valuable assets inside. As it is not feasible to have eyes everywhere, you have positioned your guards where they can listen for odd sounds in key egress pathways. You have also trained your guards to notice anomalous noises. You are told that shinobi have specially made sandals with soft, fabric-stuffed soles so they can walk on tile or stone without making noise.

How could you use this information to detect a ninja in your castle? What evidence might these special sandals leave behind? What countermeasures could you deploy to mitigate the threat these sandals pose? How would you train your guards to react when they see a person in the castle walking suspiciously quietly?

Recommended Security Controls and Mitigations

Where relevant, recommendations are presented with applicable security controls from the NIST 800-53 standard. Each should be evaluated in terms of the light, noise, and litter that might accompany an attack.

1. Determine your organization's detection capabilities by simulating network infiltration by both loud-and-fast and low-and-slow adversaries. Document which logs are associated with which observable activity and where you may have sensory dead spots. [AU-2: Audit Events; CA-8: Penetration Testing; SC-42: Sensor Capability and Data]
2. Correlate incident logs, alerts, and observables with documented threat actions to better educate your staff and test your perception of how threats will "sound" on the network. [IR-4: Incident Handling | (4) Information Correlation]
3. Tune your sandboxes and detonation chambers to look for indicators of a threat actor who is attempting to exercise the cyber equivalent of light, noise, and litter discipline. [SC-44: Detonation Chambers]
4. Use non-signature-based detection methods to look for covert disciplined activity designed to avoid signature identification. [SI-3: Malicious Code Protection | (7) Nonsignature-Based Detection]
5. Deploy information system monitoring to detect stealth activity. Avoid placing oversensitive sensors in high-activity areas. [SI-4: Information System Monitoring]

Debrief

In this chapter, we reviewed the precautions shinobi took and the tools they used to hide evidence of their activity—for example, measuring how much noise they could make before alerting the guards and learning what the target was likely to do if shinobi activity were discovered. We discussed several cyber tools that adversaries have used and how they might be understood as the equivalent of light and noise—evidence that can be detected by defenders. Lastly, we reviewed potential countermeasures that defenders can take.

In the next chapter, we will discuss circumstances that assist shinobi in infiltration because they mitigate the problems of light, noise, and litter. For example, a strong rainstorm would mask noise, obscure visibility, and clear away evidence of their presence. A cyber defender can consider analogous circumstances to protect their systems.

21

CIRCUMSTANCES OF INFILTRATION

You should infiltrate at the exact moment that the enemy moves and not try when they do not move—this is a way of principled people.

In heavy rainfall, when the rain is at its most, you should take advantage of it for your shinobi activities and night attacks.
—Yoshimori Hyakushu #1

The *Ninpiden* and *Bansenshūkai* both advise that when moving against a target, shinobi should use cover to go undetected. They may wait for circumstances in which cover exists or, if necessary, create those circumstances themselves. The scrolls provide a wide range of situations that can aid infiltration, from natural occurrences (strong winds and rain) to social gatherings (festivals, weddings, and religious services) to shinobi-initiated activity (releasing horses, causing fights, and setting fire to buildings).[1] Regardless of their source, a canny shinobi should be able to capitalize on distractions, excitement, confusion, and other conditions that divert the target's focus.

Shinobi were able to turn inclement weather into favorable infiltration circumstances. For instance, heavy rainstorms meant empty streets, poor visibility, and torrents to muffle any sounds the shinobi made.[2] Of course, bad weather is bad for everyone, and the second poem of the *Yoshimori Hyakushu* notes that too strong a storm can overpower a shinobi, making it difficult to execute tactics and techniques: "In the dead of night, when the wind and rain are raging, the streets are so dark that shinobi cannot deliver a night attack easily."[3]

Shinobi also capitalized on other, more personal circumstances, such as a tragic death in the target's family. The scrolls point out that while a target is in mourning, they may not sleep well for two or three nights, meaning the shinobi may approach unnoticed during the funeral or bereavement disguised as a mourner, or wait to infiltrate until the target finally sleeps deeply on night three or four.[4]

Of course, a shinobi's mission did not always coincide with providence. In some cases, shinobi took it upon themselves to cause severe illness at the target fortification. Sick people were ineffective defenders, and their worried caregivers were preoccupied and denied themselves sleep to tend to the ill. When the afflicted began to recover, the relieved caregivers slept heavily, at which point shinobi infiltrated. Alternatively, shinobi could destroy critical infrastructure, such as a bridge, and then wait for the target to undertake the large and difficult reconstruction project in the summer heat before infiltrating an exhausted opponent.[5]

Effective distractions could also be more directly confrontational. *Bansenshūkai* describes a technique called *kyonin* ("creating a gap by surprise") that employs the assistance of military forces or other shinobi. These allies make the target think an attack is underway, perhaps by firing shots, beating war drums, or shouting, and the shinobi can slip in during the confusion. When the shinobi wanted to exit safely, this technique was simply repeated.[6]

In this chapter, we will review how using situational factors to aid in infiltration as described in the shinobi scrolls apply to the digital era. The use of situational factors depends on defenders, security systems, and organizations having finite amounts of attention. Overloading, confusing, and misdirecting that limited attention creates opportunities a threat actor can exploit. We will identify various opportunities that can be found in modern networked environments and explain how they parallel the circumstances described in the shinobi scrolls. Finally, we will review how organizations can incorporate safeguards and resiliency to prepare for circumstances that may weaken their defenses.

Adversarial Opportunity

Cybersecurity adversaries may distract their targets and create conditions that make detecting infiltration as widely—and wisely—as shinobi once did. For example, when cyberdefenders detect a sudden distributed denial of service (DDoS) attack, standard operating procedures require evaluating the strength and duration of the DDoS and creating a security incident ticket to log the activity. Defenders may not immediately suspect a DDoS as cover for a threat actor's attack on the network. So when the attack overwhelms the target's security sensors and packet capture (pcap) and intrusion detection or prevention systems (IDS/IPS) fail to open—in other words, when there is too much communication to inspect—defensive systems might naturally rush the packet along without searching it for malicious content. When the DDoS ceases, the defenders will note that there was no significant downtime and return their status to normal, not realizing that, while the DDoS lasted only 10 minutes, the packet flood gave the adversary enough time and cover to compromise the system and establish a foothold in the network. (As in *Yoshimori Hyakushu* 2, which warned that a strong storm could hinder both target and attacker, the adversary is unlikely to deploy an overly intense DDoS. Doing so could cause networking gear to drop packets and lose communication data—including their own attacks. Instead, an attacker will likely throttle target systems to overwhelm security without disrupting communication.)

Adversaries have many other ways to create favorable circumstances in the infiltration target; they are limited only by their ingenuity. It could be advantageous to attack service and infrastructure quality and reliability, such as by disrupting ISPs or interconnections. Patient attackers could wait for commercial vendors to release faulty updates or patches, after which the target's security or IT staff temporarily creates "permit any-any" conditions or removes security controls to troubleshoot the problem. Threat actors might monitor a company's asset acquisition process to determine when it moves new systems and servers to production or the cloud—and, hence, when these targets might be temporarily unguarded or not properly configured against attacks. Threat actors might also track a corporate merger and attempt to infiltrate gaps created when the different companies combine networks. Other adversaries might use special events hosted in the target's building, such as large conferences, vendor expos, and third-party meetings, to mingle in the crowd of strangers and infiltrate the target. They might even pick up a swag bag in the process.

Adversarial Adversity

It is considered infeasible to guarantee 100 percent uptime of digital systems, and it should be considered even harder to guarantee 100 percent assurance of security at all times for those same digital systems. Furthermore, it is almost certainly impossible to prevent disasters, hazards, accidents, failures and unforeseen changes—many of which will create circumstances in which opportunistic threat actors can infiltrate. Being overly cautious to avoid these circumstances can hamper a business's ability to be bold in strategy and execute on goals. A solution to this dilemma may be to redundantly layer systems to reduce infiltration opportunities. Security teams might put in place the equivalent of high-availability security—security that is layered redundantly where systems are weaker. *Practice awareness and preparation.* As part of security staff protocols for change management, events, incidents, crises, natural disasters, and other distracting or confusing circumstances, train your security team to look for indications that an event was created or is being used by adversaries to infiltrate the organization. Document role responsibilities in organizational policies and procedures. Use threat modeling, tabletop exercises, and risk management to identify potential distractions, then consider safeguards, countermeasures, and protections for handling them.

CASTLE THEORY THOUGHT EXERCISE

Consider the scenario in which you are the ruler of a medieval castle with valuable assets inside. You have noticed that during especially cold and windy ice storms, your gate guards hunker down in their posts, cover their faces, and keep themselves warm with small, unauthorized fires—fires that reduce their night vision and make their silhouette visible.

How might a shinobi take advantage of extreme conditions, such as a blizzard or ice storm, to infiltrate your castle? How would they dress? How would they approach? How freely could they operate with respect to your guards? What physical access restrictions and security protocols could your guards apply during a blizzard? Could you change the guard posts so your soldiers could effectively watch for activity during such conditions? Besides weather events, what other distracting circumstances can you imagine, and how would you handle them?

Recommended Security Controls and Mitigations

Where relevant, recommendations are presented with applicable security controls from the NIST 800-53 standard. They should be evaluated with the concept of circumstances of infiltration in mind.

1. Identify and document how different security controls and protocols—for example, authentication—might be handled during emergencies or other extreme circumstances to mitigate adversary infiltration. [AC-14: Permitted Actions Without Identification or Authentication]
2. Establish controls and policies around the conditions for using external information systems, particularly during extenuating circumstances. [AC-20: Use of External Information Systems]
3. Launch penetration testing exercises during contingency training for simulated emergencies, such as fire drills, to test defensive and detection capabilities. [CA-8: Penetration Testing; CP-3: Contingency Training; IR-2: Incident Response Training]
4. Enforce physical access restrictions for visitors, as well as for circumstances in which it is not possible to escort a large number of uncontrolled persons—for example, firefighters responding to a fire—but unauthorized system ingress and egress must still be prevented. [PE-3: Physical Access Control]
5. Develop a capability to shut off information systems and networks in the event of an emergency, when it is suspected that an adversary has compromised your defenses. [PE-10: Emergency Shutoff]
6. Consider how your organization can incorporate adversary awareness and hunting into contingency planning. [CP-2: Contingency Plan]
7. Evaluate whether a sudden transfer or resumption of business operations at fallback sites will create opportune circumstances for adversary infiltration. Then consider appropriate defensive safeguards and mitigations. [CP-7: Alternate Processing Site]

Debrief

In this chapter, we reviewed the tactic of creating and/or waiting for circumstances that provide cover for infiltrating a target. We looked at several examples of how shinobi would create an opportunity when a target was well defended, and we explored how this tactic could play out in modern networked environments. We covered various methods for managing security during times of weakness, and through the thought exercise, we looked at preparing for circumstances where risk cannot be avoided, transferred, or countered.

In the next chapter, we will discuss the zero-day, or a means of infiltration so novel or secret that no one has yet thought about how to defend against it. Shinobi had exploits and techniques similar to zero-days; they were so secret, it was forbidden to write them down, and the scrolls only allude to them indirectly. We are left only with cryptic clues—clues provided to remind a shinobi of a secret technique they had learned, but not to teach it. Even so, the scrolls provide insight around how to create new zero-days, procedures to defend against them, and tradecraft in executing them. Furthermore, the scrolls describe several historical zero-day techniques that had been lost due to their disclosure, giving us insight into modern zero-day exploits and a potential forecast of zero-days of the future.

22

ZERO-DAYS

A secret will work if it is kept; you will lose if words are given away.

You should be aware that you shouldn't use any of the ancient ways that are known to people because you will lose the edge of surprise.
—Shōninki, "Takaki wo Koe Hikuki ni Hairu no Narai"[1]

One of the shinobi's key tactical advantages was secrecy. The scrolls repeatedly warn shinobi to prevent others from learning the details of their capabilities, since if knowledge of a technique leaked to the public, the consequences could be disastrous. Not only could the techniques be invalidated for generations, but the lives of shinobi using a leaked technique could be in danger. Both *Shōninki* and the *Ninpiden* describe the hazards of exposing secret ninja tradecraft to outsiders, with some scrolls going so far as to advise killing targets who discover tradecraft secrets or bystanders who observe a shinobi in action.[2]

Both *Shōninki* and the *Ninpiden* cite ancient techniques that were spoiled due to public exposure. For instance, when ancient ninjas (*yato*)[3] conducted reconnaissance, they sometimes traveled across farm fields;

they avoided detection by, among other means, dressing like a scarecrow and snapping into a convincing pose when people approached.[4] Once this technique was discovered, however, locals regularly tested scarecrows by rushing them or even stabbing them. No matter how convincing the shinobi's disguise or how skillful their pantomime, the technique became too risky, and shinobi had to either develop new ways to hide in plain sight or avoid fields altogether. The skill was lost.

Similarly, some shinobi became master imitators of cat and dog sounds, so that if they accidentally alerted people to their presence during a mission, they could bark or mew to convince the target that the disturbance was just a passing animal and there was no need for further inspection. This technique was also discovered eventually. Guards were trained to investigate unfamiliar animal noises, putting shinobi at risk of discovery.[5]

The scrolls also describe situations in which a fortification was protected by dogs that shinobi could not kill, kidnap, or befriend without rousing suspicion from security guards. In this situation, the scrolls tell shinobi to wear the scent of whale oil and then either wait for the dog to stray away from the guards or lure the dog away. They then beat the dog, and they do this several nights in a row. With its pungency and rarity, the scent of whale oil conditions the dog to associate pain and punishment with the odor, and the dog is then too afraid to attack shinobi wearing the distinctive scent. When this technique was disclosed, guards were trained to notice the unique scent of whale oil or when their dog's behavior suddenly changed.[6]

Of course, most shinobi secrets went unexposed until the formal publication of the scrolls many years after the shinobi were effectively a historical relic. Therefore, defenders of the era had to create techniques to thwart attacks of which they had no details—potentially even attacks that the attackers themselves had not yet considered.

For shinobi acting as defenders, the scrolls offer some baseline advice. *Bansenshūkai*'s "Guideline for Commanders"[7] volumes recommend various security best practices, including passwords, certification stamps, identifying marks, and secret signs and signals. The scroll also advises commanders to contemplate the reasoning behind these security stratagems; pair them with other standard protocols, such as night watches and guards; take advanced precautions, such as setting traps; and develop their own secret, custom, dynamic security implementations. Together, these techniques defended against attackers of low or moderate skill but not against the most sophisticated shinobi.[8]

To that end, *Bansenshūkai*'s most pragmatic security advice is that defenders will never be perfectly secure, constantly alert, or impeccably disciplined. There will always be gaps that shinobi can exploit. Instead, the scroll emphasizes the importance of understanding the philosophy, mindset, and thought processes of one's enemies, and it implores shinobi to be open to trying new techniques, sometimes on the fly: "It is hard to tell exactly how to act according to the situation and the time and the place. If you have a set of fixed ways or use a constant form, how could even the greatest general obtain a victory?"[9]

Shinobi defenders used creative mental modeling, such as by imagining reversed scenarios and exploring potential gaps. They drew inspiration from nature, imagining how a fish, bird, or monkey would infiltrate a castle and how they could mimic the animal's abilities.[10] They derived new techniques by studying common thieves (*nusubito*). Above all, they trusted the creativity of the human mind and exercised continuous learning, logical analysis, problem solving, and metacognitive flexibility:

> Although there are millions of lessons for the shinobi, that are both subtle and ever changing, you can't teach them in their entirety by tradition or passing them on. One of the most important things for you to do is always try to know everything you can of every place or province that is possible to know. . . . If your mind is in total accordance with the way of things and it is working with perfect reason and logic, then you can pass through "the gateless gate." . . . The human mind is marvelous and flexible. It's amazing. As time goes by, clearly or mysteriously, you will realize the essence of things and understanding will appear to you from nowhere. . . . On [the path of the shinobi] you should master everything and all that you can . . . you should use your imagination and insight to realize and grasp the way of all matters. [11]

A forward-thinking shinobi with a keen mind and a diligent work ethic could build defenses strong enough to withstand unknown attacks, forcing enemies to spend time and resources developing new attack plans, testing for security gaps, and battling hidden defenses—only to be thwarted once again when the whole security system dynamically changed.

In this chapter, we will explore the modern threat landscape of zero-days and understand what of the philosophy and tradecraft described in the shinobi scrolls we can apply to cybersecurity. In addition, we will explore various proposed defenses against zero-days. The castle thought exercise in this chapter presents the challenge of addressing unknown and potential zero-days hidden in modern computing hardware, software, clouds, and networks—all in the hope of provoking new insights.

Zero-Day

Few terms in the cybersecurity lexicon strike fear into the hearts of defenders and knowledgeable business stakeholders like *zero-day* (or *0-day*), an exploit or attack that was previously unknown and that defenders may not know how to fight. The term comes from the fact that the public has known about the attack or vulnerability for zero days. Because victims and defenders have not had the opportunity to study the threat, a threat actor with access to a zero-day that targets a common technology almost always succeeds. For example, STUXNET used four zero-day exploits to sabotage an air-gapped nuclear enrichment facility in Iran, demonstrating the power of zero-days to attack even the most secure and obscure targets.[12]

A zero-day attack derives its value from the fact that it is unknown. As soon as a threat actor uses a zero-day, the victim has the chance to capture evidence of the attack via sensors and monitoring systems, forensically examine that evidence, and reverse engineer the attack. After the zero-day appears in the wild, security professionals can quickly develop mitigations, detection signatures, and patches, and they will publish CVE numbers to alert the community. Not everyone pays attention to such advisories or patches their systems, but the 0-day is increasingly less likely to succeed as it becomes a 1-day, 2-day, and so on.

Zero-days are deployed in different ways depending on the attacker's motivations. Cybercriminals interested in a quick, lucrative score might immediately burn a zero-day in a massive and highly visible attack that maximizes their immediate return. More advanced threat actors establish procedures to delete artifacts, logs, and other observable evidence of a zero-day attack, extending its useful life. Truly sophisticated attackers reserve zero-days for hardened, valuable targets, as zero-days that target popular technologies can sell for thousands of dollars to cybercriminals on the black market—or more than $1 million to governments eager to weaponize them or build a defense against them.

While some zero-days come from legitimate, good-faith security gaps in software code, threat actors can introduce zero-days into a software application's source code maliciously through agreements or covert human plants. Targeted attacks can also compromise software libraries, hardware, or compilers to introduce bugs, backdoors, and other hidden vulnerabilities for future exploitation, in much the same way a ninja joining a castle construction team might compromise the design by creating secret entrances that only the ninja knows about (the scrolls tell us this happened).[13]

Traditionally, zero-day discoveries have come from security researchers with deep expertise studying code, threat hunters thinking creatively about vulnerabilities, or analysts accidentally discovering the exploit being used against them in the wild. While these methods still work, recent technologies such as "fuzzing" have helped automate zero-day detection. Fuzzers and similar tools automatically try various inputs—random, invalid, and unexpected—in an attempt to discover previously unknown system vulnerabilities. The advent of AI-powered fuzzers and AI defenders signals a new paradigm. Not unlike the way that the invention of the cannon, which could pierce castle walls, led to new defense strategies, AI offers the possibility that defenses may someday evolve almost as quickly as the threats themselves. Of course, attack systems may also learn how to overwhelm any defensive capability, altering not just how the industry detects and fights zero-days but how the world looks at cybersecurity as a whole.

For now, though, the pattern of exploit and discovery is cyclical. Threat actors become familiar with a subset of exploits and vulnerabilities, such as SQL injection, XSS, or memory leaks. As defenders become familiar with combatting those threats, attackers move to exploiting different techniques and technologies, and the cycle continues. As time goes by and these defenders and attackers leave the workforce, we will likely observe a new generation of threat actors rediscovering the same common weaknesses in new software and technologies, resulting in the reemergence of old zero-days—the cycle will begin anew.

Zero-Day Defense

Zero-day detection and protection are often the go-to claim for new entrants to the cybersecurity market, as they like to promise big results from their solution. That isn't to say none of them work. However, this topic can easily fall into snake-oil territory. Rest assured that I am not trying to sell you anything but practical guidance on the threat, as detailed below.

1. *Follow best practices.* Just because zero-days are maddeningly difficult to defend against does not mean that you should give up on security. Follow industry best practices. While they may not fully neutralize zero-days, they do make it harder for threat actors to conduct activities against your environment, and they give your organization a better chance to detect and respond to zero-day attacks. Rather than idly worrying about potential zero-days, patch and mitigate 1-days, 2-days, 3-days, and so on, to minimize the time your organization remains vulnerable to known attacks.

2. *Use hunt teams and blue teams.* Form or contract a hunt team and a blue team to work on zero-day defense strategies.

   The hunt team comprises specialized defenders who do not rely on standard signature-based defenses. Instead, they constantly develop hypotheses about how adversaries could use zero-days or other methods to infiltrate networks. Based on those hypotheses, they hunt using honeypots, behavioral and statistical analysis, predictive threat intelligence, and other customized techniques.

   The blue team comprises specialized defenders who design, test, and implement real defenses. First, they document the information flow of a system or network, and then they build threat models describing real and imagined attacks that could succeed against the current design. Unlike with the hunt team, it is not the blue team's job to find zero-days. Instead, they evaluate their information and threat models in terms of zero-days to determine how they could effectively mitigate, safeguard, harden, and protect their systems. The blue team exists apart from normal security, operations, and incident response personnel, though the team should review existing incident response reports to determine how defenses failed and how to build proactive defenses against similar future attacks.

3. *Implement dynamic defenses . . . with caution.* In recent years, security professionals have made concerted efforts to introduce complex and dynamic defense measures that:

   - Attempt to make a network a moving target—for example, nightly updates
   - Introduce randomization—for example, address space layout randomization (ASLR)
   - Dynamically change on interaction—for example, quantum cryptography
   - Initiate erratic defense conditions or immune response systems

   Some of these dynamic defenses were quite successful initially, but then adversaries developed ways to beat them, rendering them effectively static from a strategic perspective.

   Talk to cybersecurity vendors and practitioners and explore the literature on state-of-the-art dynamic defenses to determine what would work for your organization. Proceed with caution, however, as today's dynamic defense can become tomorrow's standard-issue, easily circumvented security layer.

4. *Build a more boring defense.* Consider utilizing "boring" systems, coding practices, and implementations in your environment where possible. Started by Google's BoringSSL open source project,[14] the boring defense proposes that simplifying and reducing your code's attack surface, size, dependency, and complexity—making it boring—will likely eliminate high-value or critical vulnerabilities. Under this practice—which can be effective on a code, application, or system level—code is not elaborate or artful but rather tediously secured and unvaried in structure, with dull and simple implementations. In theory, making code easier for humans and machines to read, test, and interpret makes it less likely that unexpected inputs or events will unearth zero-day vulnerabilities.
5. *Practice denial and deception (D&D).* D&D prevents adversaries from obtaining information about your environment, systems, network, people, data, and other observables, and it can deceive them into taking actions that are advantageous to you. Making adversaries' reconnaissance, weaponization, and exploit delivery harder forces them to spend more time testing, exploring, and verifying that the gap they perceive in your environment truly exists. For example, you could deceptively modify your systems to advertise themselves as running a different OS with different software, such as by changing a Solaris instance to look like a different SELinux OS. (Ideally, you would actually migrate to SELinux, but the logistics of legacy IT systems may keep your organization reliant on old software for longer than desired.) If your deception is effective, adversaries may try to develop and deliver weaponized attacks against your SELinux instance—which will, of course, fail because you're not actually running SELinux.

   Note that D&D should be applied on top of good security practices to enhance them rather than leveraged on its own to achieve security through obscurity. D&D is a security endgame for extremely mature organizations looking for additional ways to defend systems from persistent threat actors, similar to the "hush-hush tactics" described in *Bansenshūkai*.[15]

6. *Disconnect to protect.* In its discussion of the disconnect defense, *Shōninki* teaches you to disconnect from the enemy mentally, strategically, physically, and in every other way.[16] In cybersecurity, this means creating a self-exiled blue team that turns completely inward, working in isolation from the world and ignoring all security news, threat intelligence, patches, exploits, malware variations,

new signatures, cutting-edge products—anything that could influence their reason, alter their state of mind, or provide a connection with the enemy. If undertaken correctly, the disconnect skill forks the defenders' thinking in a direction far from the industry standard. Adversaries have trouble thinking the same way as the disconnected defenders, and the defenders develop unique, secret defense strategies that the adversary has not encountered, making it exceedingly difficult for a zero-day attacks to work.

Like D&D, this method is recommended only if you already possess elite cybersecurity skills. Otherwise, it can be counterproductive to alienate yourself from the enemy and operate in the dark.

CASTLE THEORY THOUGHT EXERCISE

Consider the scenario in which you are the ruler of a medieval castle with valuable assets inside. You hear rumors that a shinobi infiltrated the construction crew when it was building your castle and installed one or more backdoors or other gaps in the castle's security. Shinobi who know the locations and mechanisms of these vulnerabilities can slip in and out of your castle freely, bypassing the guards and security controls. You have sent guards, architects, and even mercenary shinobi to inspect your castle for these hidden vulnerabilities, but they have found nothing. You do not have the money, time, or resources to build a new, backdoor-free castle.

How would you continue castle operations knowing that there is a hidden flaw a shinobi could exploit at any time? How will you safeguard the treasure, people, and information inside your castle? How can you hunt for or defend against a hidden weakness without knowing what it looks like, where it is located, or how it is used? How else could you manage the risk of this unknown vulnerability?

Recommended Security Controls and Mitigations

Where relevant, recommendations are presented with applicable security controls from the NIST 800-53 standard. Each should be evaluated with the concept of zero-days in mind.

1. Create custom, dynamic, and adaptive security protections for your organization to fortify security best practices. [AC-2: Account Management | (6) Dynamic Privilege Management; AC-4: Information Flow Enforcement | (3) Dynamic Information

Flow Control; AC-16: Security and Privacy Attributes | (1) Dynamic Attribute Association; IA-10: Adaptive Authentication; IR-4: Incident Handling | (2) Dynamic Reconfiguration; IR-10: Integrated Information Security Analysis Team; PL-8: Security and Privacy Architectures | (1) Defense-in-Depth; SA-20: Customized Development of Critical Components; SC-7: Boundary Protection | (20) Dynamic Isolation and Segregation; SI-14: Non-persistence]

2. Keep records of zero-days, including when and how they are discovered, what technology they target, vulnerability scan results, and their correlation with predicted future zero-days. [AU-6: Audit Review, Analysis, and Reporting | (5) Integrated Analysis of Audit Records; SA-15: Development Process, Standard, and Tools | (8) Reuse of Threat and Vulnerability Information]
3. Conduct specialized vulnerability scanning, validation, and system testing to assess zero-day security. [CA-2: Assessments | (2) Specialized Assessments]
4. Contract specialized penetration testers to find zero-days in your software, systems, and other technologies so you can proactively defend against these exploits. [CA-8: Penetration Testing; RA-6: Technical Surveillance Countermeasures Survey]
5. Threat-model your systems and software to evaluate potential zero-days and assess how you can proactively redesign to mitigate them. Consider implementing "boring" code. [SA-11: Developer Testing and Evaluation | (2) Threat Modeling and Vulnerabilities Analyses; SA-15: Development Process, Standard, and Tools | (5) Attack Surface Reduction; SI-10: Information Input Validation | (3) Predictable Behavior]
6. Implement custom, diverse, and unique security defenses to mitigate a zero-day's ability to exploit your systems. [SC-29: Heterogeneity]
7. Deploy denial and deception campaigns to reduce adversaries' ability to perform reconnaissance or weaponize and deliver zero-day attacks against your organization. [SC-30: Concealment and Misdirection]
8. Establish hunt teams and security teams to search for indicators of zero-day attacks and exploits. [SI-4: System Monitoring | (24) Indicators of Compromise]
9. Conduct regular automated vulnerability scanning to check for 1-days, 2-days, 3-days, and so on. Patch, mitigate, or remediate the vulnerabilities as appropriate. [RA-5: Vulnerability Scanning; SI-2: Flaw Remediation]

Debrief

In this chapter, we reviewed shinobi tradecraft and the secrecy surrounding the exploit techniques they cultivated over centuries. We explored how many of these secret shinobi techniques closely parallel the zero-day exploits and vulnerabilities we observe today. We reviewed the current state of the art and the potential future of zero-day attacks in terms of cybersecurity, cyberwar, and information dominance. This chapter touched on how talking about zero-days can feel pointless but is actually critical to confronting the threat.

In the next chapter, we will discuss hiring the right kind of talent to combat zero-days and threat actors of all kinds. We will review the guidelines the shinobi scrolls offer for recruiting shinobi and explore how we can apply that guidance to attracting cybersecurity talent. There are persistent claims that the cybersecurity industry has a talent shortage problem, and I suspect there was a similar shinobi shortage problem during periods of strife in medieval Japan. The shinobi scrolls explain how to identify who could be trained to be a shinobi operative, a role that was much higher stakes than the office jobs of today. A poor recruitment choice would likely soon die, thus wasting the investment in training while jeopardizing missions and team members' lives.

23

HIRING SHINOBI

In order to defend against enemy plans or shinobi, or should an emergency arise, you may think it more desirable to have a large number of people. However, you should not hire more people into your army without careful consideration.

A shinobi should have three major principles:
skillful speech, boldness, and strategy.
—Yoshimori Hyakushu #38

We know many of the jobs that shinobi performed in feudal Japan, such as committing espionage and sabotage, leading raids, gathering information, carrying out assassinations, and—perhaps the most useful of all—defending against enemy shinobi. But to use shinobi for these purposes, lords and commanders first had to do the same thing that executives and managers still do today: recruit and hire staff.

Scattered but large portions of *Bansenshūkai* and *Yoshimori Hyakushu* are dedicated to advising lords why they should hire shinobi, how and when to use them, and the qualities that make a successful candidate—and, eventually, an effective shinobi. According to the scrolls, an ideal shinobi should be:[1]

Intelligent A strong-minded, logical, strategic thinker with a good memory, keen observation skills, and an aptitude for learning quickly

Patient A deliberate but decisive operative with exemplary willpower and self-control

Capable Resourceful, creative, and courageous in the field, with a demonstrable record of achievement and the vision to see victory even in dire situations

Loyal Sincere, honorable, and benevolent to others; someone who takes personal responsibility for their actions

Eloquent Able to communicate effectively with lords and persuasively with employees

In addition to those qualities, shinobi sought for leadership positions must be able to prioritize effectively, execute complex tactics successfully, and demonstrate sound judgment under duress.[2]

The scrolls also flag certain traits that disqualify candidates, including selfishness and stupidity; immorality (for example, using one's skills for personal gain); and being likely to overindulge in alcohol, lust, or greed.[3] Nepotism might have been a problem as well. While one's chances of becoming a successful shinobi might increase with the early expectations, opportunities, and grooming that came with being born into a shinobi village (most notably Iga and Koka), being born to shinobi parents did not guarantee success. Such children could, in fact, become low-quality candidates who possessed any number of the negative qualities mentioned above.[4]

Importantly, in that lengthy list of desirable and undesirable attributes, there are no mentions of specific required skills, past experiences, educational credentials, social pedigrees, ranks, or titles—or for that matter, ages or genders. It seems that being a shinobi was merit based, dependent on the individual's character, values, qualifications, and abilities.

While the scrolls don't offer any specific guidance on recruiting, interviewing, or assessing candidates, *Shōninki* does provide advice on how to understand a person's deeper nature—their knowledge, modes of thought, beliefs, desires, flaws, and character. Though typically used for spying and targeting, these methods could be usefully adapted for interviewing recruits.

For instance, *Shōninki* recommends visiting the target's frequent hangouts to collect information from locals who know the target well.

The best information comes from places where the target seems comfortable or has relationships with the proprietors or clientele and therefore is more likely to reveal secrets.[5]

There is also the skill of *hito ni kuruma wo kakeru*—"to get people carried away by praising them." This involves asking the target questions and praising their answers; such flattery makes you seem less intelligent and seems to demonstrate awe in the candidate's abilities. Done convincingly, this technique loosens up your target, boosts their confidence, and makes them enjoy telling you about themselves, which could lead to all manner of valuable intelligence. For instance, once they're comfortable, you can change conversational topics and see how they react to unexpected inquiries. Do they have their own opinions, or are they simply parroting other people's wisdom?[6]

Recruiting allies and sussing out enemies bore the weight of life and death for shinobi. They often had to decide whether to entrust a person with their life or whether that person would let them down during a perilous mission. As a result, shinobi likely internalized these techniques and other rubrics to become expert people readers, able to quickly and unobtrusively size up someone's capability, knowledge, and character.[7]

In this chapter, we will look at the common hiring practices of modern organizations and identify opportunities to incorporate the wisdom of the shinobi into recruiting and training talent. Many hiring managers and even the historical shinobi seem to believe that they can assess the suitability of a person after a thorough interview. While this may work some of the time, many candidates never get the opportunity to attend such an interview due to the various signaling steps, proxy prerequisites, and human resource checkboxes that may erroneously screen them out. We explore these hiring processes in terms of why they may not achieve the desired outcome.

Cybersecurity Talent

The explosive growth of the cybersecurity sector has led to problems recruiting enough people—and the right people—to perform all the necessary work. While part of this stems from the fact that cybersecurity is a relatively new field with a high technical barrier to entry, current candidate assessment methods are also problematic. Too many private-sector companies place too much value on recruiting candidates who check the right résumé boxes or do well on whiteboard puzzles, but cannot perform the job's day-to-day functions. Candidates, recruiters, and training programs have noted what it takes to get a job and are positioning themselves accordingly, lessening the effectiveness of traditional methods of candidate evaluation. Universities churn out computer science graduates who cannot solve the FizzBuzz problem, designed to test basic programming skills. Candidates provide potential employers with biased or made-up references. Employees pursue meaningless job titles that look good on a résumé but rarely correlate with their work experience or capabilities. Career climbers attain IT or security certifications by cramming for tests (and often forget that information almost immediately); publish shallow, pointless articles for the visibility; and file for patents by adding their names to projects they had almost nothing to do with.

Measures to combat these hiring loopholes, such as take-home tests, are easily bypassed with online help or outright plagiarism. On-the-spot interview whiteboard puzzles, while once novel, are now routine. Candidates come in having practiced for them and may have even gotten the exact exercises from leaks at the company. Even if they weren't easily compromised, none of these assessments accurately gauge a candidate's ability to do the work of cybersecurity.

To be fair, candidates have just as much reason to be suspicious of cybersecurity employers. Even if an organization hires an incredible professional worthy of the title "cyber ninja," there is no guarantee that the employer will use them effectively. While this risk exists in any industry, it's compounded for cybersecurity companies for numerous reasons, including the obscurity of the highly technical profession, the evolution of technology, leadership's lack of awareness or exposure to an employee's more advanced capabilities, and the importance of nondemarcated creativity to success. To perform well and influence organizational security, employees need leadership buy-in and the green light to exercise their skills without fear of punishment or outright sabotage of their abilities.

One of the biggest recruiters, employers, and trainers of cyber professionals is the US military, who can take nearly computer-illiterate high school dropouts and, over the span of 18 months, train them to become capable cyber warfare specialists. Of course, not every recruit makes it through the training, as multiple layers of requirements filter out poor candidates—a practice that aligns closely with those described for shinobi recruits in *Bansenshūkai*.[8]

One distinctive tool in military recruiting is the Armed Services Vocational Aptitude Battery test (ASVAB).[9] Unlike corporate recruiting, which emphasizes past accomplishments and professional credentials, the ASVAB assesses recruits' learning potential, aptitude, and general technical ability. The scores are used to assign candidates to occupational specialties in which they are likely to thrive if successfully trained. The ASVAB has been highly effective for the military, but it's worth noting that certain cyber jobs have reported unexpectedly high rates of training failure and poor field performance, likely due to the jobs' demanding attributes that the ASVAB does not always test for. In the structured world of the military, it can be difficult to identify or train people who want to approach challenges with creative, fearless, independent, problem solving–based thinking—a skill set closely associated with hackers.

Talent Management

Everyone wants to hire cybersecurity professionals for their organization, but the supply is limited. So how does everyone get their hands on some cybersecurity talent? Organizations should first determine whether they intend to develop raw talent themselves or compete against other organizations for the limited supply of experienced cybersecurity experts. Many of the recommendations below are suited for developing talent but may be suitable for a hybrid approach as well. Many cybersecurity professionals may agree that current hiring practices are broken and it's time to move past all the proxy signals to try something new. As an alternative, consider the below approaches to hiring and maintaining talent.

1. *Start using practical interview capability assessments.* Instead of interview quizzes, random whiteboard puzzles, live coding exercises, or take-home projects, ask candidates to perform functions of the actual job for which they are being evaluated. Have them audition in the same environment and conditions they will work in if hired. Test and validate assessments by giving the exercises to current employees and reviewing the results, measuring the correlation between performance on the test and actual job performance. Keep the assessments modular and regularly alter them so candidates cannot benefit from obtaining a leaked exercise or coaching. Regularly integrate recent challenges your employees have faced to keep the test current with the demands of the job. Ideally, the assessment should be able to determine an applicant's competence in 30 minutes or less, with time enough for the candidate to learn through online research and/or rapid trial and error.
2. *Implement a black-box aptitude battery.* Give the candidate a modular, semirandom pseudo-technology and ask them to discover how it works so they can then attempt to hack and/or secure it. This exercise is similar to the Department of Defense's DLAB (Defense Language Aptitude Battery) test.[10] Instead of testing a candidate's proficiency with an existing language, the DLAB uses a fake

language to test the ability to learn a new language. This approach is likely even more useful for technology than spoken languages, as new technologies and frameworks appear all the time. Key criteria of the black-box test would measure a candidate's ability to:

- Quickly memorize technology specifications, commands, or manuals of the fake technology
- Use logic and critical thinking to solve problems or navigate scenarios in the fake technology
- Display resourcefulness to achieve specific outcomes with artificial barriers, such as bypassing the fake technology's local security

You may find and hire a promising candidate who has high aptitude but lacks the necessary technical skill to do the job. In this case, know that you must make an expensive long-term investment in teaching the candidate actual technical skills. Otherwise, their high aptitude will not help you.

3. *Be able to spot disqualifiers.* Go beyond the typical drug tests, reference checks, background and criminal histories, and credit reports that most organizations perform, as these do not always paint an accurate picture of someone's character—for better or worse. Devote serious effort to identifying candidates who constantly make poor decisions that harm themselves and others. These "harmful-stupid" people can have degrees, certifications, good credit scores, clean drug tests, and solid work history by virtue of other qualities such as fortitude, ambition, diligence, raw talent, and luck. During the interview, probe their desires and motivations to disqualify the wrong type of people. (Of course, past harmful-stupid decisions may not represent the candidate's current mindset and character, so give the candidate opportunities to demonstrate whether they're likely to make harmful-stupid decisions in the future.)
4. *Train staff and establish a culture of excellence.* Technical skills can be taught, but other character attributes take outsized effort to hone. Identify staff who want to become "cyber ninjas" and help them improve the personal qualities described in *Bansenshūkai* by constantly challenging, conditioning, and training them. Instruct your staff to take the following steps:

- Strive to solve progressively harder cyber problems every day.

- Hone their mind with memory drills, self-discipline challenges, and exercises in patience centered on technology.
- Learn ingenuity by creating limited cyber operational situations governed by self-imposed rules, then trying to accomplish goals while following those rules.

CASTLE THEORY THOUGHT EXERCISE

Consider the scenario in which you are the ruler of a medieval castle with valuable assets inside. You post public notice of your intention to hire and train shinobi to defend against enemy ninja. You receive a huge number of applications. You know of no academies, guilds, or other organizations that can attest to a candidate's credentials, and given the covert nature of the trade, you cannot verify candidates' experience with previous employers. You don't understand a shinobi's skills fully enough to test or quantify them yourself, and when you request that an applicant demonstrate the shinobi arts, the candidate either refuses or asks for payment.

How could you determine whether a self-proclaimed shinobi will ably defend your castle? How might you identify and hire a high-aptitude candidate with no shinobi experience if you don't know exactly what a shinobi does? How would you train those high-aptitude candidates without access to real shinobi?

Recommended Security Controls and Mitigations

These recommendations are presented with the NIST 800-53 standard and NIST 800-16 Cyber Workforce Framework in mind.[11] Consider these recommendations when evaluating potential hires who will implement security controls.

1. Define the knowledge, skills, and abilities needed to perform cybersecurity duties at your organization. Address these needs—along with competency benchmarks, workforce skills, and mission requirements—during talent recruitment, hiring, and training. [PM-13 Security and Privacy Workforce]
2. Define hiring requirements for "cyber ninja" positions by reviewing and documenting required knowledge units, such as:
   - Advanced network technology and protocols
   - Digital forensics

- Software development
- Compliance
- Computer network defense
- Configuration management
- Cryptography and encryption
- Data security
- Databases
- Identity management/privacy
- Incident management
- Industrial control systems
- Information assurance
- Information systems
- IT systems and operations
- Network and telecommunications security
- Personnel security
- Physical and environmental security
- Architecture, systems, and application security
- Security risk management
- Web security

3. Consider the following training, certifications, and protocols: OV-6, ANTP-*, ARCH-*, COMP-1/5/9/10, CND-*, CM-*, CR-*, DS-*, DB-*, DF-*, IM-*, IR-*, ICS-*, IA-*, WT-*, SI-*, ITOS-*, NTS-*, PS-*, PES-1, RM-*, SW-*, SAS-*.

Debrief

In this chapter, we reviewed the qualities that the shinobi believed were necessary to be successful in their tradecraft. In addition, we described some of the back-channel interview methods used by shinobi. We also explored many of the current hiring processes used by modern organizations and why they not are as effective as desired. We listed some novel approaches to identifying suitable candidates. The thought exercise in this chapter is as relevant today as it was for the medieval commanders who needed to hire shinobi to protect themselves from enemy shinobi. Hiring hacker-like people who may not have a good GPA or a solid work history, or who may not wear professional attire, will likely be more effective in countering cybercriminals than hiring the typical person who colors between the lines.

Once you have hired these talented and/or skilled defenders, it is important to establish standards and processes so they can defend your organization in a disciplined manner. Without leadership that sets clear expectations, the defenders may become lax and thus less than worthless. In the next chapter, we will discuss guardhouse behavior.

24

GUARDHOUSE BEHAVIOR

Do not let your guard down, even if you are not confronting the enemy.

In a guardhouse, it is warned that you should not talk in loud voices, drink booze, sing, have prostitutes, or gamble.
—Yoshimori Hyakushu #65

The shinobi scrolls are filled with details about how to bypass a target's security personnel. To a shinobi in the field, no defensive impediment is quite as pressing—or as complicated—as an enemy's guards. While the scrolls instruct shinobi to work in blind spots that guards cannot monitor or protect easily, the most exploitable gaps stem not from poor military strategy or lack of manpower but from guards' negligence and lack of discipline.

The scrolls advise seeking out guards who are observably tired, lazy, poorly organized, ignorant of shinobi techniques, or complacent. There are any number of ways to assess and exploit guard capabilities. Among other techniques, *Bansenshūkai* recommends:[1]

- Whispering near guards to test their attentiveness, then monitoring their reaction for at least one hour to gauge their response methods and capabilities
- Identifying negligent guards who act on signals from hidden guards, exposing the presence of embedded defenders such as listening or smelling scouts
- Targeting guardhouses where guards speak loudly, converse incessantly, or drink or party to excess, all of which indicates inexperience or negligence
- Waiting for or causing an event that compels guards to abandon their post

The same scroll also advises shinobi to observe guards' conduct, movements, bearings, and actions to infer more about their discipline. For instance, if the moat and surrounding perimeter of a castle are kept clean, clear, and well lit, then the guards are likely vigilant and practice defensive hygiene. But if commonly known castle entry points such as corners, spillways, and sewage outlets are not protected, it could be a sign that the guards or their commanders neglect their duties.[2]

Infiltrating enemy guardhouses gave shinobi crucial insight into improving guard discipline, behavior, and capability in their own defenses. Again, the scrolls cite guards' negligence and laziness as the biggest obstacles to a successful defense, and they put the onus for overcoming those vices on lords or commanders, whose strict discipline, tough training, and thorough attention to detail could give their guards the requisite mental toughness to defend against enemy threats, including other shinobi.[3] "Every single thing is decided by your own mind and by the way that you think," say the ninja poems. "If you always assume that you are facing the enemy, you will never drop your guard in any way."[4]

In this chapter, we will compare the guardhouses of shinobi times to the security operations centers (SOCs) of today. We will touch on the modernization of security, which has shifted security responsibility to all employees instead of just security personnel. We'll review methods by which an external threat actor can detect poor security controls/practices on networks. In addition, we'll present some theory around the direct interaction between security staff and adversaries—particularly if the adversary can infiltrate SOC/IR ticket systems—as well as other ideas about how adversaries may be able to judge the vigilance of the SOC.

Most importantly, we discuss why security staff behavior is so important, why it may degrade over time, and how to establish a culture of security excellence.

Security Operations Center Issues and Expectations

It is especially easy for cybersecurity and IT personnel to become lazy, complacent, negligent, tired, or burned out in their jobs. Why? There are myriad reasons.

One of the biggest is an unfortunate reality of human nature: if no one is looking over their shoulder, many workers simply shirk their duties. Lazy cybersecurity professionals have ample cover. Their tasks are largely invisible to their colleagues—even their supervisors. Many operation centers are isolated behind locked doors where employees work, relax, or even sleep without anyone knowing the difference. Their networks and machines exist on separate VLANs or "research" boxes that allow them to freely browse the internet without logging, inspection, or filtering.

The industry's heavy reliance on process can also lull employees into a state of negligence or complacency. Through procedural repetition, security staff develop familiarities, habits, and narrowed ideas of what it means to defend their organization. While this tendency stems from the necessary routines of everyday work, it also results in highly specialized single-tool or single-approach defenders who don't consider attackers' techniques and tools outside the scope of their own daily experience. Such a limited mindset leaves an organization with considerable security gaps.

Driven employees have the opposite problem. For them, working in a competitive field that demands deep specialized knowledge, ability, and ambition raises the risk of burnout. After tiresome months spent hunting for threats and incidents, it becomes easy to lose focus, rely on known concepts, wait to act until there is a security systems or software alert, or learn only what is necessary to report or remediate specific security incidents as they appear.

Cyber professionals aren't the sole arbiters of computer literacy and security awareness; all employees share this responsibility. Unfortunately, this means the laziness and negligence of nontechnical employees is often a bigger security threat to an organization than a malicious external actor. These employees may inadvertently expose their company's network or systems to threats by carelessly clicking on phishing emails or plugging in foreign USB drives they find in the parking lot. If management does not enforce security vigilance and discipline when appropriate, then conscientious employees are forced to operate in a culture in which careless employees abound and may even be rewarded. Success at these organizations becomes a game of attrition, wherein employees are promoted for surviving the longest without burning out or quitting. This environment compromises the work ethic, discipline, and integrity of the effective workers and degrades the entire workforce, allowing threat actors to exploit the many gaps these nonvigilant employees create.

Leadership buy-in and competency significantly boost employee morale and security vigilance, just as poor leadership decisions or organizational strategies can weaken security posture and degrade employee trust. Attempts to improve defensive blind spots or weaknesses typically require interdepartmental cooperation, shared budgets, weekend hours, and inconveniences that lead employees to complain and resist the initiatives. As a result, worn down, defeated security engineers become cynical about security improvements and turn a blind eye to existing deficiencies. Some may even wait for an incident to occur, knowing their organization's reactive security posture means they won't be allowed to make improvements unless something bad happens first.

It can be easy for threat actors to assess an organization's security vigilance from externally observable indicators, such as:

- Too much information leaked through error messages on websites
- Password policy details leaked upon login
- Lack of security policy header content
- Improperly self-signed certificates
- Misconfigured email Domain-Based Message Authentication, Reporting and Conformance (DMARC)/Sender Policy Framework (SPF)
- Poorly configured DNS records
- Exposed management interfaces on internet-facing servers, security devices, or networking hardware
- Disclosure of technology versions or security used

To counteract a tendency toward lack of vigilance, defenders must constantly self-assess and strive for improvement. While managers don't always praise or reward staff who implement additional security, ongoing vigilance sends a message to adversaries that an organization's first line of defense is strong and hints that interior defenses may be even stronger.

Influencing Behavior

How employees respond in the workplace is influenced by their own beliefs, the culture at work, and conditioning over time from their learned experiences. Shaping work culture by reinforcing behavior selectively and implementing meaningful work-feedback loops will encourage employees toward excellence. The lack of feedback, especially of positive feedback, may be the most challenging issue to address in security, as it can be easy for a defender's behavior to slide into a low-energy state of security nihilism. This can result from a lack of positive reinforcement for good behavior. Perhaps the only inputs received by the security staff are compliance audits and KPI numbers, which don't represent the utility of their actions. The results of good performance, like stopping adversaries from robbing the organization of intellectual property or money, can take years to manifest and thus can be hard to build on. Listed below is guidance on how to improve and sustain good security behaviors.

1. *Set standards and develop your culture.* The US Department of Defense (DoD) has fostered a culture that prioritizes security vigilance. Ex-DoD employees who move to other organizations regularly describe experiencing culture shock when they encounter security negligence in their new workplace (and unfortunately eventually reduce their standards, accepting the new culture). Review the DoD's *Cybersecurity Culture and Compliance Initiative*[5] and determine which of its elements could help your organization establish a culture of security vigilance. Some possible attributes to call out explicitly include:

   Integrity Encourage staff to report mistakes when they happen. For instance, an employee who accidentally compromises the security of a network should not feel a need to hide the incident for fear of losing their job. Rather, they should feel safe enough to admit their mistake and help the organization fortify the security gap.

   Competence Establish baseline educational standards for everyone who operates in cyberspace. These should inform all employees' daily behavior, empower people to identify security risks, and facilitate smart decision making through ongoing cybersecurity education. Note that establishing a core competency for your organization could mean preventing those who do not demonstrate competency from holding certain positions.

   Professionalism To maintain a standard of excellence and a culture of vigilance, require that staff hold themselves accountable for their work and not take shortcuts.

   Questioning attitudes Hire people who do not accept things as they are but rather question, analyze, and interpret their observations. Ensure that staff feel safe to speak up without being quickly dismissed or made to feel stupid.

2. *Enforce discipline.* Security negligence affects more than one person's work performance or product. It puts entire organizations at risk. *Bansenshūkai*'s "Six Points on Behavior in the Guardhouse" says, "Strict rules should be adhered to, and in the case where there is someone who is not vigilant, he should be punished severely."[6] Establish a formal procedure to identify and punish cybersecurity violations and nonvigilant practices by users, security, IT, and leadership. Avoid the temptation to scapegoat the chief information security officer (CISO) or other personnel when there is a security incident, as doing so sabotages a culture in which everyone feels accountable.
3. *Establish formal processes, procedures, and compliance.* Identify, document, and disseminate the tasks, rules, and policies you want your security team to follow and enforce. Determine ways to measure whether employees are complying with these standards. Avoid using shallow key performance indicators (KPIs) such as how many tickets are filed or how many security incidents are investigated, as these metrics do not meaningfully judge work. Install leadership that understands and cares about security, dedicates time to build vigilance, and identifies noncompliance.
4. *Drive agency and engagement.* Many corporate employees do not feel engaged at work. They don't take part in decisions, don't act in the interests of the organization, and aren't invested in the company's success (or their own). Boredom is a common issue in security—one that can often be alleviated by removing obstacles that deter or demotivate staff from taking proactive security actions. Empower security staff by allowing them to:

    - Experiment with new security controls, routines, and concepts
    - Learn new technologies, techniques, and tools
    - Find meaning in their work
    - Experience positive outcomes, such as a path for career development or promotions
    - Participate in strategic risk decisions
    - Conduct blue team, red team (for example, purple teaming), or other simulations and exercises so they can provide positive input to each other
    - Celebrate success in finding security flaws

CASTLE THEORY THOUGHT EXERCISE

Consider the scenario in which you are the ruler of a medieval castle with valuable assets inside. While patrolling your castle, you notice that spears are oddly arranged in some of the guardhouses, and you suspect that some of the night watch guards have devised a way to prop themselves up on supporting spears, allowing them to relax or sleep while appearing upright and awake at their posts. You have received no reports of sleeping guards—or of any other guard staff misconduct—nor are you aware of any recent security incidents.

What evidence, if any, do you need before you take measures to improve security, processes, and personnel? How might you gauge the alertness of your guards? What security information could you have guards study during their shift to ensure they do not sleep? How would you solicit honest feedback from guards on how to improve their attentiveness and engagement? How would you punish a single guard who sleeps during night watch, and how would you punish an entire regiment that does the same? How do you establish a culture of trust and integrity so your guards feel they can tell you when something is wrong without fear of punishment?

Recommended Security Controls and Mitigations

Where relevant, recommendations are presented with applicable security controls from the NIST 800-53 standard. Each should be evaluated with the concept of guardhouse behavior in mind.

1. Develop, document, and provide security training, procedures, and rules of behavior to all staff. Create specific training and procedures for roles with significant security responsibilities, such as development, IT, security, and leadership positions. Enforce strict disciplinary measures for failure to comply with security policy and procedures. [AT-1: Awareness and Training Policy and Procedures; AT-2: Awareness Training; AT-3: Role-Based Training; IR-2: Incident Response Training; PL-4: Rules of Behavior; SA-16: Developer-Provided Training]
2. Conduct performance-based tests of security responsiveness, posture, and tool capability with specialized security assessments, scans, pen tests, and red teams. This activity identifies processes or procedures not being followed, security blind spots, and unvigilant staff members. [CA-2: Assessments | (2) Specialized Assessments; CA-8: Penetration Testing; IR-3: Incident Response

Testing; RA-5: Vulnerability Scanning; SC-7: Boundary Protection | (10) Test Exfiltration; SI-4: System Monitoring | Testing of Monitoring Tools and Mechanisms; SI-6: Security and Privacy Function]

3. Create training programs and exercises to continually improve your security staff's knowledge, skill set, and competency. [CA-8: Penetration Testing; IR-3: Incident Response Testing | (3) Continuous Improvement; PM-12: Insider Threat Program; PM-13: Security and Privacy Workforce; PM-14: Testing, Training, and Monitoring; PM-16: Threat Awareness Program]
4. Allow security staff to determine which configurations and controls should be changed to improve security. Put the burden on system owners, maintainers, and developers to provide strong, evidence-based arguments as to why changes recommended by security staff cannot be implemented. [CM-3: Configuration Change Control]
5. Implement a policy and process for addressing security staff complaints. This feedback helps security improve processes by revising or rolling back improper controls. It also provides users with a way to identify security concerns and alert security staff without fear of repercussions. [PM-28: Complaint Management]
6. Require that security personnel practice OPSEC to protect key operational, configuration, and deployment information, while taking care not to reveal OPSEC to adversaries who may be testing security defenses. [SC-38: Operations Security]

Debrief

In this chapter, we looked at the ways in which shinobi probed guards and guardhouses to assess infiltration opportunities based on their target's security standards (or lack thereof). We reviewed how hundreds of years ago, as today, it was commonplace for guards to become complacent in their duties and how skilled infiltrators were able to take advantage of this complacency. In addition, we touched on the ways culture can shape an organization's ability to defend itself; this concept was given paramount importance in the philosophy of shinobi. Shinobi culture was then compared to modern SOCs and InfoSec work cultures, which have issues that today's cyber adversaries are likely to exploit. We also described several methods and best practices for establishing and maintaining a culture of security excellence.

In the next chapter, we will discuss the shinobi principal of "stranger danger"—of not allowing anyone suspicious to approach. Repeating this message to create a culture of security, while also implementing strict controls to prevent suspicious events from becoming malicious, is a demonstration of organizational security excellence.

25

ZERO-TRUST THREAT MANAGEMENT

If you enter a room from the rear and if there is someone in the room who is not asleep, then they will not suspect you as an intruder. It is because those who come from the rear are not considered possible thieves or assailants.

You should never allow anyone from outside your province to come close to the guardhouse, even if he or she is a relative.
—Yoshimori Hyakushu #93

In feudal Japan, it was typical for traveling merchants, monks, priests, performers, entertainers, beggars, and other outsiders to operate in or near an active military camp or castle, as the encamped soldiers made frequent use of their services.[1] However, some of these outsiders were secret operatives paid to collect information for the soldiers' enemies. Some were even disguised shinobi who took advantage of being near the castle to study or engage their targets, gather intelligence, and even infiltrate or attack the camp.[2]

Bansenshūkai describes how military commanders can block such threats. The most effective approach is to disallow suspicious activities and fraternization near the camp. Discussing a policy "strictly brought home to everyone by repetition," the scroll warns that anybody who looks suspicious should not be allowed into the castle or camp at any time, mitigating the opportunity for suspicious activity to become a malicious threat.[3] Trained, disciplined troops allowed only trusted merchants to operate in or near their encampment, and they actively blocked unknown or untrusted merchants from offering services in the area. Shinobi had the broader operational philosophy to distrust anyone they didn't know.[4] Furthermore, *Bansenshūkai* recommends that shinobi help trusted merchants and vendors fortify their huts and shops against fire to mitigate the risk that fire would spread from those shops to the encampment, whether by accident or arson.[5]

In this chapter, we will review the "block malicious only" mode—a mode that can become an endless chasing down of new domains, IPs, URLs, and files that are shown to be malicious. We will explore some of the reasons why many organizations (and the security industry) choose to chase this never-ending threat feed rather than adopt a "block all suspicious" mode of operation. We'll also outline strategies and guidance for dealing with the technical problems of this inverted approach. Furthermore, in this chapter's Castle Theory Thought Exercise, we'll explore the ways internal staff may attempt to bypass this "block all suspicious" security control.

Threat Opportunity

In terms of cybersecurity, imagine the encampment is your organization and the merchants, entertainers, and everyone else beyond your perimeter are the many external services and applications available on the internet. All the legitimate business interconnections to external sites that help your staff do their jobs—not to mention the news, social media, and entertainment sites that your employees check during their breaks—allow suspicious entities to connect to your organization and operate under the guise of normal business. Threat actors seeking to perform initial access, delivery, and exploitation often require these external communication capabilities to go unchallenged, uninspected, and unfiltered. Their ensuing offensive tactics include perpetrating drive-by compromises on websites your staff visits, sending spear-phishing emails with links and attachments to your employees, performing network scans of your environment from untrusted IPs, and using command and control (C2) sites to obtain information and send instructions to malware implants on compromised machines, to name just a few.

To combat these attacks, the cybersecurity industry has established functional security controls, policies, and systems that whitelist appropriate communications to known and trusted associates, partners, and other verified, third-party business entities. Organizations can create whitelists of domain names, IP blocks, name servers, email addresses, websites, and certificate authorities that allow staff to communicate only with trusted partners and vice versa. Under these strict whitelisting conditions, before attempting to breach an organization, threat actors must first devote the time, resources, and focus to infiltrating trusted partners.

However, while the technical problem has been solved, the human problem remains. It is part of the human condition to seek stimulation through outside relationships as well as entertainment and news. Consequently, enforcing a "block suspicious" policy can be challenging for management, as it requires the willpower to lead significant cultural and behavioral change across all parts of an organization.

For example, suppose you notice that most of your organization's internet traffic comes from your employees' streaming videos on entertainment sites. You note that this activity is not in line with their job duties, and you decide to block all the major entertainment sites from entering your network using layer-7 detection tools.

While this reasonable measure is in line with your business needs and perhaps even documented IT policy, many organizations that have gone through this process have come to regret it. Employees will likely complain or put social pressure on you to unblock the offending traffic, with some surely attempting to circumvent the policy via encryption or tunneling technology, proxy avoidance, or visiting entertainment sites that contain similar content but avoid your filters—putting your network and systems at greater risk.

One popular solution is to provide a non-business internet—or bring your own device (BYOD) network—on which employees can stream videos on their personal devices. You could even set up separate machines that employees use for internet research and on breaks, but not for business functions. The US Department of Defense (DoD) uses this approach, providing employees with a separate, dedicated system for nonclassified internet (NIPRnet) access; network guards physically and logically segregate this system for information flow control.[6] The DoD takes further measures on NIPRnet to whitelist all known non-malicious internet resources and deny large IP blocks and ASNs it deems suspicious, or at least unnecessary.

For the past decade or more, organizations have constantly consumed threat feeds of known malicious IPs, domains, and URLs, so blocking known *malicious* (blacklisting) is easy enough. Blocking *suspicious* prevents unknown malicious traffic from infiltrating but is considerably harder for organizations, often for valid reasons. It can be extremely difficult to create a master whitelist of all known safe internet resources, sites, and IPs that you know your staff will use. Once again, the DoD is an ideal practitioner, as the organization proactively establishes a policy to block and prevent these threat scenarios. It also constantly reminds staff—through OPSEC posters, required training, terms of use on systems, and clear system warning labels—to not circumvent its policies or controls, as doing so could compromise network, system, and information security.

Blocking the Suspicious

"Stranger danger" is a simple concept many children learn at a young age. Potential threats to the child are averted by having zero tolerance for approach by any strangers. Stranger danger is not a perfect strategy, but it can be effective, assuming any known entities (non-strangers) are verified as trustworthy. An advantage of this strategy is that it does not depend on additional security layers to respond to a threat previously recognized as suspicious. Because children and many organizations are defenseless once a malicious threat is permitted to interact with them, applying a "block all suspicious" security policy may be the first and only defense they will get. Listed below is guidance on how to apply these concepts in your environment.

1. *Practice identification, awareness, and understanding.* Demonstrate for stakeholders the idea that suspicious sites must be blocked. A good starting point may be to ping or perform an external DNS query against a server in Iran, North Korea (175.45.178.129), or another recognized but unlikely threat to your organization. If you receive a successful response, your network allowed you to communicate with a suspicious system without a valid business reason. This network probe usually works. Organizations tend to conduct block malicious rather than block suspicious, and because no known IPs have hosted malware or conducted attacks from internet space in those countries, they have not been placed on known bad threat feeds.

   Now that you have evidence of something that should be blocked, your organization can block that single IP, or possibly the netblock it belongs to (/24) if you request a firewall change from your security team. However, note that more than 14.3 million IPv4 /24 subnets would need to be evaluated and blocked, and naturally, your organization might not have the time, will, or resources to enforce a block suspicious list that comprehensively covers the internet. In lieu of that approach, start documenting a whitelist, with the understanding that this will produce false positives but will also block malicious, suspicious, and future/unknown malicious.

2. *Join or create an information sharing and analysis center (ISAC).* To reduce the burden of creating a master whitelist for your organization, join or create an ISAC to share information with other companies in the same industry regarding what trusted sites, IPs, and domains their employees use for business functions. There is a business opportunity for a company that develops a profiling system to create master internet whitelists; organizations could use these whitelists to limit the number of suspicious sites encountered, making secure networks easier to build and maintain.
3. *Seek mutual assurance.* Conduct reciprocal vulnerability scanning and red teaming of trusted external entities your organization does business with; this approach aligns with the recommendation of *Bansenshūkai*, which advises helping to fireproof trusted merchants' buildings for mutual protection. Reserve this measure for organizations that belong in a trusted extranet, have direct interconnections, or use other direct tunnel technologies that bypass normal security controls.

CASTLE THEORY THOUGHT EXERCISE

Consider the scenario in which you are the ruler of a medieval castle with valuable assets inside. You notice various strangers camping out, loitering, and conducting business next to your castle walls. You don't recognize many of these merchants, and your guards have complained that their presence, in addition to being a distraction, makes it hard to identify potential enemy agents operating near the castle. You ban any camps near the castle and create a large, clear perimeter, but in the weeks that follow, your commanders report that soldiers feel isolated. Furthermore, in hopes of bypassing the ban, the merchants approach the castle at night to quickly sell wares to your soldiers in hidden areas. This causes several incidents when soldiers are out past curfew or unknown individuals approach the castle stealthily, making it even harder for guards to discern friend from foe.

What adjustments could you make to your ban to prevent these late-night interactions? What additional policies or punishments could you implement to better enforce your "block suspicious" policy without harming your organization? How could you allow strangers near the castle without providing the opportunity for enemy shinobi to covertly infiltrate or attack?

Recommended Security Controls and Mitigations

Where relevant, recommendations are presented with applicable security controls from the NIST 800-53 standard. Each should be evaluated with the concept of blocking suspicious in mind.

1. Implement a bring your own device (BYOD) policy for when users want to connect to the internet for non-business reasons or provide staff with an additional dedicated workstation for external internet connections. [CA-3: System Interconnections | (1) Unclassified National Security System Connections; SC-7: Boundary Protection | (1) Physically separated subnetworks]
2. For both incoming and outgoing connections, establish whitelists that are deny-all, except for documented exceptions. [CA-3: System Interconnections | (4) Connections to Public Networks | (5) Restrictions on External System Connections; SC-7: Boundary Protection | (5) Deny by Default—Allow by Exception]
3. Share information with similar organizations to create a master whitelist. [PA-4: Information Sharing with External Parties]

Debrief

In this chapter, we looked at how shinobi commanders of fortifications adopted security policies that would make the jobs of enemy shinobi much harder. We also discussed how difficult it can be for modern organizations to adopt a similar strategy, including the challenges that organizations would need to overcome to try a similar approach with network security. We explored several ideas for how to apply the "block suspicious" concept as guidance.

In the next chapter, we will bring together concepts learned from previous chapters in order to apply them to threat intelligence. This final chapter is the capstone of the book, tying together everything you've learned about shinobi with the real cyber threats you've encountered in the previous chapters.

26

SHINOBI TRADECRAFT

Secret techniques to infiltrate without fail are deceptive, and they are varied and flexible and are done according to opportunity. Thus, as a basis, you should embrace the old ways of the shinobi who served under ancient great generals, but remember not only to keep to these ways but to adapt them, each dependent on the situation and the moment.

Even if there is a din outside, be aware that the guardhouse should not be left completely empty. Also, you should listen for any sounds.
—Yoshimori Hyakushu #66

While shinobi were sometimes hired to guard castles and other fortifications (as described in *Shōninki*[1]), non-shinobi soldiers or mercenaries—warriors trained to repel common invaders—occupied most guard stations in feudal Japan. But *Bansenshūkai* and the *Gunpo Jiyoshu* manual advise commanders defending against shinobi to hire their own, as these warriors could train ordinary guards to identify secret shinobi tactics, techniques, and procedures (TTPs).[2] Though many are described in the scrolls, TTPs were constantly being developed and refined, and different clans had their own secret techniques that other shinobi did not know.

Shinobi TTPs were clever and elegant, and they often served multiple purposes. For example, a shinobi might covertly stick a common umbrella in the ground and open it within sight of a castle's guards. Not only could the shinobi hide things from the guards' view by placing them under the umbrella, but also the obvious sign of human activity might draw guards away from their posts.[3] This technique also leveraged a prevailing superstition of the time: the idea that forgotten or lost umbrellas became possessed and haunted their previous owner, a phenomenon variously referred to as *tsukumogami*, *kasa-obake*, and *yokai*.[4]

Shinobi hired to instruct guards faced a unique pedagogical challenge: it was taboo or outright forbidden to write down TTPs or share them with outsiders, as doing so would compromise the integrity of the skill and put other shinobi's lives at risk. Some passages in the scrolls even advise shinobi to kill any observer or victim who discovered a TTP.[5]

So, instead of giving away specific techniques, shinobi stressed adopting the proper mindset, having a high level of awareness, and exercising the degree of scrutiny necessary to catch a shinobi.[6] This mental stance was bolstered by a risk assessment performed on the guards' camp, knowledge of the enemy, and the most probable and impactful threat scenarios the enemy could deploy. It seems shinobi did provide guards with a general sense of a shinobi's operating capabilities and examples of different threat scenarios, but probably described them in a manner that did not fully disclose trade secrets.[7] They taught guards the indicators of potential shinobi activity—the sights, sounds, and other observables to look for on watch—and established rules to avoid mistakes.[8]

Because of the innumerable techniques to learn, and because many of the guards in training lacked formal education, shinobi transmitted knowledge via poems to make the information easier to remember. (This explains the high number of poems about guard awareness found in the "100 Ninja Poems" of *Yoshimori Hyakushu*. These were not for shinobi per se but rather for shinobi to relay to guards.) Again, the poems provided just enough detail to describe shinobi tactics, and they provided realistic guidance but not so much as to overwhelm the guards with information. For instance, poem 66 (cited at the beginning of this chapter) provides straightforward advice: do not leave your post empty and listen for any sounds, including but not limited to the din that initially drew attention, such as footsteps approaching from the rear.[9] The poems were grouped thematically. Poems 64–67, 78, 79, 91, 93, and 94 all deal with examples of maintaining awareness and avoiding blunders. Examples include how to keep watch at night when tired; which direction to face; and why drinking, singing, and soliciting prostitutes on duty are bad ideas.

Of course, if an adversary shinobi observed that guards were actively searching for shinobi TTPs, then the adversary deployed countermeasures. A clear example that appears in all three major scrolls involves a shinobi's hiding in bushes or tall grass or crawling through a field. The shinobi's activity disturbs the surrounding insects, who freeze and remain quiet to hide themselves. For a trained guard, the absence of buzzing, humming, or chirping indicates that a hidden person is approaching. Typically, if the guard suddenly becomes alert and starts searching for the intruder, and the shinobi knows they are exposed, the shinobi quietly withdraws.[10] That's where the countermeasure comes in. Before the next attempt, the shinobi captures some crickets in a box. The crickets, untroubled to the presence of the shinobi carrying them, chirp away freely, filling any silence around the shinobi approaching the guard post. The guards now have no reason to suspect the shinobi's approach.[11]

Poem 68 vividly illustrates the challenges of TTP detection and countermeasures: "You should conduct a thorough search, following behind the party of a night patrol. This is called *kamaritsuke* [ambush detection]."[12] At night, the commander would dispatch a primary search party to patrol the perimeter with the usual lanterns and other equipment, but the leader would also send a covert search party in the main group's wake.[13] Guards on perimeter patrol were told by their shinobi advisers to look for anything out of place—especially sounds, movement, and people.[14] Of course, enemy shinobi were aware of this guidance. The scrolls describe how attacking shinobis could hide in bushes, ditches, or other dark places while a patrol passed before they continued working.[15] However, in some cases, the enemy might follow the patrol party, their own movements covered by the sound and light of the defenders; the infiltrators might even attack the patrol from behind.[16] Thus, having a second, covert patrol behind the first could catch hidden enemy shinobi. This group of heavily armed troops searched likely hiding spots and stayed alert for an enemy also following the main patrol party.[17] However, as a counter to the counter, the attacking shinobi who was aware of the *kamaritsuke* technique might wait in the shadows for the second hidden patrol to pass or move to a place that the second patrol would not search. To combat this—the counter to the counter to the counter—poems 69 and 70 were added:[18]

> 69: "After the night patrol is conducted, it is important to conduct *kamaritsuke* over and over again."
>
> 70: "When undertaking *kamaritsuke*, it is said that you should make multiple rounds at intervals to enable you to find the enemy's shinobi agents."

This guidance encouraged an inconsistent cadence of *kamaritsuke* patrols to interfere with the adversary's ability to operate freely. Frequent, semiunpredictable patrols with one or more following *kamaritsuke* parties left little opportunity for enemy shinobi to execute actions confidently against either the fortification or the defenders' patrol parties.[19]

A best-effort approach with TTP detection and countermeasures can quickly escalate, but eventually, it becomes too dangerous or impractical to attack the fortification. This result is often the best defenders can hope for against enemy shinobis.

In this chapter, we will discuss how the philosophy behind shinobi tradecraft is applicable to understanding cyber threat actor TTPs. We will touch on how cyber threat intelligence could guide incident responders, security engineers, and threat hunters so they can better defend their organizations, much as the shinobi were able to improve the effectiveness of common castle guards and soldiers with intelligence-driven defense. We explore several of the prevailing frameworks used to describe cyber threat TTPs. Blending those frameworks with the knowledge of the shinobi makes it easier to understand both threats and why TTPs are useful. We will go over why the P in TTPs is often a mystery and will likely remain unknown, but we'll also theorize about the procedures a rational adversary would likely take, based on how we know the shinobi acted. Lastly, we'll explore guidance for how to incorporate cyber threat intelligence into your organization's defense strategy and touch on why this can be so difficult to do.

Techniques, Tactics, and Procedures

In cybersecurity, TTPs describe approaches for analyzing a specific threat actor's or group's patterns of behavior, activities, and methods. *Tactics* describe the adversary's operational maneuvers, such as reconnaissance, lateral movement, and backdoor deployment. *Techniques* are the detailed technical methods the adversary uses to accomplish tasks, such as using a specific tool or software to execute weaponization or exploitation. *Procedures* detail standard policies and courses of action to perform, such as confirming whether an exploited target system has any active users logged in before conducting additional tasks, running malware through string analysis for tradecraft errors before deploying, or implementing precautionary self-cleanup after verifying connectivity on a target box.

Once TTPs are identified and defined, defenders can search for indicators of them in their environment. They can even predict which TTPs could be used against them to support planning and implementing preemptive mitigations or countermeasures. To establish and communicate a common definition of cyber adversary TTPs, the industry has developed multiple concepts, models, analyses, and sharing methods, including:

- Pyramid of Pain[20]
- ATT&CK™ framework[21]
- Attack LifeCycle model[22]
- Cyber Kill Chain framework[23]
- Diamond Model of Intrusion Analysis[24]
- STIX (Structured Threat Information eXpression)[25]

Pyramid of Pain

The Pyramid of Pain (see Figure 26-1) is an excellent model for visualizing how awareness of an adversary's indicators, tools, and TTPs can affect the defender's security posture. It also shows how the difficulty of implementing measures and countermeasures increases for both defenders and attackers.

The name Pyramid of Pain refers to the idea that, while there is no way to guarantee absolute security or prevent all attacks, an adversary is less likely to target your organization if you make it extremely painful for them to expend the time, resources, and effort to do so.

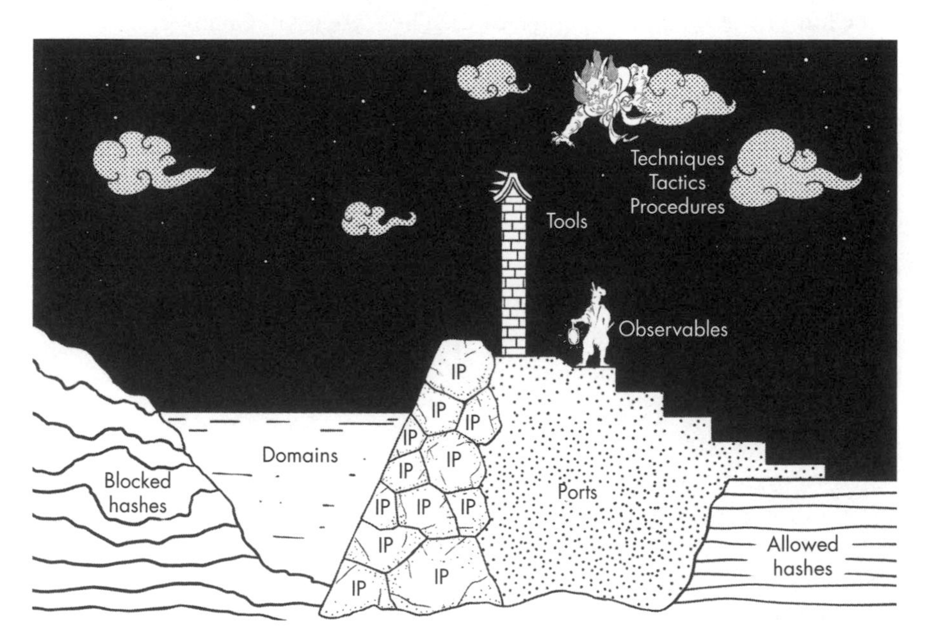

Figure 26-1: Fortification of indicators of compromise (adapted from David Bianco's Pyramid of Pain[26])

At the bottom of the pyramid are indicators of compromise (IoC)—such as domains, IPs, file hashes, and URLs—that can positively identify known malicious indicators. Defenders can block these indicators or raise alerts around them, but the adversary can also change them.

Above the atomic indicators are host-based indicators, such as registry keys, dropped files, and artifacts. These can be detected or responded to, but threat detection or mitigation may not be automatic, and the adversary can alter them based on the target or operation.

The next level is tools—software or devices with which the adversary conducts or supports offensive actions. By searching for, removing access to, or disabling the functionality of known malicious tools in an environment, defenders may be able to detect and prevent the adversary from operating effectively.

At the top of the pyramid are the adversary's tactics, techniques, and procedures. If you can identify or mitigate against these methods, it becomes difficult for the adversary to create or learn new TTPs to use against you—though of course, it is also painful for you as the defender to develop safeguards or countermeasures.

ATT&CK Framework

MITRE's Adversarial Tactics, Techniques, and Common Knowledge (ATT&CK) framework derives many tactics from Lockheed Martin's Cyber Kill Chain framework (see Figure 26-2). The Cyber Kill Chain framework outlines seven stages of the attack lifecycle: reconnaissance, weaponization, delivery, exploitation, installation, command and control, and actions on objectives. Each tactic identified in the ATT&CK framework lists techniques and methods, with examples, to detect or mitigate against.

Note that "Procedures" is missing from the ATT&CK framework. This is understandable, as identifying these would likely require stealing and analyzing a nation-state's or military's book of offensive cyber operations. This is why the *Bansenshūkai*, *Ninpiden*, and *Shōninki* texts, which describe the procedures of a sophisticated espionage threat group, so greatly enrich the discussion.

Threat Intelligence

When your security team understands these tactics and techniques—and has identified your attack surfaces, evaluated your current security controls, and performed analysis of previous incidents to determine your organization's defensive effectiveness—it is possible to start predicting where adversaries are likely to target your environment. With a good set of threat predictions, you can then start threat hunting—looking for indicators and evidence threat actors left behind that may indicate compromise.

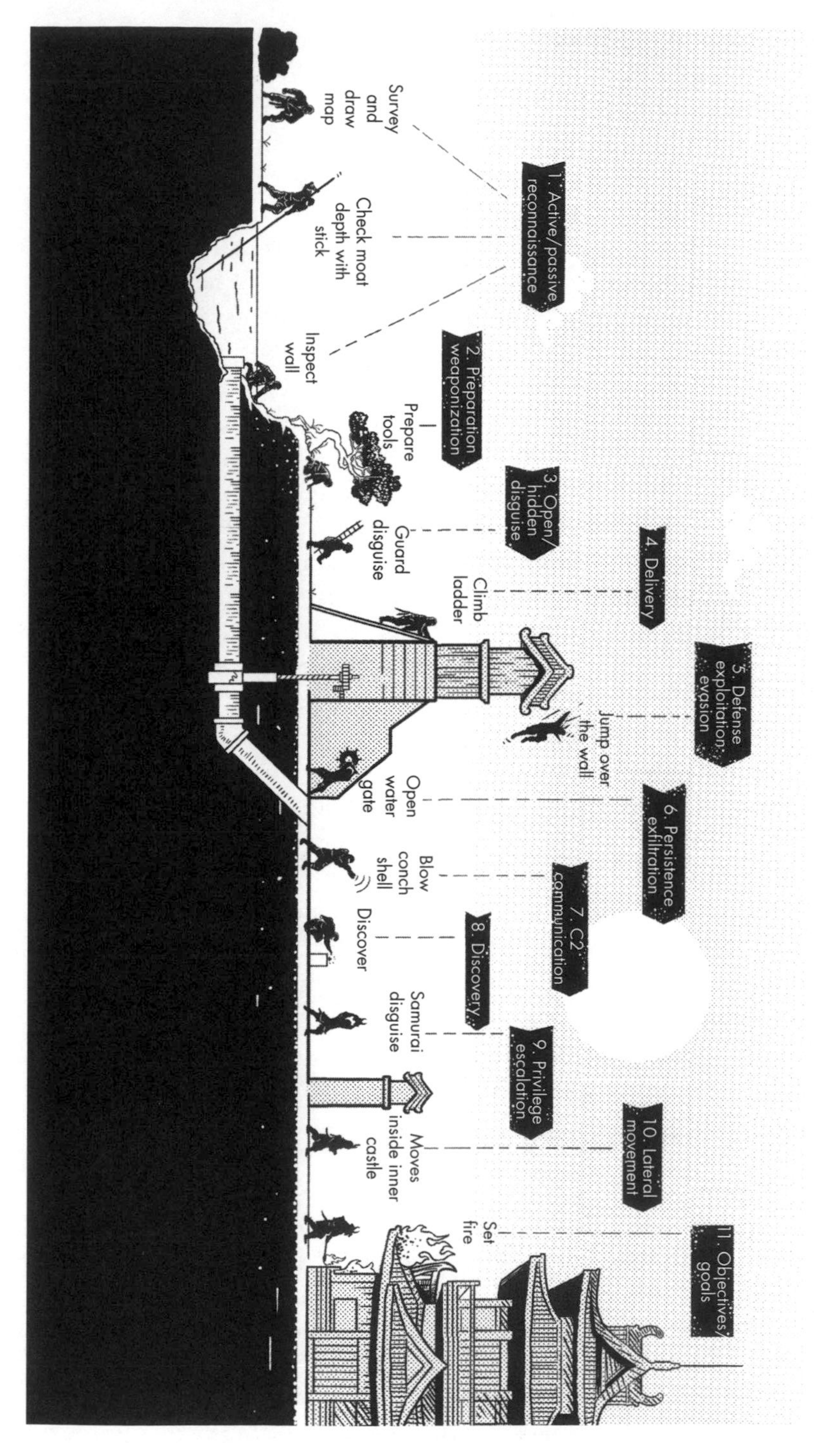

Figure 26-2: Ninja attack chain (adapted from MITRE's ATT&CK framework[27])

However, without a deep understanding of exactly how threat actors operate, it is difficult to effectively hunt or detect their presence.

Here, threat intelligence shows its value. *Threat intelligence* does not necessarily mean feeds such as lists of new IPs, domains, URLs, and file hashes associated with malware, hacking infrastructure, or threat groups. Rather, *cyber threat intelligence (CTI)* refers to traditional intelligence that collects and analyzes cyber threats such as malware, hacktivists, nation-states, criminals, DDoS attacks, and more. When consumed correctly, CTI provides actionable intelligence on and assessment of what the threat is doing, its motivations, and its TTPs. Simply put, CTI is one of the best ways to effectively understand and defend against threats because it requires decision makers to inform themselves and take defensive actions.

Unfortunately, many CTI consumers pay attention only to the IoCs, as they can easily be ingested into SIEMs, firewalls, and other security devices to block or detect threats. Operating this way negates CTI's real value, as detailed observations and assessments by CTI analysts describe behaviors, patterns, methods, attribution, and context. While CTI producers may not always reveal how they collect intelligence on a threat, they often strive to be transparent in their assessments of what they know and why they believe the threat conducts certain actions.

Of course, consuming intelligence reports with the intention of understanding a threat while also developing a deep understanding of your environment can be demanding. This process requires a broad skill set—one that includes the ability to quickly learn and make strategic decisions. But if a CTI consumer can dedicate the time to understand a threat's every step, code, tactic, and technique, they can make decisions that allow them to successfully mitigate, detect, respond to, and even predict future threat movements.

Cyber Threat Intelligence

Having already bought dozens of security solutions and employed full-time security staff to handle numerous threat vectors, some may regard CTI as the final cost layer to top off their already "expense-in-depth" security model. CTI, though, may allow you to improve your security strategies, and it can amplify the effectiveness of all other security layers, thus justifying its cost. Unfortunately, in many cases, effectively using CTI can be akin to reading reports of the newest scientific discoveries in a given field, as it requires you to understand the implications of the discovery and then rapidly change culture, business strategies, and technologies in response. While possible, this intensity of consumption, synthesis, and action seems excessively demanding. This is the biggest challenge of CTI: it's not a crystal ball that offers easy answers that are easy to follow through on. Review the guidance below to make sound decisions about your CTI program.

1. *Develop cyber threat intelligence and threat hunting.* Consider subscribing your organization to a free or paid CTI report. Also, start developing your own internal CTI by collecting evidence of threats currently attacking your environment. Establish a CTI team to collect and analyze findings and analysis and report these findings to IT, security, and business stakeholders. These parties should understand who's targeting the organization, how they're infiltrating, what they'll do once on the network, their assumed goals, and how they're executing those goals. Implement strategic and operational safeguards, mitigations, and countermeasures in your information systems to defend against the specific tactics observed.

   Train your security and intelligence staff to threat hunt. Because not every threat can be engineered or blocked, a dedicated hunt team must constantly search for traces of threats in your network, guided by intelligence from your CTI partner, vendor, or team. Threat hunting can be augmented with purple team exercises, in which the red team performs adversarial activity on your network while your blue team attempts to hunt them, thereby learning how to counter a threat.

2. *Consume and leverage CTI.* Run a tabletop exercise with your email, IT, and security teams to simulate a threat's TTPs and gauge your reaction. Suppose, for instance, you receive intelligence that a phishing campaign is targeting organizations like yours that use Google link shorteners (*http://goo.gl/*). You cannot simply block Google's IPs, URLs, or domain without hindering business operations, and many organizational staff use link shorteners for legitimate purposes. Your CTI assesses that the adversary likely uses the goo.gl link because your antivirus software, proxy, or phishing protocol does not properly evaluate it as malicious. The security systems recognize that Google is a whitelisted site.

   First, attempt to hunt for evidence of that link in your current emails. Many organizations hit an early barrier here, as their email administrator is not cooperative or does not have the necessary visibility or resources to search incoming email containing goo.gl hyperlinks. Additional barriers could include quarantining potential phishes, alerting non-IT and non-security staff to the presence of the threat, and training them on how to detect and avoid this threat.

Just as the adversary has different tools, tactics, and techniques to target your organization, your own tools require contemplation, understanding, ingenuity, and engineering to effectively block and respond to threats in a holistic, effective way. For example, your email administrator may create a rule to detect the goo.gl link shortener, but what about others? Hopefully, your CTI team would identify the threat from phishing with links and link shortening and recommend methods to detect, block, or mitigate those links. In addition, the team should keep people in your organization aware of this TTP. In other words, they should be looking not only for goo.gl but also for *all* link shorteners. Finally, decision makers have to strategically address this threat with new architecture, policies, or controls.

Going through this process, however painful it may be, is necessary to identify where your organization needs to improve in detecting, mitigating, and responding to threats.

CASTLE THEORY THOUGHT EXERCISE

Consider the scenario in which you are the ruler of a medieval castle with valuable assets inside. You receive intelligence that a security awareness protocol you've taught your guards—that the sudden silence of insects may indicate the presence of an intruder—has been countered by shinobi who carry cricket boxes. The crickets carried by the attackers deceive guards into thinking nothing is amiss.

Consider how you might handle retraining your guards to deal with the confusing reality that both silence and noise could indicate a shinobi intruder nearby. What additional hunting or monitoring methods could help your guards detect approaching shinobi? How would you detect the presence of a cricket box or deploy countermeasures against it? Finally, how might enemy shinobi respond to your new countermeasures and safeguards?

Recommended Security Controls and Mitigations

These recommendations are presented with NIST 800-53 standards and should be evaluated with the idea of security awareness, TTPs, and CTI in mind.

1. Provide security awareness training to personnel in all roles within your organization to help employees determine how to rapidly respond to threats they encounter. [AT-2: Security Awareness Training; PM-13: Information Security Workforce]
2. Dedicate a team to analyzing threats, incidents, intelligence, and adversary TTPs, as well as developing countermeasures and safeguards to combat those threats. [IR-10: Integrated Information Security Analysis Team]
3. Partner with external security groups and threat-sharing institutions to receive intelligence on threats relevant to your organization. [PM-15: Contacts with Security Groups and Associations]
4. Implement a threat awareness program that shares details about threat intelligence, how to mitigate threats, and indicators of compromise. [PM-16: Threat Awareness Program]
5. Use credible threat intelligence and information to hunt for and monitor activity, behaviors, patterns, and other observables indicative of a threat. [SI-4: Information System Monitoring]

Debrief

In this chapter, we reviewed several shinobi TTPs, in particular how *kamaritsuke* TTPs co-evolved with countertactics by both defender and adversary until a fault-tolerant security system emerged. We explored other cyber threat tactics, which may also develop as each side tries to counter the other, until resiliency emerges. We discussed cyber threat intelligence and why just knowing what the adversary is doing, how they are doing it, and what they are going to do is not enough. To be useful, CTI must be consumed with an eye toward addressing the threat in some way. In the Castle Theory Thought Exercise, we looked at a clear example of defenders discovering an observable, followed by a shift in tactics regarding the threat. This thought exercise could be compared to spoofing system/network logs to deceive threat hunters, anomaly detectors, and even machine learning systems—and it could reemerge in modern times. The most important lesson of this chapter—perhaps even the book—is that it is critical to consume threat intelligence and respond against dynamic threats in innovative ways.

NOTES

Introduction

1. "SP 800-53 Rev. 5 (DRAFT): Security and Privacy Controls for Information Systems and Organizations," Computer Security Resource Center, National Institute of Standards and Technology, published August 2017, *https://bit.ly/3hX2MUf*.
2. Antony Cummins and Yoshie Minami, *True Path of the Ninja* (North Clarendon, VT: Tuttle Publishing, 2017), 30.
3. Antony Cummins, *In Search of the Ninja: The Historical Truth of Ninjutsu* (Stroud, England: The History Press: 2013), 37.
4. Stephen Turnbull, *Ninja AD 1460–1650* (Oxford, England: Osprey Publishing, 2003), 5.
5. Cummins and Minami, *True Path*, 23.
6. Antony Cummins and Yoshie Minami, *The Secret Traditions of the Shinobi* (Berkeley, CA: Blue Snake Books, 2012), 8.
7. Cummins and Minami, *True Path*, 36.
8. Turnbull, *Ninja AD 1460–1650*, 9.
9. Oscar Ratti and Adele Westbrook, *Secrets of the Samurai: The Martial Arts of Feudal Japan* (North Clarendon, VT: Tuttle Publishing, 2016), 281.
10. Cummins and Minami, *True Path*, 41.
11. Antony Cummins and Yoshie Minami, *The Book of Ninja* (London: Watkins Publishing, 2013), 206.
12. Turnbull, *Ninja AD 1460–1650*, 17.
13. Turnbull, *Ninja AD 1460–1650*, 12.
14. Cummins and Minami, *The Book of Ninja*, 32.
15. Cummins and Minami, *True Path*, 162.
16. Cummins and Minami, *True Path*, 107–109, 168.
17. Cummins and Minami, *True Path*, 162.
18. Cummins and Minami, *The Book of Ninja*, 102–103, 122, 148, 194.
19. Cummins and Minami, *True Path*, 72.

20. Cummins and Minami, *True Path,* 82.
21. Cummins and Minami, *True Path,* 88.

Chapter 1, Mapping Networks

1. Antony Cummins and Yoshie Minami, *The Book of Ninja* (London: Watkins Publishing, 2013), 55.
2. Poems 6–10, 24
3. Cummins and Minami, "*Shochi I*—A Guideline for Commanders I," in *The Book of Ninja,* 55–65.
4. Gordon Lyon, "Nmap: The Network Mapper," Insecure.org, updated March 18, 2018, *https://nmap.org.*
5. Cummins and Minami, *The Book of Ninja,* 168.
6. Cummins and Minami, *The Book of Ninja,* 148.

Chapter 2, Guarding with Special Care

1. Antony Cummins and Yoshie Minami, *The Book of Ninja* (London: Watkins Publishing, 2013), 93.
2. Cummins and Minami, *The Book of Ninja,* 183.
3. Cummins and Minami, *The Book of Ninja,* 146.
4. *Cybersecurity Framework,* National Institute of Standards and Technology, updated September 2018, *https://www.nist.gov/cyberframework/.*
5. Adam Shostack, "STRIDE chart," *Microsoft Secure* (blog), Microsoft Corporation, September 11, 2007, *https://bit.ly/39aeOWy.*

Chapter 3, Xenophobic Security

1. Antony Cummins and Yoshie Minami, *The Secret Traditions of the Shinobi* (Berkeley, CA: Blue Snake Books, 2012), 41.
2. Cummins and Minami, *Secret Traditions,* 48.
3. Cummins and Minami, *Secret Traditions,* 41–43, 47.

Chapter 4, Identification Challenge

1. Antony Cummins and Yoshie Minami, *The Book of Ninja* (London: Watkins Publishing, 2013), 91.
2. Cummins and Minami, *The Book of Ninja,* 92.
3. Cummins and Minami, *The Book of Ninja,* 126.

Chapter 5, Double-Sealed Password

1. Antony Cummins and Yoshie Minami, *The Secret Traditions of the Shinobi* (Berkeley, CA: Blue Snake Books, 2012), 100.
2. Cummins and Minami, *Secret Traditions,* 192.
3. Cummins and Minami, *The Book of Ninja,* 127.
4. Cummins and Minami, *The Book of Ninja,* 127.

5. Antony Cummins and Yoshie Minami, *True Path of the Ninja* (North Clarendon, VT: Tuttle Publishing, 2017), 80.
6. Fans of the HBO series *The Wire* might remember this as the "jump the 5" code broken in season 1, episode 5 ("The Pager").

Chapter 6, Hours of Infiltration

1. Antony Cummins and Yoshie Minami, *True Path of the Ninja* (North Clarendon, VT: Tuttle Publishing, 2017), 78.
2. Antony Cummins and Yoshie Minami, *The Secret Traditions of the Shinobi* (Berkeley, CA: Blue Snake Books, 2012), 158.
3. Cummins and Minami, *True Path*, 79.
4. Cummins and Minami, *True Path*, 79.
5. Antony Cummins and Yoshie Minami, "*Tenji I*—Opportunities Bestowed by Heaven I," in *The Book of Ninja* (London: Watkins Publishing, 2013), 268–293.
6. "SP 800-154 (DRAFT): Guide to Data-Centric System Threat Modeling," Computer Security Resource Center, National Institute of Standards and Technology, March 2016, *https://bit.ly/3bjQofW.*

Chapter 7, Access to Time

1. Antony Cummins and Yoshie Minami, *The Book of Ninja* (London: Watkins Publishing, 2013), 313.
2. Cummins and Minami, *The Book of Ninja*, 169.
3. Antony Cummins and Yoshie Minami, *True Path of the Ninja* (North Clarendon, VT: Tuttle Publishing, 2017), 85.
4. Richard Kayser, "Die exakte Messung der Luftdurchgängigkeit der Nase," *Arch. Laryng. Rhinol.* 8 (1895), 101.
5. Symantec Security Response, "The Shamoon Attacks," *Symantec Official Blog*, Symantec Corporation, August 16, 2012, *https://bit.ly/2L2Az2z.*

Chapter 8, Tools

1. Antony Cummins and Yoshie Minami, *The Secret Traditions of the Shinobi* (Berkeley, CA: Blue Snake Books, 2012), 17.
2. Antony Cummins and Yoshie Minami, *The Book of Ninja* (London: Watkins Publishing, 2013), 188, 342.
3. Antony Cummins and Yoshie Minami, *True Path of the Ninja* (North Clarendon, VT: Tuttle Publishing, 2017), 101.
4. Cummins and Minami, *True Path*, 112.
5. Cummins and Minami, *The Book of Ninja*, 317.
6. "Sword hunt," Wikipedia, Wikimedia Foundation, last modified November 26, 2018, *https://en.wikipedia.org/wiki/Sword_hunt/.*
7. Cummins and Minami, *The Book of Ninja*, 189.
8. Cummins and Minami, *The Book of Ninja*, 342.

Chapter 9, Sensors

1. Antony Cummins and Yoshie Minami, *The Book of Ninja* (London: Watkins Publishing, 2013), 96.
2. Cummins and Minami, *The Book of Ninja*, 96.
3. Cummins and Minami, *The Book of Ninja*, 97.
4. Cummins and Minami, *The Book of Ninja*, 90.
5. Cummins and Minami, *The Book of Ninja*, 91.

Chapter 10, Bridges and Ladders

1. Antony Cummins and Yoshie Minami, *The Book of Ninja* (London: Watkins Publishing, 2013), 183.
2. Cummins and Minami, "Ninki I—Ninja Tools I," in *The Book of Ninja*, 317–325.
3. Antony Cummins and Yoshie Minami, *The Secret Traditions of the Shinobi* (Berkeley, CA: Blue Snake Books, 2012), 104–105.
4. Cummins and Minami, *The Book of Ninja*, 318–320.
5. Cummins and Minami, *The Book of Ninja*, 317.
6. Antony Cummins and Yoshie Minami, *True Path of the Ninja* (North Clarendon, VT: Tuttle Publishing, 2017), 82.
7. Cummins and Minami, *The Book of Ninja*, 29.
8. TEMPEST Equipment Selection Process, NCI Agency, accessed September 25, 2018, *https://bit.ly/2LfB3SK.*

Chapter 11, Locks

1. Antony Cummins and Yoshie Minami, *The Book of Ninja* (London: Watkins Publishing, 2013), 354–355.
2. Cummins and Minami, "A Short Introduction to Japanese Locks and the Art of Lock-picking" in *The Book of Ninja*, xxix–xxxii.
3. Cummins and Minami, *The Book of Ninja*, 342.
4. Antony Cummins and Yoshie Minami, *The Secret Traditions of the Shinobi* (Berkeley, CA: Blue Snake Books, 2012), 34.
5. Antony Cummins and Yoshie Minami, *True Path of the Ninja* (North Clarendon, VT: Tuttle Publishing, 2017), 102.

6. While locks on information systems and data are certainly worth discussing, in this chapter, *locks* refers to physical locks used to block access to information systems and environments.

Chapter 12, Moon on the Water

1. Antony Cummins and Yoshie Minami, *The Book of Ninja* (London: Watkins Publishing, 2013), 133.
2. Cummins and Minami, *The Book of Ninja*, 133.
3. Cummins and Minami, *The Book of Ninja*, 134.

4. Cummins and Minami, *The Book of Ninja*, 134.
5. Daniel Kahneman, *Thinking, Fast and Slow* (New York: Farrar, Straus and Giroux, 2013).

Chapter 13, Worm Agent

1. Antony Cummins and Yoshie Minami, *The Book of Ninja* (London: Watkins Publishing, 2013), 109–110.
2. Cummins and Minami, *The Book of Ninja*, 109–110.
3. Cummins and Minami, *The Book of Ninja*, 109–110.
4. Cummins and Minami, *The Book of Ninja*, 110.
5. Cummins and Minami, *The Book of Ninja*, 110.

Chapter 14, Ghost on the Moon

1. Antony Cummins and Yoshie Minami, *The Book of Ninja* (London: Watkins Publishing, 2013), 104.
2. Cummins and Minami, *The Book of Ninja*, 104–106.
3. R. E. Smith, "A Contemporary Look at Saltzer and Schroeder's 1975 Design Principles," *IEEE Security & Privacy* 10, no. 6 (2012): 20–25.

Chapter 15, The Art of the Fireflies

1. Antony Cummins and Yoshie Minami, *The Book of Ninja* (London: Watkins Publishing, 2013), 111.
2. Antony Cummins and Yoshie Minami, *True Path of the Ninja* (North Clarendon, VT: Tuttle Publishing, 2017), 122.
3. Cummins and Minami, *The Book of Ninja*, 112.
4. Cummins and Minami, *The Book of Ninja*, 114.
5. Cummins and Minami, *The Book of Ninja*, 112.
6. This is described more thoroughly in Cliff Stoll's book, *The Cuckoo's Egg: Tracking a Spy Through the Maze of Computer Espionage* (New York: Pocket Books, 2005).
7. Cameron H. Malin et al., *Deception in the Digital Age: Exploiting and Defending Human Targets Through Computer-Mediated Communications* (London: Elsevier, 2017), 221; Brandon Valeriano et al., *Cyber Strategy: The Evolving Character of Power and Coercion* (New York: Oxford University Press, 2018), 138.
8. For further reading, see Richards J. Heuer Jr. and Randolph H. Pherson's book *Structured Analytic Techniques for Intelligence Analysis* (Los Angeles: CQ Press, 2015).

Chapter 16, Live Capture

1. Antony Cummins and Yoshie Minami, *The Book of Ninja* (London: Watkins Publishing, 2013), 96.

2. Antony Cummins and Yoshie Minami, *The Secret Traditions of the Shinobi* (Berkeley, CA: Blue Snake Books, 2012), 102.
3. Cummins and Minami, *The Book of Ninja*, 160, 420, 464, 467.
4. Cummins and Minami, *The Book of Ninja*, 161.
5. Cummins and Minami, *The Book of Ninja*, 213, 219, 221.
6. Cummins and Minami, *The Book of Ninja*, 216.
7. Cummins and Minami, *Secret Traditions*, 154.

Chapter 17, Fire Attack

1. Antony Cummins and Yoshie Minami, *The Book of Ninja* (London: Watkins Publishing, 2013), 62.
2. Antony Cummins and Yoshie Minami, *The Secret Traditions of the Shinobi* (Berkeley, CA: Blue Snake Books, 2012), 31–34, 87–91, 167.
3. Cummins and Minami, *Secret Traditions*, 90.
4. Cummins and Minami, *The Book of Ninja*, 61.
5. Motoo Hinago and William Coaldrake, *Japanese Castles* (New York: Kodansha USA, 1986), 98.
6. Cummins and Minami, *Secret Traditions*, 119.
7. Cummins and Minami, *The Book of Ninja*, 75–76.
8. Cummins and Minami, *Secret Traditions*, 162.
9. Pierluigi Paganini, "BAE Systems report links Taiwan heist to North Korean LAZARUS APT," *Cyber Defense Magazine* (website), October 18, 2017, *https://bit.ly/3s3PCcS*.
10. Symantec Security Response, "Shamoon: Back from the dead and destructive as ever," *Symantec Official Blog*, November 30, 2016, *https://bit.ly/3oqdkxK*.
11. Kim Zetter, "A Cyberattack Has Caused Confirmed Physical Damage for the Second Time Ever," *WIRED*, January 8, 2015, *https://bit.ly/3nqx0Aj*.
12. Andy Greenberg, "'Crash Override': The Malware That Took Down a Power Grid," *WIRED*, June 12, 2017, *https://bit.ly/38oMhgz*.
13. Sharon Weinberger, "How Israel Spoofed Syria's Air Defense System," *WIRED*, October 4, 2017, *https://bit.ly/35i67Za*.
14. Kim Zetter, "An Unprotected Look at STUXNET, the World's First Digital Weapon," *WIRED*, November 3, 2014, *https://bit.ly/3ooEULS*.
15. For more information, see "Chaos Monkey," GitHub, Inc., Lorin Hochstein, last modified July 31, 2017, *https://bit.ly/3noAJhL*.
16. Allan Liska and Timothy Gallo, *Ransomware: Defending Against Digital Extortion* (Sebastopol, CA: O'Reilly Media, 2017), 73.

Chapter 18, Covert Communication

1. Antony Cummins and Yoshie Minami, *The Book of Ninja* (London: Watkins Publishing, 2013), 67–69, 102.
2. Cummins and Minami, *The Book of Ninja*, 70.

3. Antony Cummins and Yoshie Minami, *The Secret Traditions of the Shinobi* (Berkeley, CA: Blue Snake Books, 2012), 96.
4. Cummins and Minami, *The Book of Ninja*, 70–72.
5. "APT17," Advanced Persistent Threat Groups, FireEye Inc., last accessed February 7, 2020, *https://bit.ly/2Xl1QQ7*.

Chapter 19, Call Signs

1. Antony Cummins and Yoshie Minami, *The Secret Traditions of the Shinobi* (Berkeley, CA: Blue Snake Books, 2012), 84.
2. Dmitri Alperovitch, "CrowdStrike's work with the Democratic National Committee: Setting the record straight," *CrowdStrike Blog*, CrowdStrike, last modified January 22, 2020, *https://bit.ly/3rYVHr3*.
3. Charlie Osborne, "Create a single file to protect yourself from the latest ransomware attack," *Zero Day* (blog), ZDNet, CBS Interactive, June 28, 2017, *https://bit.ly/35lPQ5d*.

Chapter 20, Light, Noise, and Litter Discipline

1. Antony Cummins and Yoshie Minami, *The Book of Ninja* (London: Watkins Publishing, 2013), 209.
2. Cummins and Minami, *The Book of Ninja*, 211.
3. Antony Cummins and Yoshie Minami, *The Secret Traditions of the Shinobi* (Berkeley, CA: Blue Snake Books, 2012), 54.
4. Antony Cummins and Yoshie Minami, *True Path of the Ninja* (North Clarendon, VT: Tuttle Publishing, 2017), 63–64.
5. Cummins and Minami, *Secret Traditions*, 55.
6. Cummins and Minami, *The Book of Ninja*, 178–179.
7. Cummins and Minami, *The Book of Ninja*, 188.
8. "Nmap: The Network Mapper," Insecure.org, Gordon Lyon, updated August 10, 2019, *https://nmap.org*.
9. "Software: China Chopper," ATT&CK, The MITRE Corporation, last modified April 24, 2019, *https://bit.ly/3q019YR*.
10. Wireshark, The Wireshark Corporation, last accessed February 7, 2020, *https://www.wireshark.org*.

Chapter 21, Circumstances of Infiltration

1. Antony Cummins and Yoshie Minami, *The Book of Ninja* (London: Watkins Publishing, 2013), 174, 199, 201.
2. Cummins and Minami, *The Book of Ninja*, 175.
3. Antony Cummins and Yoshie Minami, *The Secret Traditions of the Shinobi* (Berkeley, CA: Blue Snake Books, 2012), 133.
4. Cummins and Minami, *The Book of Ninja*, 201.
5. Cummins and Minami, *The Book of Ninja*, 200–201.
6. Cummins and Minami, *The Book of Ninja*, 74.

Chapter 22, Zero-Days

1. Antony Cummins and Yoshie Minami, *True Path of the Ninja* (North Clarendon, VT: Tuttle Publishing, 2017), 105.
2. Antony Cummins and Yoshie Minami, *The Book of Ninja* (London: Watkins Publishing, 2013), 67.
3. Cummins and Minami, *True Path*, 166.
4. Antony Cummins and Yoshie Minami, *The Secret Traditions of the Shinobi* (Berkeley, CA: Blue Snake Books, 2012), 51.
5. Cummins and Minami, *The Book of Ninja*, 212.
6. Cummins and Minami, *True Path*, 175.
7. Cummins and Minami, "*Shochi* I: A Guideline for Commanders I" to "*Shochi* V: A Guideline for Commanders V" in *The Book of Ninja*.
8. Cummins and Minami, *The Book of Ninja*, 502.
9. Cummins and Minami, *The Book of Ninja*, 98.
10. Cummins and Minami, *The Book of Ninja*, 56.
11. Cummins and Minami, *True Path*, 43, 148.
12. "W32.Stuxnet," Symantec Security Center, Symantec Corporation, last modified September 16, 2017, *https://bit.ly/3bfoW2R*.
13. Cummins and Minami, *The Book of Ninja*, 185.
14. "BoringSSL," Git repositories on boringssl, last accessed September 26, 2018, *https://bit.ly/3s1mrHk*.
15. Cummins and Minami, *The Book of Ninja*, 98.
16. Cummins and Minami, *True Path*, 154.

Chapter 23, Hiring Shinobi

1. Antony Cummins and Yoshie Minami, *The Book of Ninja* (London: Watkins Publishing, 2013), 77–79.
2. Cummins and Minami, *The Book of Ninja*, 37.
3. Cummins and Minami, *The Book of Ninja*, 33, 36, 40.
4. Cummins and Minami, *The Book of Ninja*, 79–80.
5. Antony Cummins and Yoshie Minami, *True Path of the Ninja* (North Clarendon, VT: Tuttle Publishing, 2017), 74.
6. Cummins and Minami, *True Path*, 125.
7. Cummins and Minami, *True Path*, 158.
8. Cummins and Minami, *The Book of Ninja*, 79.
9. "The ASVAB Test," Military.com, Military Advantage, last accessed February 7, 2020, *https://bit.ly/2Xle3Eu*.
10. "Entering the Military: DLAB," Military.com, Military Advantage, last accessed February 7, 2020, *https://bit.ly/39fvNXc*.
11. "SP 800-16: Information Technology Security Training Requirements: A Role- and Performance-Based Model," Computer Security Resource Center, National Institute of Standards and Technology, published April 1998, *https://bit.ly/3otA9QY*.

Chapter 24, Guardhouse Behavior

1. Antony Cummins and Yoshie Minami, *The Book of Ninja* (London: Watkins Publishing, 2013), 128, 178–180, 259.
2. Cummins and Minami, *The Book of Ninja*, 93, 222.
3. Cummins and Minami, *The Book of Ninja*, 93.
4. Antony Cummins and Yoshie Minami, *The Secret Traditions of the Shinobi* (Berkeley, CA: Blue Snake Books, 2012), 164.
5. "Department of Defense Cybersecurity Culture and Compliance Initiative (DC3I)," U.S. Department of Defense, published September 2015, *https://bit.ly/3s1npTY.*
6. Cummins and Minami, *The Book of Ninja*, 93.

Chapter 25, Zero-Trust Threat Management

1. Antony Cummins and Yoshie Minami, *The Book of Ninja* (London: Watkins Publishing, 2013), 83.
2. Cummins and Minami, *The Book of Ninja*, 84.
3. Cummins and Minami, *The Book of Ninja*, 83.
4. Cummins and Minami, *The Book of Ninja*, 84.
5. Cummins and Minami, *The Book of Ninja*, 84.
6. "Sensitive but Unclassified IP Data," Network Services, Defense Information Systems Agency, last accessed February 7, 2020, *https://bit.ly/2Xl9s57.*

Chapter 26, Shinobi Tradecraft

1. Antony Cummins and Yoshie Minami, *True Path of the Ninja* (North Clarendon, VT: Tuttle Publishing, 2017), 19.
2. Antony Cummins and Yoshie Minami, *The Secret Traditions of the Shinobi* (Berkeley, CA: Blue Snake Books, 2012), 77.
3. Antony Cummins and Yoshie Minami, *The Book of Ninja* (London: Watkins Publishing, 2013), 202.
4. *Classiques de l'Orient*, 5 (1921), 193.
5. Cummins and Minami, *The Book of Ninja*, 67.
6. Cummins and Minami, *Secret Traditions*, 81.
7. Cummins and Minami, *The Book of Ninja*, 66.
8. Cummins and Minami, *The Book of Ninja*, 93.
9. Cummins and Minami, *Secret Traditions*, 159.
10. Cummins and Minami, *The Book of Ninja*, 208.
11. Donn F. Draeger, *Ninjutsu: The Art of Invisibility* (North Clarendon, VT: Tuttle Publishing, 1989), 65.
12. Cummins and Minami, *Secret Traditions*, 160.
13. Cummins and Minami, *The Book of Ninja*, 95.
14. Cummins and Minami, *Secret Traditions*, 161.
15. Cummins and Minami, *The Book of Ninja*, 95.

16. Cummins and Minami, *Secret Traditions*, 160.
17. Cummins and Minami, *The Book of Ninja*, 95.
18. Cummins and Minami, *Secret Traditions*, 160–161.
19. Cummins and Minami, *Secret Traditions*, 161.
20. Sqrrl Team, "A Framework for Cyber Threat Hunting Part 1: The Pyramid of Pain," *Threat Hunting Blog*, Sqrrl, July 23, 2015, *https://www.threathunting.net/sqrrl-archive.*
21. Blake E. Strom, "Adversarial Tactics, Techniques & Common Knowledge," ATT&CK, The MITRE Corporation, September 2015, *https://bit.ly/38oSrNJ.*
22. "APT1: Exposing One of China's Cyber Espionage Units," Mandiant, FireEye, FireEye Inc., February 2013, *https://bit.ly/2LbnPqg.*
23. "The Cyber Kill Chain," Lockheed Martin, Lockheed Martin Corporation, last accessed February 7, 2020, *https://bit.ly/2XjYrRN.*
24. Cris Carreon, "Applying Threat Intelligence to the Diamond Model of Intrusion Analysis," *Recorded Future Blog*, Recorded Future Inc., July 25, 2018, *https://bit.ly/39kPe1c.*
25. "Structured Threat Information eXpression (STIX) 1.x Archive Website," STIX, The MITRE Corporation, last accessed February 7, 2020, *https://stixproject.github.io.*
26. David Bianco, "The Pyramid of Pain," *Enterprise Detection & Response* (blog), last updated January 17, 2014, *https://bit.ly/3s31prV.*
27. "Adversarial Tactics, Techniques, & Common Knowledge Mobile Profile," ATT&CK, The MITRE Corporation, last modified May 2, 2018, *https://attack.mitre.org.*

INDEX

C

D

M

N

O

P

R

U

W

X

Y

Z

RESOURCES

Visit *https://nostarch.com/cyberjutsu/* for errata and more information.